*The*

*Elements*

*of*

*Typographic*

*Style*

ALSO BY ROBERT BRINGHURST

POETRY:

*The Shipwright's Log* · 1972
*Cadastre* · 1973
*Bergschrund* · 1975
*Tzuhalem's Mountain* · 1982
*The Beauty of the Weapons: Selected Poems 1972–82* · 1982
*The Blue Roofs of Japan* · 1986
*Pieces of Map, Pieces of Music* · 1986
*Conversations with a Toad* · 1987

PROSE:

*Visions: Contemporary Art in Canada*
(with Geoffrey James, Russell Keziere & Doris Shadbolt) · 1983
*Ocean/Paper/Stone* · 1984
*The Raven Steals the Light* (with Bill Reid) · 1984
*Shovels, Shoes and the Slow Rotation of Letters* · 1986
*The Black Canoe* (with photographs by Ulli Steltzer) · 1991

# The
# Elements
# of
# Typographic
# Style

Robert

Bringhurst

HARTLEY & MARKS
*Publishers*

HARTLEY & MARKS, PUBLISHERS
79 Tyee Drive, Point Roberts, WA 98281
3661 West Broadway, Vancouver, BC
V6R 2B8

*Library of Congress Cataloging in Publication Data:*

Bringhurst, Robert.
    Elements of typographic style / Robert Bringhurst. – 1st ed.    p.    cm.
    Includes bibliographical references and index.
    ISBN 0-88179-110-5 (cloth): $24.95. – ISBN 0-88179-033-8 (pbk): $14.95
    1. Printing, Practical – Layout. 2. Type and type-founding. 3. Book design.
    I. Title.
Z246.B74  1992
686.2'24 – dc20                                                    92-7746
                            CIP

*Canadian Cataloguing in Publication Data:*

Bringhurst, Robert, 1946–
    The elements of typographic style
    ISBN 0-88179-110-5 (bound). – ISBN 0-88179-033-8 (pbk)
    1. Printing, Practical – Layout. 2. Type and type-founding. 3. Book design.
    I. Title.
Z246.B75  1992      686.2'24    C92-091423-3

Typeset in Canada; printed & bound in the USA.

∾

*for my colleagues & friends*

*in the worlds of letters:*

*writers & editors,*

*type designers, typographers,*

*printers & publishers,*

*shepherding words and books*

*on their lethal and innocent ways*

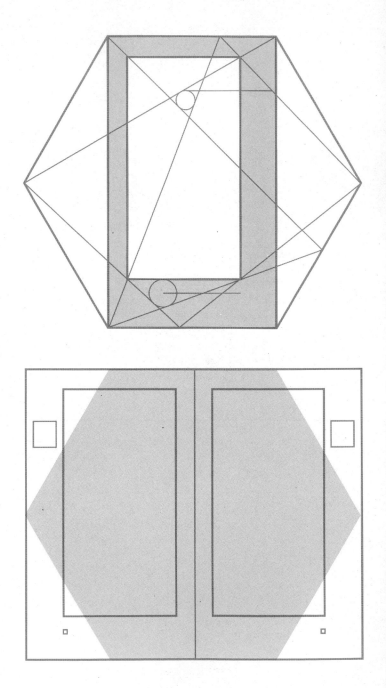

# CONTENTS

— Everything written symbols can say has already passed by. They are like tracks left by animals. That is why the masters of meditation refuse to accept that writings are final. The aim is to reach true being by means of those tracks, those letters, those signs – but reality itself is not a sign, and it leaves no tracks. It doesn't come to us by way of letters or words. We can go toward *it,* by following those words and letters back to what they came from. But so long as we are preoccupied with symbols, theories and opinions, we will fail to reach the principle.

— But when we give up symbols and opinions, aren't we left in the utter nothingness of being?

— Yes.

KIMURA KYŪHO, *Kenjutsu Fushigi Hen*
[*On the Mysteries of Swordsmanship*],
1768


A true revelation, it seems to me, will only emerge from stubborn concentration on a solitary problem. I am not in league with inventors or adventurers, nor with travellers to exotic destinations. The surest – also the quickest – way to awake the sense of wonder in ourselves is to look intently, undeterred, at a single object. Suddenly, miraculously, it will reveal itself as something we have never seen before.

CESARE PAVESE, *Dialoghi con Leucò,*
1947

There are many books about typography, and some of them are models of the art they teach. But when I set myself to compile a simple list of working principles, one of the benchmarks I first thought of was William Strunk and E.B. White's small master-piece, *The Elements of Style*. Brevity, however, is the essence of Strunk & White's manual of literary technique. This book is longer than theirs, and for that there is a cause.

Typography makes at least two kinds of sense, if it makes any sense at all. It makes visual sense and historical sense. The visual side of typography is always on display, and materials for the study of its visual form are many and widespread. The history of letterforms and their usage is visible too, to those with access to manuscripts, inscriptions and old books, but from others it is largely hidden. This book has therefore grown into something more than a short manual of typographic eti-quette. It is the fruit of a lot of long walks in the wilderness of letters: in part a pocket field guide to the living wonders that are found there, and in part a meditation on the ecological prin-ciples, survival techniques and ethics that apply. The principles of typography as I understand them are not a set of dead con-ventions but the tribal customs of the magic forest, where an-cient voices speak from all directions and new ones move to unremembered forms.

One question, nevertheless, has been often in my mind. When all right-thinking human beings are struggling to re-member that other men and women are free to be different, and free to become more different still, how can one honestly write a rulebook? What reason and authority exist for these com-mandments, suggestions and instructions? Surely typogra-phers, like others, ought to be at liberty to follow or to blaze the trails they choose.

Typography thrives as a shared concern – and there are no paths at all where there are no shared desires and directions. A typographer determined to forge new routes must move, like other solitary travellers, through uninhabited country and against the grain of the land, crossing common thoroughfares in the silence before dawn. The subject of this book is not typographical solitude, but the old, well-travelled roads at the core of the tradition: paths that each of us is free to follow or not, and to enter and leave when we choose – if only we know the paths are there and have a sense of where they lead. That freedom is denied us if the tradition is concealed or left for dead. Originality is everywhere, but much originality is blocked if the way back to earlier discoveries is cut or overgrown.

If you use this book as a guide, by all means leave the road when you wish. That is precisely the use of a road: to reach individually chosen points of departure. By all means break the rules, and break them beautifully, deliberately and well. That is one of the ends for which they exist.

Letterforms change constantly, yet differ very little, because they are alive. The principles of typographic clarity have also scarcely altered since the second half of the fifteenth century, when the first books were printed in roman type. Indeed, most of the principles of legibility and design explored in this book were known and used by Egyptian scribes writing hieratic script with reed pens on papyrus in 1000 BC. Samples of their work sit now in museums in Cairo, London and New York, still lively, subtle and perfectly legible thirty centuries after they were made.

Writing systems vary, but a good page is not hard to learn to recognize, whether it comes from Táng Dynasty China, the Egyptian New Kingdom or Renaissance Italy. The principles that unite these distant schools of design are based on the structure and scale of the human body – the eye, the hand and the forearm in particular – and on the invisible but no less real, no less demanding, no less sensuous anatomy of the human mind. I don't like to call these principles universals, because they are largely unique to our species. Dogs and ants, for example, read and write by more chemical means. But the underlying principles of typography are, at any rate, stable enough to weather any number of human fashions and fads.

It is true that typographers' tools are presently changing with considerable force and speed, but this is not a manual in the use of any particular typesetting system or medium. I suppose that most readers of this book will set most of their type in digital form, using computers, but I have no preconceptions about which brands of computers, or which versions of which proprietary software, they may use. The essential elements of style have more to do with the goals typographers set for themselves than with the mutable eccentricities of their tools. Typography itself, in other words, is far more device-independent than PostScript, which is the computer language used to render these particular letters, and the design of these pages, into typographic code. If I have succeeded in my task, this book should be as useful to artists and antiquarians setting foundry metal by hand and pulling proofs on a flat-bed press, as to those who check their work on a screen or laser printer, then ship it to high-resolution digital output devices by floppy disk or long-distance telephone line.

Typography is the craft of endowing human language with a durable visual form, and thus with an independent existence. Its heartwood is calligraphy – the dance, on a tiny stage, of the living, speaking hand – and its roots reach into living soil, though its branches may be hung each year with new machines. So long as the root lives, typography remains a source of true delight, true knowledge, true surprise.

As a craft, typography shares a long common boundary and many common concerns with writing and editing on the one side and with graphic design on the other; yet typography itself belongs to neither. This book in its turn is neither a manual of editorial style nor a textbook on design, though it overlaps with both of these concerns. The perspective throughout is first and foremost typographic – and I hope the book will be useful for that very reason to those whose work or interests may be centered in adjacent fields.

This book owes much to the conversation and example, over the years, of several friends and master craftsmen – Stan Bevington, Crispin Elsted, Glenn Goluska, Vic Marks and George Payerle – and to the practice of two artists and exemplars: the late Adrian Wilson, and Hermann Zapf. It owes as much, in other ways, to another friend and colleague, E.M. Ginger. Artists and scholars around the world have shared their knowledge freely. James Mosley and his staff at the St Bride Printing Library, London, have been particularly helpful. I am grateful to them all.

R.B.

11

*aperture:* the
opening in letters
such as a, c, e, s

RENAISSANCE (15th & 16th centuries): modulated stroke, humanist [oblique] axis; crisp, pen-formed terminals; large aperture; italic equal to and independent of roman

BAROQUE (17th century): modulated stroke, variable axis; modelled serifs and terminals; moderate aperture; italic subsidiary to roman and closely linked with it

# abpfoe

*abpfoe*

NEOCLASSICAL (18th century): modulated stroke, rationalist [vertical] axis; refined, adnate serifs; lachrymal terminals; moderate aperture; italic fully subjugated to roman

*adnate:* flowing into the stem
*lachrymal:* teardrop-shaped

# abpfoe

*abpfoe*

ROMANTIC (18th & 19th centuries): high contrast, intensified rationalist axis; abrupt, thin serifs; round terminals; small aperture; fully subjugated italic

13

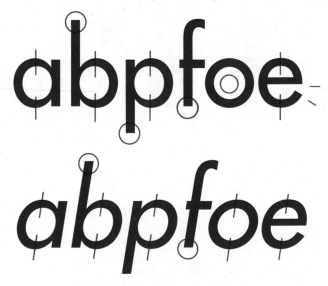

abpfoe

abpfoe

REALIST (19th & early 20th centuries): unmodulated stroke, implied vertical axis; small aperture; serifs absent or abrupt and of equal weight with main strokes; italic absent or replaced by sloped roman

abpfoe

abpfoe

GEOMETRIC MODERNIST (20th century): unmodulated stroke; bowls often circular (no axis); moderate aperture; serifs absent or of equal weight with main strokes; italic absent or replaced by sloped roman

14

LYRICAL MODERNIST (20th century): rediscovery of Renaissance form: modulated stroke, humanist axis; pen-formed serifs and terminals; large aperture; italic partially liberated from roman

POSTMODERNIST (late 20th century): frequent parody of Neoclassical and Romantic form; rationalist axis; sharply modelled serifs and terminals; moderate aperture; italic subjugated to roman

15

rigo Habraam numerā

ı a moſaica lege(ſeptim

r)ſed naturalı fuit ratio

idit enim Habraam de‹

m quoq; gentium patr

ːs oés gentes hoc uıdelı‹

m eſt:cuius ille iuſtıtiæ

us eſt:qui poſt multas ‹

ïmum omnium diuin‹

ɔ naſcerétur tradidit:u‹

gnum:uel ut hoc quaſ

ſuos imitari conaret':au

um nobis modo eſt. Po

Roman type cut in 1469 by Nicolas Jenson, a French typographer working
in Venice. The original is approximately 16 pt. The type is shown here as
Jenson printed it, but at twice actual size. This is the ancestor of the type
(Bruce Rogers's Centaur) shown at the top of page 12.

# THE GRAND DESIGN

## 1.1 FIRST PRINCIPLES

### 1.1.1 *Typography exists to honor content.*

Like oratory, music, dance, calligraphy – like anything that lends its grace to language – typography is an art that can be deliberately misused. It is a craft by which the meanings of a text (or its absence of meaning) can be clarified and honored, or knowingly disguised.

In a world rife with unsolicited messages, typography must often draw attention to itself before it will be read. Yet in order to be read, it must relinquish the attention it has drawn. Typography with anything to say therefore aspires to a kind of statuesque transparency. Its other traditional goal is durability: not immunity to change, but a clear superiority to fashion. Typography at its best is a visual form of language linking timelessness and time.

One of the principles of durable typography is always legibility; another is something more than legibility: some earned or unearned interest that gives its living energy to the page. It takes various forms and goes by various names, including serenity, liveliness, laughter, grace and joy.

These principles apply, in different ways, to the typography of business cards, instruction sheets and postage stamps, as well as to editions of religious scriptures, literary classics and other books that aspire to join their ranks. Within limits, the same principles apply even to stock market reports, airline schedules, milk cartons, classified ads. But laughter, grace and joy, like legibility itself, all feed on meaning, which the writer, the words and the subject, not the typographer, must generally provide.

In 1770, a bill was introduced in the English Parliament with the following provisions:

*… all women of whatever age, rank, profession, or degree, whether virgins, maids, or widows, that shall … impose upon, seduce, and betray into matrimony, any of His Majesty's subjects, by the scents, paints, cosmetic washes, artificial teeth, false hair, Spanish wool, iron stays, hoops, high heeled shoes [or] bolstered hips shall incur*

*the penalty of the law in force against witchcraft ... and ... the marriage, upon conviction, shall stand null and void.*

The function of typography, as I understand it, is neither to further the power of witches nor to bolster the defences of those, like this unfortunate parliamentarian, who live in terror of being tempted and deceived. The satisfactions of the craft come from elucidating, and perhaps even ennobling, the text, not from deluding the unwary reader by applying scents, paints and iron stays to empty prose. But humble texts, such as classified ads or the telephone directory, may profit as much as anything else from a good typographical bath and a change of clothes. And many a book, like many a warrior or dancer or priest of either sex, may look well with some paint on its face, or indeed with a bone in its nose.

### 1.1.2 *Letters have a life and dignity of their own.*

Letterforms that honor and elucidate what humans see and say deserve to be honored in their turn. Well-chosen words deserve well-chosen letters; these in their turn deserve to be set with affection, intelligence, knowledge and skill. Typography is a link, and it ought as a rule to be as strong as the others in the chain.

Writing begins with the making of footprints, the leaving of signs. Like speaking, it is a perfectly natural act which humans have carried to complex extremes. The typographer's task has always been to add a somewhat unnatural edge, a protective shell of artificial order, to the power of the writing hand. The tools have altered over the centuries, and the exact degree of unnaturalness desired has varied from place to place and time to time, but the character of the essential transformation between manuscript and type has scarcely changed.

The original purpose of type was simply copying. The job of the typographer was to imitate the scribal hand in a form that permitted exact and fast replication. Dozens, then hundreds, then thousands of copies were printed in less time than a scribe would need to finish one. This excuse for setting texts in type has disappeared. In the age of photolithography, digital scanning and offset printing, it is as easy to print directly from handwritten copy as from text that is typographically composed. Yet the typographer's task is little changed. It is still to give the illusion of superhuman speed and stamina – and of superhuman patience and precision – to the writing hand.

Typography is just that: idealized writing. Writers themselves now rarely have the calligraphic skill of earlier scribes, but they evoke countless versions of ideal script by their varying voices and literary styles. To these blind and often invisible visions, the typographer must respond in visible terms.

In a badly designed book, the letters mill and stand like starving horses in their field. In a book designed by rote, they sit like stale bread and mutton on the page. In a well-made book, where designer, compositor and printer have all done their jobs, no matter how many thousands of lines and pages, the letters are alive. They dance in their seats. Sometimes they rise and dance in the margins and aisles.

Simple as it may sound, the task of creative non-interference with letters is a rewarding and difficult calling. In ideal conditions, it is all that typographers are really asked to do – and it is enough.

### 1.1.3  *There is a style beyond style.*

Literary style, says Walter Benjamin, "is the power to move freely in the length and breadth of linguistic thinking without slipping into banality." Typographic style, in this large and intelligent sense of the word, does not mean any particular style – my style or your style, or Neoclassical or Baroque style – but the power to move freely through the whole domain of typography, and to function at every step in a way that is graceful and vital instead of banal. It means typography that can walk familiar ground without sliding into platitudes, typography that responds to new conditions with innovative solutions, and typography that does not vex the reader with its own originality in a self-conscious search for praise.

Typography is to literature as musical performance is to composition: an essential act of interpretation, full of endless opportunities for insight or obtuseness. Much typography is far removed from literature, for language has many uses, including packaging and propaganda. Like music, it can be used to manipulate behavior and emotions. But this is not where typographers, musicians or other human beings show us their finest side. Typography at its best is a slow performing art, worthy of the same informed appreciation that we sometimes

From Part 2 of Benjamin's essay on Karl Kraus, in *Illuminationen* (Frankfurt, 1955). There is an English translation in Walter Benjamin, *Reflections*, ed. Peter Demetz (New York, 1978).

give to musical performances, and capable of giving similar nourishment and pleasure in return.

The same alphabets and page designs can be used for a biography of Mohandas Gandhi and for a manual on the use and deployment of biological weapons. Writing can be used both for love letters and for hate mail, and love letters themselves can be used for manipulation and extortion as well as to bring delight to body and soul. Evidently there is nothing inherently noble and trustworthy in the written or printed word. Yet generations of men and women have turned to writing and printing to house and share their deepest hopes, perceptions, dreams and fears. It is to them, and not to the extortionist, that the typographer must answer.

1.2 TACTICS

1.2.1 *Read the text before designing it.*

The typographer's one essential task is to interpret and communicate the text. Its tone, its tempo, its logical structure, its physical size, all determine the possibilities of its typographic form. The typographer is to the text as the theatrical director to the script, or the musician to the score.

1.2.2 *Discover the outer logic of the typography in the inner logic of the text.*

A novel often purports to be a seamless river of words from beginning to end, or a series of unnamed scenes. Research papers, textbooks, cookbooks and other works of nonfiction rarely look so smooth. They are often layered with chapter heads, section heads, subheads, block quotations, footnotes, endnotes, lists and illustrative examples. Such features may be obscure in the manuscript, even if they are clear in the author's mind. For the sake of the reader, each requires its own typographic identity and form. Every layer and level of the text must be consistent, distinct, yet harmonious in form.

The first task of the typographer is therefore to read and understand the text; the second task is to analyze and map it. Only then can typographical interpretation begin.

If the text has many layers or sections, it may need not only heads and subheads but running heads as well, reappearing on every page or two-page spread, to remind readers which intellectual neighborhood they happen to be visiting.

Novels seldom need such signposts, but they often require typographical markers of other kinds. Peter Mathiessen's novel *Far Tortuga* (New York, 1975; designed by Kenneth Miyamoto) uses two sizes of text, three different margins, free-floating block paragraphs and other typographical devices to separate thought, speech and action. Ken Kesey's novel *Sometimes a Great Notion* (New York, 1964) seems to flow like conventional prose, yet it shifts repeatedly in mid-sentence between roman and italic to distinguish what characters say to each other from what they say in silence to themselves.

In poetry and drama, a larger typographical palette is sometimes required. Some of Douglass Parker's translations from classical Greek and Dennis Tedlock's translations from Zuni use roman, italic, bold, small caps and full caps in various sizes to emulate the dynamic markings of music. Robert Massin's typographical performances of Eugène Ionesco's plays use intersecting lines of type, stretched and melted letters, inkblots, pictograms, and a separate typeface for each character. In the works of artists like Guillaume Apollinaire and Guy Davenport, boundaries between author and designer sometimes vanish. Writing merges with typography, and the text becomes its own illustration.

See for example Aristophanes, *Four Comedies* (Ann Arbor, MI, 1969); Dennis Tedlock, *Finding the Center* (Lincoln, NE, 1972); Eugène Ionesco, *La Cantatrice chauve* (Paris, 1964) and *Délire à deux* (Paris, 1966). There are samples of Massin's work in *Typographica* n.s. 11 (June 1965).

The typographer must analyze and reveal the inner order of the text, as a musician must reveal the inner order of the music he performs. But the reader, like the listener, should in retrospect be able to close her eyes and see what lies inside the words she has been reading. The typographic performance must reveal, not replace, the inner composition. Typographers, like other artists and craftsmen – musicians, composers and authors as well – must as a rule do their work and disappear.

1.2.3 *Make the visible relationship between the text and other elements (photographs, captions, tables, diagrams, notes) a reflection of their real relationship.*

If the text is tied to other elements, where do they belong? If there are notes, do they go at the side of the page, the foot of the page, the end of the chapter, the end of the book? If there are photographs or other illustrations, should they be embedded in the text or do they belong in a special section of their own? And if the photographs have captions or credits or labels, should these be exhibited together with the photographs or confined to a separate section?

If there is more than one text – as in countless publications issued in Canada, Switzerland, Belgium and other multilingual countries – how will the separate but equal texts be arrayed? *Tactics* Will they run side by side to emphasize their equality (and perhaps to share in a single set of illustrations), or will they be printed back-to-back, to emphasize their distinctness?

No matter what their relation to the text, photos or maps must sometimes be grouped apart from it because they require a separate paper or different inks. If this is the case, what typographical cross-references will be required?

These and similar questions, which confront the working typographer on a daily basis, must be answered case by case. The typographic page is a map of the mind; it is frequently also a map of the social order from which it comes. And for better or for worse, minds and social orders change.

1.2.4 *Choose a typeface or a group of faces that will honor and elucidate the character of the text.*

This is the beginning, middle and end of the practice of typography: choose and use the type with sensitivity and intelligence. Aspects of this principle are explored throughout this book and considered in detail in chapters 6 and 7.

Letterforms have tone, timbre, character, just as words and sentences do. The moment a text and a typeface are chosen, two streams of thought, two rhythmical systems, two sets of habits, or if you like, two personalities, intersect. They need not live together contentedly forever, but they must not as a rule collide.

The root metaphor of typesetting is that the alphabet (or in Chinese, the entire lexicon) is a system of interchangeable parts. The word *form* can be surgically revised, instead of rewritten, to become the word *farm* or *firm* or *fort* or *fork* or *from*, or with a little more trouble, to become the word *pineapple*. The old compositor's typecase is a partitioned wooden tray holding hundreds of such interchangeable bits of information. These sub-semantic particles, these bits – called *sorts* by letterpress printers – are letters cast on standardized bodies of metal, waiting to be assembled into meaningful combinations, then dispersed and reassembled in a different form. The compositor's typecase is one of the primary ancestors of the computer – and it is no surprise that while typesetting was one of the last crafts to be mechanized, it was one of the first to be computerized.

But the bits of information handled by typographers differ in one essential respect from the computer programmer's bits. Whether the type is set in hard metal by hand, or in softer metal by machine, or in digital form on paper or film, every comma, every parenthesis, every *e*, and in context, even every empty space, has style as well as bald symbolic value. Letters are microscopic works of art as well as useful symbols. They mean what they *are* as well as what they say.

Typography is the art and craft of handling these doubly meaningful bits of information. A good typographer handles them in intelligent, coherent, sensitive ways. When the type is poorly chosen, what the words say linguistically and what the letters imply visually are disharmonious, dishonest, out of tune.

1.2.5 *Shape the page and frame the text block so that it honors and reveals every element, every relationship between elements, and every logical nuance of the text.*

Selecting the shape of the page and placing the type upon it is much like framing and hanging a painting. A cubist painting in an eighteenth-century gilded frame, or a seventeenth-century still-life in a slim chrome box, will look no sillier than a nineteenth-century English text set in a seventeenth-century French typeface asymmetrically positioned on a German modernist page.

If the text is long or the space is short, or if the elements are many, multiple columns may be required. If illustrations and text march side by side, does one take prominence over the other? And does the order or degree of prominence change? Does the text suggest perpetual symmetry, perpetual asymmetry, or something in between?

Again, does the text suggest the continuous unruffled flow of justified prose, or the continued flirtation with order and chaos evoked by flush-left ragged-right composition? (The running heads and sidenotes on the odd-numbered pages of this book are set flush left, ragged right. On the even numbered pages, they are ragged left. Leftward-reading alphabets, like Arabic and Hebrew, are perfectly at home in ragged-left text, but with rightward-reading alphabets like Latin, Greek or Thai, ragged-left setting emphasizes the end, not the beginning, of the line. This makes it a poor choice for extended composition.)

Shaping the page goes hand in hand with choosing the type, and both are permanent typographical preoccupations. The subject of page shapes and proportions is addressed in greater detail in Chapter 8.

*Tactics*

### 1.2.6 *Give full typographical attention even to incidental details.*

Some of what a typographer must set, like some of what any musician must play, is simply passage work. Even an edition of Plato or Shakespeare will contain a certain amount of routine text: page numbers, scene numbers, textual notes, the copyright claim, the publisher's name and address, and the hyperbole on the jacket, not to mention the passage work or background writing that is implicit in the text itself. But just as a good musician can make a heart-wrenching ballad from a few banal words and a trivial tune, so the typographer can make poignant and lovely typography from bibliographical paraphernalia and textual chaff. The ability to do so rests on respect for the text as a whole, and on respect for the letters themselves.

Perhaps the rule should read: Give full typographical attention *especially* to incidental details.

### 1.3 SUMMARY

There are always exceptions, always excuses for stunts and surprises. But perhaps we can agree that, as a rule, typography should perform these services for the reader:

- invite the reader into the text;
- reveal the tenor and meaning of the text;
- clarify the structure and the order of the text;
- link the text with other existing elements;
- induce a state of energetic repose, which is the ideal condition for reading.

While serving the reader in this way, typography, like a musical performance or a theatrical production, should serve two other ends. It should honor the text for its own sake – always assuming that the text is worth a typographer's trouble – and it should honor and contribute to its own tradition: that of typography itself.

# RHYTHM *&* PROPORTION

---

## 2.1 HORIZONTAL SPACE

An ancient metaphor: thought is a thread, and the raconteur is a spinner of yarns – but the true storyteller, the poet, is a weaver. The scribes made this old and audible abstraction into a new and visible fact. After long practice, their work took on such an even, flexible texture that they called the written page a *textus,* cloth.

The typesetting device, whether it happens to be a computer or a composing stick, functions like a loom. And the typographer, like the scribe, normally aims to weave the text as evenly as possible. Good letterforms are designed to give a lively, even texture, but careless spacing of letters, lines and words can tear this fabric apart.

Another ancient metaphor: the density of texture in a written or typeset page is called its *color.* This has nothing to do with red or green ink; it refers only to the darkness or blackness of the letterforms in mass. Once the demands of legibility and logical order are satisfied, *evenness of color* is the typographer's normal aim. And color depends on four things: the design of the type, the spacing between the letters, the spacing between the words, and the spacing between the lines. None is independent of the others.

2.1.1 *Define the word space to suit the size and natural letterfit of the font.*

Type is normally measured in picas and points (explained in detail on p 236), but horizontal spacing is measured in *ems,* and the em is a sliding measure. One em is a distance equal to the type size. In 6 point type, an em is 6 points; in 12 pt type it is 12 points, and in 60 pt type it is 60 points. Thus a one-em space is *proportionately* the same in any size.

| | | | |
|---|---|---|---|
| 12 pt em | 18 pt em | 24 pt em | 36 pt em |

Typesetting machines generally divide the em into units. Ems of 18, 36 or 54 units, for example, are commonly found in the older machines. In newer devices, the em may be a thousand units. Typographers are more likely to divide the em into simple fractions: half an em, a third of an em, and so on, knowing that the unit value of these fractions will vary from one machine to the next. Half an em is called an *en*.

If text is set ragged right, the *word space* (the space between words) can be fixed and unchanging. If the text is *justified* (set flush left and right, like the text in this book), the word space must be elastic. In either case, the size of the ideal word space varies from one circumstance to another, depending on factors such as letterfit, type color and size. A loosely fitted or bold face will need a larger interval between the words. At larger sizes, when letterfit is tightened, the spacing of words can be tightened as well. For a normal text face in a normal text size, a typical value for the word space is a quarter of an em, which can be written m/4. (A quarter of an em is typically about the same as, or slightly more than, the set-width of the letter t.)

Language has some effect on the word space as well. In highly inflected languages, such as Latin, most word boundaries are marked by grammatical tags, and a smaller space is therefore sufficient. In English and other uninflected languages, good word spacing makes the difference between a line that has to be deciphered and a line that can be efficiently read.

If the text is justified, a reasonable *minimum* word space is a fifth of an em (m/5), and m/4 is a good average to aim for. A reasonable *maximum* in justified text is m/2. If it can be held to m/3, so much the better. But for bold or loosely fitted faces, or text set in a small size, m/3 is often a better average to aim for, and a better minimum is m/4. In a line of widely letterspaced capitals, a word space of m/2 or more may be required.

2.1.2  *Choose a comfortable measure.*

Anything from 45 to 75 characters is widely regarded as a satisfactory length of line for a single-column page set in a serifed text face in a text size. The 66-character line (counting both letters and spaces) is widely regarded as ideal. For multiple-column work, a better average is 40 to 50 characters.

If the type is well set and printed, lines of 85 or 90 characters will pose no problem in discontinuous texts, such as bibliographies, or, with generous leading, in footnotes. But even with generous leading, a line that averages more than 75 or 80 characters is likely to be too long for continuous reading.

A reasonable working minimum for justified text in English is the 40-character line. Shorter lines may compose perfectly well with sufficient luck and patience, but in the long run, justified lines averaging less than 38 or 40 characters will lead to white acne or pig bristles: a rash of erratic and splotchy word spaces or an epidemic of hyphenation. When the line is short, the text should be set ragged right. In large doses, even ragged-right composition may look anorexic if the line falls below 30 characters, but in small and isolated patches – ragged marginal notes, for example – the minimum line (if the language is English) can be as little as 12 or 15 characters.

These line lengths are in every case averages, and they include empty spaces and punctuation as well as letters. The simplest way of computing them is with a copyfitting table like the one on page 29. Measure the length of the basic lowercase alphabet – abcdefghijklmnopqrstuvwxyz – in any font and size you are considering, and the table will tell you the average number of characters to expect on a given line. In most text faces, the 10 pt roman alphabet will run between 120 and 140 points long, but a 10 pt *italic* alphabet might be 100 points long or even less, while a 10 pt bold might run to 160. The 12 pt alphabet is, of course, about 1.2 times the length of the 10 pt alphabet – but not exactly so unless it is generated from the same master design and the letterfit is unchanged.

On a conventional book page, the *measure,* or length of line, is usually around 30 times the size of the type, but lines as little as 20 or as much as 40 times the type size fall within the expectable range. If, for example, the type size is 10 pt, the measure might be around $30 \times 10 = 300$ pt, which is $300/12 = 25$ picas. A typical lowercase alphabet length for a 10 pt text font is 128 pt, and the copyfitting table tells us that such a font set to a 25-pica measure will yield roughly 65 characters per line.

### 2.1.3 *Set ragged if ragged setting suits the text and the page.*

In justified text, there is always a trade-off between evenness of word spacing and frequency of hyphenation. The best available compromise will depend on the nature of the text as well as on the specifics of the design. Good compositors like to avoid consecutive hyphenated line-ends, but frequent hyphens are better than sloppy spacing, and ragged setting is better yet.

Narrow measures – which prevent good justification – are commonly used when the text is set in multiple columns. Setting ragged right under these conditions will lighten the page and decrease its stiffness, as well as preventing an outbreak of hyphenation.

*Horizontal*
*Space*

Many unserifed faces look best when set ragged no matter what the length of the measure. And monospaced fonts, which are common on typewriters, always look better set ragged, in standard typewriter style. A typewriter (or a computer-driven printer of similar quality) that justifies its lines in imitation of typesetting is a presumptuous machine, mimicking the outer form instead of the inner truth of typography.

❧ When setting ragged right from a computer, take a moment to refine your software's understanding of what constitutes an honest rag. Many programs are predisposed to invoke a minimum as well as a maximum line. If permitted to do so, they will hyphenate words and adjust spaces regardless of whether they are ragging or justifying the text. Ragged setting under these conditions produces an orderly ripple down the righthand side, making the text look like a neatly pinched piecrust. This approach combines the worst features of justification with the worst features of ragged setting, while eliminating the principal virtues of both. Unless the measure is excruciatingly narrow, it is usually better to set a hard rag. This means a fixed word space, no minimum line, and no hyphenation beyond what is inherent in the text. In a hard rag, hyphenated linebreaks may occur in words like *self-consciousness,* which are hyphenated anyway, but they can only occur with manual intervention in words like *hyphenation* or *pseudosophisticated,* which are not.

2.1.4 *Use a single word space between sentences.*

In the nineteenth century, which was a dark and inflationary age in typography and type design, many compositors were encouraged to stuff extra space between sentences. Generations of twentieth-century typists were then taught to do the same, by hitting the spacebar twice after every period. Your typing as well as your typesetting will benefit from unlearning this quaint Victorian habit. As a general rule, no more than a single space is

28

| | 10 | 12 | 14 | 16 | 18 | 20 | 22 | 24 | 26 | 28 | 30 | 32 | 34 | 36 | 38 | 40 |
|---|---|---|---|---|---|---|---|---|---|---|---|---|---|---|---|---|
| 80 | 40 | 48 | 56 | 64 | 72 | 80 | 88 | 96 | 104 | 112 | 120 | 128 | 136 | 144 | 152 | 160 |
| 85 | 38 | 45 | 53 | 60 | 68 | 76 | 83 | 91 | 98 | 106 | 113 | 121 | 129 | 136 | 144 | 151 |
| 90 | 36 | 43 | 50 | 57 | 64 | 72 | 79 | 86 | 93 | 100 | 107 | 115 | 122 | 129 | 136 | 143 |
| 95 | 34 | 41 | 48 | 55 | 62 | 69 | 75 | 82 | 89 | 96 | 103 | 110 | 117 | 123 | 130 | 137 |
| 100 | 33 | 40 | 46 | 53 | 59 | 66 | 73 | 79 | 86 | 92 | 99 | 106 | 112 | 119 | 125 | 132 |
| 105 | 32 | 38 | 44 | 51 | 57 | 63 | 70 | 76 | 82 | 89 | 95 | 101 | 108 | 114 | 120 | 127 |
| 110 | 30 | 37 | 43 | 49 | 55 | 61 | 67 | 73 | 79 | 85 | 92 | 98 | 104 | 110 | 116 | 122 |
| 115 | 29 | 35 | 41 | 47 | 53 | 59 | 64 | 70 | 76 | 82 | 88 | 94 | 100 | 105 | 111 | 117 |
| 120 | 28 | 34 | 39 | 45 | 50 | 56 | 62 | 67 | 73 | 78 | 84 | 90 | 95 | 101 | 106 | 112 |
| 125 | 27 | 32 | 38 | 43 | 48 | 54 | 59 | 65 | 70 | 75 | 81 | 86 | 91 | 97 | 102 | 108 |
| 130 | 26 | 31 | 36 | 41 | 47 | 52 | 57 | 62 | 67 | 73 | 78 | 83 | 88 | 93 | 98 | 104 |
| 135 | 25 | 30 | 35 | 40 | 45 | 50 | 55 | 60 | 65 | 70 | 75 | 80 | 85 | 90 | 95 | 100 |
| 140 | 24 | 29 | 34 | 39 | 44 | 48 | 53 | 58 | 63 | 68 | 73 | 77 | 82 | 87 | 92 | 97 |
| 145 | 23 | 28 | 33 | 37 | 42 | 47 | 51 | 56 | 61 | 66 | 70 | 75 | 80 | 84 | 89 | 94 |
| 150 | 23 | 28 | 32 | 37 | 41 | 46 | 51 | 55 | 60 | 64 | 69 | 74 | 78 | 83 | 87 | 92 |
| 155 | 22 | 27 | 31 | 36 | 40 | 45 | 49 | 54 | 58 | 63 | 67 | 72 | 76 | 81 | 85 | 90 |
| 160 | 22 | 26 | 30 | 35 | 39 | 43 | 48 | 52 | 56 | 61 | 65 | 69 | 74 | 78 | 82 | 87 |
| 165 | 21 | 25 | 30 | 34 | 38 | 42 | 46 | 51 | 55 | 59 | 63 | 68 | 72 | 76 | 80 | 84 |
| 170 | 21 | 25 | 29 | 33 | 37 | 41 | 45 | 49 | 53 | 57 | 62 | 66 | 70 | 74 | 78 | 82 |
| 175 | 20 | 24 | 28 | 32 | 36 | 40 | 44 | 48 | 52 | 56 | 60 | 64 | 68 | 72 | 76 | 80 |
| 180 | 20 | 23 | 27 | 31 | 35 | 39 | 43 | 47 | 51 | 55 | 59 | 62 | 66 | 70 | 74 | 78 |
| 185 | 19 | 23 | 27 | 30 | 34 | 38 | 42 | 46 | 49 | 53 | 57 | 61 | 65 | 68 | 72 | 76 |
| 190 | 19 | 22 | 26 | 30 | 33 | 37 | 41 | 44 | 48 | 52 | 56 | 59 | 63 | 67 | 70 | 74 |
| 195 | 18 | 22 | 25 | 29 | 32 | 36 | 40 | 43 | 47 | 50 | 54 | 58 | 61 | 65 | 68 | 72 |
| 200 | 18 | 21 | 25 | 28 | 32 | 35 | 39 | 42 | 46 | 49 | 53 | 56 | 60 | 63 | 67 | 70 |
| 210 | 17 | 20 | 23 | 27 | 30 | 33 | 37 | 40 | 43 | 47 | 50 | 53 | 57 | 60 | 63 | 67 |
| 220 | 16 | 19 | 22 | 25 | 29 | 32 | 35 | 38 | 41 | 45 | 48 | 51 | 54 | 57 | 60 | 64 |
| 230 | 15 | 18 | 21 | 24 | 27 | 30 | 33 | 36 | 40 | 43 | 46 | 49 | 52 | 55 | 58 | 61 |
| 240 | 15 | 17 | 20 | 23 | 26 | 29 | 32 | 35 | 38 | 41 | 44 | 46 | 49 | 52 | 55 | 58 |
| 250 | 14 | 17 | 20 | 22 | 25 | 28 | 31 | 34 | 36 | 39 | 42 | 45 | 48 | 50 | 53 | 56 |
| 260 | 14 | 16 | 19 | 22 | 24 | 27 | 30 | 32 | 35 | 38 | 41 | 43 | 46 | 49 | 51 | 54 |
| 270 | 13 | 16 | 18 | 21 | 23 | 26 | 29 | 31 | 34 | 36 | 39 | 42 | 44 | 47 | 49 | 52 |
| 280 | 13 | 15 | 18 | 20 | 23 | 25 | 28 | 30 | 33 | 35 | 38 | 40 | 43 | 45 | 48 | 50 |
| 290 | 12 | 15 | 17 | 20 | 22 | 24 | 27 | 29 | 32 | 34 | 37 | 39 | 41 | 44 | 46 | 49 |
| 300 | 12 | 14 | 17 | 19 | 21 | 24 | 26 | 28 | 31 | 33 | 35 | 38 | 40 | 42 | 45 | 47 |
| 320 | 11 | 13 | 16 | 18 | 20 | 22 | 25 | 27 | 29 | 31 | 34 | 36 | 38 | 40 | 43 | 45 |
| 340 | 10 | 13 | 15 | 17 | 19 | 21 | 23 | 25 | 27 | 29 | 32 | 34 | 36 | 38 | 40 | 42 |
| 360 | 10 | 12 | 14 | 16 | 18 | 20 | 22 | 24 | 26 | 28 | 30 | 32 | 34 | 36 | 38 | 40 |

*Read down,* in the left column: lowercase alphabet length in points. *Read across,* in the top row: line length in picas.

required after a period, a colon or any other mark of punctuation. Larger spaces (e.g., en spaces) *replace* punctuation.

The rule is usually altered, however, when setting classical Latin and Greek, romanized Sanskrit, phonetics or other kinds of texts in which sentences begin with lowercase letters. In the absence of a capital, a full *en space* (m/2) between sentences will generally be welcome.

### 2.1.5 *Add little or no space within strings of initials.*

Names such as W.B. Yeats and J.C.L. Prillwitz need only hair spaces or no spaces at all after the intermediary periods. A normal word space follows the *last* period in the string.

### 2.1.6 *Letterspace all sequences of capitals and small caps.*

Acronyms such as CIA and PLO are frequent in some texts. So are abbreviations such as Fr William Ong, SJ, or 525 BC. The normal value for letterspacing these sequences of small or full caps is 5% to 10% of the type size.

With digital fonts, it is a simple matter to assign extra width to all small capitals, so that letterspacing occurs automatically. The width values of full caps are normally based on the assumption that they will be used in conjunction with the lower case, but letterspacing can still be automated through the use of kerning tables (see p 32).

In titles and headings, extra letterspacing is usually desirable. Justified lines of letterspaced capitals are generally set by inserting a normal word space (m/5 to m/4) between letters. This corresponds to letterspacing of 20% to 25% of the type size. But the extra space between letters will also require more space between lines. A Renaissance typographer setting a multiline head in letterspaced text-size capitals would normally set blanks between the lines: the hand compositor's equivalent of the keyboard operator's extra hard return, or double spacing.

There is no generalized optimum value for letterspacing capitals in titles or display lines. The effective letterspacing of caps in good classical inscriptions and later manuscripts ranges from 5% to 100% of the nominal type size. The quantity of space is far less important than its balance. Sequences like LA or AVA may need no extra space at all, while sequences like NN and HIH beg to be pried open.

# WAVADOPATTIMMILTL

## WAVADOPATTIMMILTL

Letterspaced caps, above, and unletterspaced, below

2.1.7  *Don't letterspace normal lower case.*

A man who would letterspace lower case would steal sheep, Frederic Goudy liked to say. If this wisdom needs updating, it is chiefly to add that a woman who would letterspace lower case would steal sheep as well.

Nevertheless, like every rule, this one extends only as far as its rationale. The reason for not letterspacing lower case is that it hampers legibility. But there are some lowercase alphabets to which this principle doesn't apply.

Headings set in exaggeratedly letterspaced, condensed, unserifed capitals are now a hallmark, if not a cliché, of postmodernist typography. In this context, secondary display can be set perfectly well in more modestly letterspaced, condensed sanserif lower case. Moderate letterspacing can make a face such as lowercase Univers bold condensed *more* legible rather than less.

## wharves and wharfingers

Lowercase Univers bold condensed, letterspaced 10%

It would be possible, in fact, to make a detailed chart of lowercase letterforms, plotting their inherent resistance to letterspacing. At the top of the list (most unsuitable for letterspacing) would be Renaissance italics, such as Arrighi, whose structure strongly implies an actual linkage between one letter and the next. A little farther along would be Renaissance romans. Still farther along, we would find faces like Syntax, which echo the forms of Renaissance roman but lack the serifs. (Syntax is used for the captions in this book.) Around the middle of the list, we would find other unserifed faces, such as Helvetica, in which nothing more than wishful thinking bonds the letters to each other. Bold condensed sanserifs would appear at the bottom of the list. Letterspacing will always sabotage a Renaissance roman or italic. But when we come to the other extreme, the

31

faces with no calligraphic content, letterspacing of lowercase letters can sometimes be of genuine benefit.

### 2.1.8 *Kern consistently and modestly or not at all.*

*Horizontal Space*

Inconsistencies in letterfit are inescapable, given the forms of the Latin alphabet, and small irregularities are after all essential to the legibility of roman type. *Kerning* – altering the space between selected pairs of letters – can increase consistency of spacing in a word like Washington or Toronto, where the combinations *Wa* and *To* are kerned. But names like Wisconsin, Tübingen, Tbilisi and Los Alamos, as well as common words like The and This, remain more or less immune to alteration.

Hand compositors rarely kern text sizes, because their kerning pairs must be manually fitted, one at a time. Computerized typesetting makes extensive kerning easy, but judgement is still required, and the computer does not make good judgement any easier to come by. Too little kerning is preferable to too much, and inconsistent kerning is worse than none.

In digital type, as in foundry type, each letter has a standard width of its own. But computerized typesetting systems can modify these widths in many ways. Digital fonts are generally kerned through the use of *kerning tables,* which can specify a reduction or increase in spacing for every possible sequence of letters, numbers or symbols. By this means, space can automatically be added to combinations like HH and removed from combinations like Ty. Prefabricated kerning tables are now widely available, but a different table is required for every face, and the tables often require extensive editing to suit individual styles and requirements. If you use an automatic kerning program, test it thoroughly before trusting its decisions, and take the time to repair its inevitable shortcomings.

Kerning tables generally subtract space from the following combinations: Av, Aw, Ay, 'A, 'A, L', and all combinations in which the first element is T, V, W or Y and the second element is a, c, d, e, g, m, n, o, p, q, r, s, u, v, w, x, y or z. Not all of these combinations occur in English, but any kerning system should accommodate names like Tchaikovsky, Tmolos and Ysaÿe.

Space is generally added to f ', f), f], f?, f!, (f, [f, (J and [J. In some italics, space must also be added to *gg* and *gy.* If your text includes them, other sequences – *gf, gj, qf, qj,* for instance – may need attention as well.

Especially at larger sizes, it is common to kern combinations involving commas and periods, such as r, / r. / v, / v. / w, / w. / y, / y. But use care when kerning combinations such as F. / P. / T. / V. Capitals need their space, and some combinations are easy to misread. P.F. Barnum may be mistaken for R E Barnum if enthusiastically kerned.

Numbers (which are often omitted from kerning tables) are often worth kerning, even if you choose to kern nothing else. The digit 1 is usually thinner in form than the other numbers, but it is usually assigned the same set-width, so columns of typeset figures will align. Many fonts include an alternative version of the 1 (the so-called 'fitted one') with a narrower set-width, intended for use in text. Other combinations of digits may need more subtle adjustment, and combinations of 4, 6, 9 and 0 with the en dash generally call for extra space.

*Rhythm and Proportion*

1840–1842    **1840–1842**

Unkerned, left, and kerned, right

Whatever kerning you do, make sure it does not result in collisions with floating accents. Wolf can be kerned more than Wölfflin in many faces, and Tennyson more than Tête-a-tête. Also beware the composite effect of sequential kerns. The apostrophes in L'Hôtel and D'Artagnan can be brought up close, but in L'Anse aux Meadows, two close kerns in a row can produce a collision.

*2.1.9  Don't alter the widths or shapes of letters without cause.*

Type design is an art practiced by few and mastered by fewer – but font-editing software makes it possible for anyone to alter in a moment the widths and shapes of letters to which an artist may have devoted decades of study, years of inspiration and a rare concentration of skill. The power to destroy such a type designer's work should be used with caution. And arbitrarily condensing or expanding letterforms is the poorest of all methods for fitting uneditable copy into unalterable space.

On many fonts, characters such as ? ! ; : need greater width than manufacturers have given them, but letter widths should be altered for one purpose only: to improve the set of the type.

33

2.1.10 *Don't stretch the space until it breaks.*

*Horizontal Space*

Lists, such as contents pages and recipes, are opportunities to build architectural structures in which the space between the elements both separates and binds. The two favorite ways of destroying such an opportunity are setting great chasms of space that the eye cannot leap without help from the hand, and setting unenlightening rows of dots (*dot leaders,* they are called) that force the eye to walk the width of the page like a prisoner being escorted back to its cell.

Two among many ways of handling a list. Setting the titles flush left and the numbers flush right, with or without dot leaders, would only muffle the information.

2.2 VERTICAL SPACE

2.2.1 *Choose a basic leading that suits the typeface, text and measure.*

Time is divisible into any number of increments. So is space. But for working purposes, time in music is divided into a few proportional intervals: halves, quarters, eighths, sixteenths and so on. And time in music is measured. Add a quarter note to a bar whose time is already accounted for and, somewhere nearby, the equivalent of that quarter note must come out. Phrasing and rhythm can move in and out of phase – as they do in the singing of Billie Holiday and the trumpet solos of Miles Davis – but the force of blues phrasing and syncopation vanishes if the beat is actually lost.

Space in typography is like time in music. It is infinitely

divisible, but a few proportional intervals can be much more useful than a limitless choice of arbitrary quantities.

The metering of horizontal space is accomplished almost unconsciously in typography. You choose and prepare a font, and you choose a measure (the width of the column). When you set the type, the measure fills with the varied rhythm of repeating letter shapes, which are music to the eye.

Vertical space is metered in a different way. You must choose not only the overall measure – the depth of the column or page – but also a basic rhythmical unit. This unit is the leading, which is the distance from one baseline to the next.

Eleven-point type *set solid* is described as 11/11. The theoretical face of the type is 11 points high (from the top of *d* to the bottom of *p*, if the type is full on the body), and the distance from the baseline of line one to the baseline of line two is also 11 points. Add two points of lead (interlinear space), and the type is set 11/13. The type size has not changed, but the distance from baseline to baseline has increased to 13 points, and the type has more room to breathe.

The text of the book you are reading, to take an example, is set 10/12 × 21. This means that the type size is 10 pt, the added lead is 2 pt, giving a total leading of 12 pt, and the line length is 21 picas.

A short burst of advertising copy or a title might be set with negative leading (24/18, for example), so long as the ascenders and descenders don't collide:

# this is an example
# of negative leading

Continuous text is scarcely ever set with negative leading, and only a few text faces read well when set solid. Most text requires positive leading. Settings such as 9/11, 10/12, 11/13 and 12/15 are routine. Longer measures need more lead than short ones. Dark faces need more lead than light ones. Large sizes need more lead than smaller ones. Faces like Bauer Bodoni, with substantial color and a rigid vertical axis, need much more lead than faces like Bembo, whose color is light and whose axis is based on the writing hand. And unserifed faces often need more lead (or a shorter line) than their serifed counterparts.

Extra leading is also generally welcome where the text is

thickened by superscripts, subscripts, mathematical expressions, or the frequent use of full capitals. A text in German would ideally have a little more lead than the same text in Latin or French, purely because of the increased frequency of capitals.

### 2.2.2 Add and delete vertical space in measured intervals.

For the same reason that the tempo must not change arbitrarily in music, leading must not change arbitrarily in type.

Pages and columns are set most often to uniform depth, but ragged depths are better in some situations. A collection of short texts, such as catalog entries, set in multiple-column pages, is likely to look better and read more easily if the text is not sawed into columns of uniform depth. A collection of short poems is bound to generate pages of varying depth as well.

Continuous prose offers no such excuse for variation. It is therefore usually set in pages of uniform depth, designed in symmetrical pairs. The lines and blocks of text on facing pages in this format should align, and the lines on the front and back of the leaf (the recto and verso pages) should align as well. Typographers check their reproduction proofs by holding them up to the light in pairs, to see that the text and crop marks match from page to page. Press proofs are checked in the same way, by holding them up to the light to see that textblocks *back each other up* when the sheet is printed on both sides.

Headings, subheads, block quotations, footnotes, illustrations, captions and other intrusions into the text create syncopations and variations against the base rhythm of regularly leaded lines. These variations can and should add life to the page, but the main text should also return after each variation precisely on beat and in phase. This means that the total amount of vertical space consumed by each departure from the main text should be an even multiple of the basic leading. If the main text runs 11/13, intrusions to the text should equal some multiple of 13 points: 26, 39, 52, 65, 78, 91, 104 and so on.

Subheads in this book are leaded in the simplest possible way, with a *white line* (that is, in keyboard terms, a hard return) before and after. They could just as well be leaded asymmetrically, with more space above than below, so long as the total additional lead is equivalent to an even number of text lines.

If you happen to be setting a text 11/13, subhead possibilities include the following:

- subheads in 11/13 small caps, with 13 pt above the head and 13 pt below;
- subheads in 11/13 bold u&lc (upper and lower case), with 8 pt above the head and 5 pt below, since 8 + 5 = 13;
- subheads in 11/13 caps with 26 pt above and 13 pt below;
- one-line subheads in 14/13 italic u&lc, with 16 pt above the head and 10 pt below. (The negative leading is merely to minimize coding in this case. If the heads are one line long, no cramping will occur.)

## 2.3 PARAGRAPHS & BLOCK QUOTATIONS

### 2.3.1  *Set opening paragraphs flush left.*

The function of a paragraph indent is to mark a pause, setting the paragraph apart from what precedes it. If a paragraph is preceded by a title or subhead, the indent is superfluous and can therefore be omitted, as it is here.

### 2.3.2  *In continuous text, mark all paragraphs after the first with an indent of at least one em.*

Typography like other arts, from cooking to chorcography, involves a balance between the familiar and the unfamiliar, the dependably consistent and the unforeseen. Typographers generally take pleasure in the unpredictable length of the paragraph while accepting the simple and reassuring consistency of the paragraph indent. The prose paragraph and its verse counterpart, the stanza, are basic units of linguistic thought and literary style. The typographer must articulate them enough to make them clear, yet not so strongly that the form instead of the content steals the show. If the units of thought, or the boundaries between thoughts, look more important than the thoughts themselves, the typographer has failed.

 Ornaments can be placed in the paragraph indents, but few texts actually profit from ornamentation.

Paragraphs can also be marked, as this one is, by drop lines, but dropline paragraphs grow tiresome in long texts. They also increase the labor of revisions and corrections. ¶ Fleurons, boxes and bullets can be used to mark the breaks in a stream of continuous text, sometimes with excellent results. This format is more economical of

37

space than conventional indented paragraphs, but again, extra labor and expense may arise with emendations and corrections. Outdented paragraphs and indented paragraphs are the two most obvious possibilities that remain. And outdented paragraphs bring with them other possibilities, such as the use of enlarged marginal letters.

All these variants, and others, have their uses, but the plainest, most unmistakable yet unobtrusive way of marking paragraphs is the simple indent: a white square.

How much indent is enough? The minimum normal indent is one em. Another standard value is *one lead.* If your text is set 11/13, the indent would then be either 11 pt (one em) or 13 pt (one lead).

Where the line is long and margins are ample, an indent of 1½ or 2 ems may look more luxurious than one em, but paragraph indents larger than three ems are generally counterproductive. Short last lines followed by new lines with large indents produce a tattered page.

Block paragraphs open flush left and are separated vertically from their neighbors by extra lead, usually a white line. Block paragraphs are common in business letters and memos, and because they suggest precision, crispness and speed, they can be useful in short documents of other kinds. In long sequences, they may seem soulless and uninviting.

2.3.3   *Add extra lead before and after block quotations.*

Block quotations can be distinguished from the main text in many ways, for instance: by a change of face (usually from roman to italic); by a change in size (as from 11 pt down to 10 pt or 9 pt); or by indention.

Combinations of these methods are often used, but one device is enough. If your paragraph indent is modest, you may for consistency's sake want to use the same indent for quotations. And even if your block quotations are set in a size smaller than normal text, you may want to leave the leading unchanged. If the main text runs 10/12, the block quotations might run 10/12 italic or 9/12 roman. If you prefer greater density or are eager to save space, you might set them 9/11 or 9/10½.

However the block quotations are set, there must be a visible break between main text and quotation, and again between the quotation and subsequent text. This means a blank line or half-line at the beginning and end of the block. But if the leading of the block quotation differs from that of the main text, these blanks before and after the quotation must be elastic. They afford the only opportunity for bringing the text back into phase.

Suppose your main text is 11/13 and a five-line block quotation set 10/12 intervenes. The depth of the quotation is $5 \times 12 = 60$. This must be bulked up to a multiple of 13 to bring the text back into phase. The nearest multiple of 13 is $5 \times 13 = 65$. The remaining space is $65 - 60 = 5$, and $5/2 = 2.5$, which is not enough. Adding 2.5 points before and after the quotation will not give adequate separation. The next multiple of 13 is $6 \times 13 = 78$, which is better: $78 - 60 = 18$, and $18/2 = 9$. Add 9 pt lead before and after the quotation, and the text will realign.

2.3.4  *Indent or center verse quotations.*

Verse is usually set flush left and ragged right, and verse quotations within prose should not be deprived of their chosen form. But to distinguish verse quotations from surrounding prose, they should be indented or centered on the longest line. Centering is preferable when the prose measure is substantially longer than the verse line. The following passage, for example, is centered on the first and longest line.

> *God guard me from those thoughts men think*
> *In the mind alone;*
> *He that sings a lasting song*
> *Thinks in a marrow bone....*

William Butler Yeats, "A Prayer for Old Age."

Suppose your main text is set on a 24-pica measure and you have decided to set verse quotations in italic at the text size. Suppose that the longest line in your quotation measures 269 points. The indent for this quotation might be computed as follows: $24 \times 12 = 288$ pt, which is the full prose measure, and $288 - 269 = 19$ pt, which is the difference between the measure and the longest verse line. The theoretically perfect left indent for the verse quotation is $19/2 = 9.5$ pt – but if another indent close to 9.5 pt is already in use, either for block quotations in prose, or as a paragraph indent, the verse quotation might just as well be indented to match.

Suppose however that the longest line in the verse is 128

points. The measure, again, is 288 points. 288 – 128 = 160, and half of 160 is 80 points. No other indent in the vicinity of 80 points is likely to be in use. The verse quotation would then be indented by precisely that amount.

## 2.4 ETIQUETTE OF HYPHENATION & PAGINATION

The rules listed below are traditional craft practice for the setting of justified text. All are programmable, but the operation of these rules necessarily affects the spacing of words and thus the texture and color of the page. If decisions are left to the software, they should be checked by a trained eye – and no typesetting program should be permitted to compress, expand or letterspace the text arbitrarily as a means of fitting the copy. Copyfitting problems should be solved by creative design, not fobbed off on the reader and the text.

2.4.1 *At hyphenated line-ends, leave at least two characters behind and take at least three forward.*

Fi-nally is conventionally acceptable line-end hyphenation, but final-ly is not, because it leaves too little of the word on the second line.

2.4.2 *Avoid leaving the stub-end of a hyphenated word, or any word shorter than four letters, as the last line of a paragraph.*

2.4.3 *Avoid more than three consecutive hyphenated lines.*

2.4.4 *Hyphenate proper names only as a last resort unless they occur with the frequency of common nouns.*

2.4.5 *Hyphenate according to the conventions of the language.*

*Hart's Rules for*
*Compositors*
includes a good,
brief guide to
hyphenation and
punctuation rules
for the major
European
languages.

In English one hyphenates *cab-ri-o-let* but in French *ca-brio-let*. In German, when *Glockenspiel* is broken at the k it is spelled *Glok-kenspiel*. In Spanish the double consonants *ll* and *rr* are not divided. (Thus the only possible hyphenations in the phrase *arroz con pollo* are *a-rroz con po-llo* – and *a-rroz* is unacceptable because it leaves too little behind.) The conventions of the individual language should, ideally, be followed even for single foreign words or brief quotations.

40

2.4.6 *Link short numerical and mathematical expressions with hard spaces.*

Digital fonts include several invisible characters: the word space, fixed spaces of various sizes (em space, en space, thin space, figure space, etc) and a *hard space* or *no-break space*. The hard space will stretch, like a normal word space, when the line is justified, but it will not convert to a linebreak. Hard spaces are useful for preventing linebreaks within phrases such as *6.2 mm, 3 in., 4 × 4,* or in phrases like *page 3* and *Chapter 5.*

When it is necessary to break longer algebraic or numerical expressions, such as $a + b = c$, the break should come at the equal sign or another clear logical pause.

2.4.7 *Avoid beginning more than two consecutive lines with the same word.*

2.4.8 *Never begin a page with the last line of a multi-line paragraph.*

The typographic terminology is telling. Isolated lines created when paragraphs begin on the last line of a page are known as *orphans.* They have no past, but they do have a future, and they trouble few typographers. The stub-ends left when paragraphs end on the first line of a page are called *widows.* They have a past but not a future, and they look foreshortened and forlorn. It is the custom to give them at least one additional line for company. This rule is applied in close conjunction with the next.

2.4.9 *Balance facing pages by moving single lines.*

Pages with more than two columns often look best with the columns set to varying depths – the vertical equivalent of ragged-right composition. Where there are only one or two main text columns per page, paired columns and facing pages (except at the end of a chapter or section) are customarily set to a uniform depth.

Balance facing pages not by adding extra lead or puffing up the word space, but by exporting or importing single lines from the preceding or following spreads. The same technique is used to avoid widows, and to extend or shorten any chapters that would otherwise end with a meager few lines on the final page. But this balancing should be performed with a gentle hand. In the end, no spread of continuous text should have to run more than a single line short or a single line long.

2.4.10   *Avoid hyphenated breaks where the text is interrupted.*

Style books sometimes insist that both parts of a hyphenated word must occur on the same page: in other words, that the last line on a page must never end with a hyphen. But turning the page is not, in itself, an interruption of the reading process. It is far more important to avoid hyphenated breaks in those locations where the reader is likely to be distracted by other information. That is, whenever a map, a chart, a photograph, a pull-quote, a sidebar or other interruption intervenes.

2.4.11   *Abandon any and all rules of hyphenation and pagination that fail to serve the needs of the text.*

## 3.1  SIZE

### 3.1.1  *Don't compose without a scale.*

The simplest scale is a single note, and sticking with a single note draws more attention to other parameters, such as rhythm and inflection. The early Renaissance typographers set each book in a single font – one face in one size supplemented by hand-drawn or specially engraved large initial letters for the openings of chapters. Their pages show what sensuous evenness of texture and variety of rhythm can be attained with a single font of type: very much greater than on a typewriter, where letters have only one width and one stroke weight as well as one size.

In the sixteenth century, a series of common sizes developed among European typographers, and the series survived with little change and few additions for 400 years. In the early days, the sizes had names rather than numbers, but measured in points, the traditional series is this:

a a a a a a a a a a a a a a a a a
6 7 8 9 10 11 12 14 18 21 24 36 48 60 72

A few examples of the many older names for type sizes:

6 pt: *nonpareil*
7 pt: *minion*
8 pt: *brevier* or *small text*
9 pt: *bourgeois* or *galliard*
10 pt: *long primer* or *garamond*
11 pt: *small pica* or *philosophy*
12 pt: *pica*
14 pt: *english* or *augustin*
18 pt: *great primer*

This is the typographic equivalent of the diatonic scale. But modern equipment makes it possible to set, in addition to these sizes, all the sharps and flats and microtonal intervals between. Twenty-point, 22-point, 23-point, and 10½-point type are all available for the asking. The designer can now choose a new scale or tone-row for every piece of work.

These new resources are useful, but rarely all at once. Use the old familiar scale, or use new scales of your own devising, but limit yourself, at first, to a modest set of distinct and related intervals. Start with one size and work slowly from there. In time, the scales you choose, like the faces you choose, will become recognizable features of personal style.

3.2.1 *If the font includes both text figures and titling figures, use titling figures only with full caps, and text figures in all other circumstances.*

*Numerals,*
*Capitals*
*and*
*Small Caps*

The date is 23 August 1832, and it is 3:00 AM in Apartment 6-B, 213-A Beacon Street; it is 27° C or 81° F; the price is $47,000 US or £28,200. The postal codes are NL 1057 JV Amsterdam; SF 00170 Helsinki 17; Honolulu 96814; London WC1 2NN; New Delhi 110 003; Toronto M5S 1E6, and Dublin 2.

BUT IT IS 1832 AND 81° IN FULL CAPITALS.

Arabic numerals – known in Arabic as Indian numerals, *arqām hindiyya,* because the Arabs obtained them from India – entered the scribal tradition of Europe in the thirteenth century. Before that (and for many purposes afterward) European scribes used roman numerals, written in capitals when they occurred in the midst of other capitals, and in lowercase in the midst of normal text. Typographers have naturally inherited this custom of setting roman numerals so that they harmonize with the words:

Number xiii lowercase AND XIII UPPERCASE
AND THE NUMBER XIII IN SMALL CAPITALS

When arabic numerals joined the roman alphabet, they too were given both lowercase and uppercase forms. Typographers call the former *text figures, hanging figures,* or *old-style figures,* and make a point of using them whenever the surrounding text is set in lowercase letters or small caps. The alternative forms are called *titling figures, ranging figures* or *lining figures,* because they range or align with one another and with the upper case.

Text 1234567890 figures
TITLING 1234567890 FIGURES
FIGURES 1234567890 WITH SMALL CAPS
*Italic text 1234567890 figures*

Text figures were the common form in European typography between 1540 and 1800. But in the mid-eighteenth century, when European shopkeepers and merchants were apt to write more numbers than letters, handwritten numerals developed proportions of their own. These quite literally middleclass figures entered the realm of typography in 1788, when a British punchcutter named Richard Austin cut a font of three-quarter-height lining figures for the founder John Bell.

## *Bell* letters and 1234567890 figures in roman *and 1234567890 italic*

In the nineteenth century, which was not a great age for typography, founders stretched these figures up to cap height, and titling figures became the norm in commercial typography. Renaissance letterforms were revived in the early twentieth century, and text figures found their way back into books. But in news and advertising work, titling figures remained routine. In the 1960s, phototypesetting machines, with their severely limited fonts, once again made text figures difficult to find. The better digital foundries now offer a wide selection of fonts with text figures and small caps. These are often sold separately and involve extra expense, but they are essential to good typography. It is better to have one good face with all its parts, including text figures and small caps, than fifty faces without.

It is true that text figures are not useful in classified ads, but they are useful for setting almost everything else, including good magazine and newspaper copy. They are basic parts of typographical speech, and they are a sign of civilization: a sign that dollars are not really twice as important as ideas, and numbers are not afraid to consort on an equal footing with words.

3.2.2 *For abbreviations and acronyms in the midst of normal text, use spaced small caps.*

This is a good rule for just about everything except two-letter geographical acronyms and acronyms that stand for personal names. Thus: 3:00 AM, 3:00 PM, the ninth century AD, 450 BC to AD 450, the OAS and NATO; World War II or WWII; but JFK and Fr J.A.S. O'Brien, OMI; the HMS *Hypothesis* and the USS *Ticonderoga*; Washington, DC, and Mexico, DF; J.S. Bach's Prelude and Fugue in B♭ minor, BWV 867.

Some typographers prefer to use small caps for postal abbreviations (San Francisco, CA 94119), and for geographical acronyms longer than two letters. Thus, the USA, or in Spanish, *los EEUU*, and Sydney, NSW. But the need for consistency intervenes when long and short abbreviations fall together. From the viewpoint of the typographer, small caps are preferable in faces with fine features and small x-height, full caps in faces with large x-height and robust form.

Genuine small caps are not simply shrunken versions of the full caps. They differ from large caps in stroke weight, letterfit, and internal proportions as well as in height. Any good set of small caps is designed as such from the ground up. Thickening, shrinking and squashing the full caps with digital modification routines will only produce a parody.

Sloped small capitals – ABCDEFG – have been designed and cut for relatively few faces in the history of type design. They can be faked with digital machinery, by sloping the roman small caps, but it is better to choose a face (such as this one, Robert Slimbach's Minion) which includes them, or to live without. Sloped (italic) text figures, on the other hand, are part of the basic requirement and are included in most good text fonts.

### 3.2.3 *Refer typographical disputes to the higher courts of speech and thinking.*

Type is idealized writing, and its normal function is to record idealized speech. Acronyms such as CD and TV or USA and IBM are set in caps because that is the way we pronounce them. Acronyms like UNESCO, ASCII and FORTRAN, which are pronounced not as letters but as words, are in the process of becoming precisely that. When a writer accepts them fully into her speech and urges readers to do likewise, it is time for the typographer to accept them into the common speech of typography by setting them in lower case: Unesco, Ascii (or ascii) and Fortran. Other acronymic words, like *laser* and *radar,* have long since travelled the same road.

Logograms pose a more difficult question. An increasing number of persons and institutions, from e.e. cummings to WordPerfect, now come to the typographer in search of special treatment. In earlier days it was kings and deities whose agents demanded that their names be written in a larger size or set in a specially ornate typeface; now it is business firms and mass-market products demanding an extra helping of capitals, or a proprietary face, and poets pleading, by contrast, to be left entirely in the vernacular lower case. But type is visible speech, in which gods and men, saints and sinners, poets and business executives are treated fundamentally alike. Logotypes push typography in the direction of hieroglyphics, which tend to be looked at rather than read. They also push it toward the realm of candy and drugs, which tend to provoke dependent responses, and away from the realm of food, which tends to promote autonomous being. Good typography is like bread: ready to be admired, appraised and dissected before it is consumed.

## 3.3 LIGATURES

*3.3.1 Use the ligatures required by the font, and the characters required by the language, in which you are setting type.*

In most roman faces the letter f reaches into the space beyond it. In most italics, the *f* reaches into the space on both sides. Typographers call these overlaps *kerns*. Only a few kerns, like those in the arm of the f and tail of the j, are implicit in a normal typefont, while others, like the overlap in the combination *To*, are optional refinements, introduced after the fact.

Reaching into the space in front of it, the arm of the f will collide with certain letters – b, f, h, i, j, k, l – and also with question marks, quotation marks or parentheses, if these are placed in its way.

Most of the early European fonts were designed primarily for setting Latin, in which the sequences fb, fh, fj and fk do not occur, but the sequences fi, ﬀ, fl, ffi and ffl are frequent. The same set of ligatures was once sufficient for English, and these five ligatures are standard in traditional roman and italic fonts. As the craft of typography spread through Europe, new regional ligatures were added. An fj and æ were needed in Norway and Denmark for words like *fjeld* and *fjord* and *nær*. In France an œ, and in Germany an ß (*eszett* or double-s) were required, along with accented and umlauted vowels. Double letters which are read as one – *ll* in Spanish, *ij* in Dutch, and *ch* in German, for example – were cast as single sorts for regional markets. New individual letters were added, like the Polish ł, the Spanish ñ, and the Danish and Norwegian ø. Purely decorative ligatures were added to many fonts as well.

*æœ as ch ct ff ffi ffl fi fl fr*
*ij is ll q̃ st sch sh si sl sp ss ß ssi ssl st sz us*

ÆŒ æ œ ß    ff fi fl ffi ffl

ct st    sh si sl ssf st

*Above:* Ligatures from an italic font cut in the 1650s by Christoffel van Dijck. *Below:* ligatures from Adobe Caslon roman, by Carol Twombly, after William Caslon, about 1750. These are Baroque typefaces. As such, they include a set of ligatures with *f* and a second set formed with the long *s*. These ligatures were normal in European typography until late in the eighteenth century. (The first font of roman type to omit the long *s* was cut in London in 1789.)

English continues to absorb and create new words – *fjord, gaffhook, halfback, hors d'œuvre* – that call for ligatures beyond the Latin list. As an international language, English must also accommodate names like *Youngfox, al-Hajji* and *Asdzą́ą́ Yoɬgai.* These sometimes make demands on the roman alphabet which earlier designers didn't foresee. In the digital world, many of these compound characters and ligatures can, in effect, take care of themselves. There is no burning need for a specially crafted fb ligature or a prefabricated ą when the digital forms can be cleanly superimposed. Recent type designers, alive to these polylingual demands on the alphabet, have often simplified the problem further by designing faces in which no sequence of letters involves a collision.

These distinctions are occasionally crucial. In Turkish, *i* with a dot and *ı* without – or in capitals, İ and I – are two different letters. A typeface whose lowercase *f* disguises the difference between the two forms of *i* is therefore, for Turkish, an unacceptable design.

This does not do away with the question of the five Latin ligatures. Older typefaces – Bembo, Garamond, Caslon, Baskerville and other distinguished creations – are, thankfully, still with us, in metal and in digital revivals. Many new faces also perpetuate the spirit of these earlier designs. These faces are routinely supplied with the five basic ligatures because they require them. And for digital typographers, typesetting programs are available that will automatically insert them.

48

# ff fi fl ffi ffl
## ff fi fl ffi ffl

Bembo, set with ligatures (above) and without (below)

    The double-f ligatures are admittedly of greater importance when setting in metal than when setting in digital form, where letters are free to overlap. In a number of faces, only two of the old ligatures, fi and fl, are crucial for digital setting. And in some faces, only the fi ligature is actually required. But true fi and fl ligatures, like true small caps, are designed instead of concocted. A fake ligature assembled from *f* and the dotless *i* will rarely have the desired form.

# fi fi fi *fi fi fi*

Adobe Caslon, set with a ligature (left), a dotless i (center) and colliding letters (right)

    Serious typographers will want an fj ligature as well, when and if they encounter a word like *fjord* – and in this case, one must generally make do. In metal, it is simple enough to pare the dot off a j and kern it under the f. In the digital world, font editing programs make the same trick nearly as easy. But font editors also bring fully customized ligatures within range. A novelist who wants an orchestra conductor to say "De*ffff*ini- tively!" can be accommodated without grievous expense, and without any serious lapse in typographical quality or speed.

3.3.2  *If you wish to avoid ligatures altogether, restrict yourself to faces that don't require them.*

It is quite possible to avoid the use of ligatures completely and still set beautiful type. All that is required is a face with non-kerning roman and italic *f* – and some of the finest twentieth-century faces have been deliberately equipped with just this

49

feature. Aldus, Melior, Palatino, Sabon, Trajanus and Trump Mediäval, for example, all set handsomely without ligatures. Full or partial ligatures do exist for these faces, and the ligatures add a touch of refinement – but when the ligatures are omitted from these faces, no unsightly collisions or near-misses occur.

*Ligatures*

fi fi *fi fi* **fi fi** *fi fi*
*fi fi*

Ligatured and unligatured combinations in Sabon (upper left), Trump (upper right) and Aldus (below)

The choice is wider still among sanserifs. Ligatures are important to the design of Eric Gill's Gill Sans, but they are irrelevant to most other unserifed faces. (Dummy ligatures, consisting of separate letters, are nevertheless included on some fonts for the sake of convenience in running standardized typesetting programs.)

3.4 TRIBAL ALLIANCES & FAMILIES

3.4.1 *To the marriage of type and text, both parties bring their cultural presumptions, dreams and family obligations. Accept them.*

Each text, each manuscript (and naturally, each language) has its own requirements and expectations. Some types are more adaptable than others in meeting these demands. But typefaces too have their individual habits and presumptions. Many of them, for instance, are rich with historical and regional connections – a subject pursued at greater length in Chapter 7. For the moment, consider just the sociology of typefaces. What kinds of families and alliances do they form?

The union of uppercase and lowercase roman letters – in which the upper case has seniority but the lower case has the power – has held firm for twelve centuries. This constitutional monarchy of the alphabet is one of the most durable of European cultural institutions.

50

Ornamental initials, small caps and arabic figures were early additions to the roman union. Italics were a separate tribe at first, refusing to associate with roman lower case, but forming an alliance of their own with roman (not italic) capitals and small caps. Italic caps developed only in the sixteenth century. Roman, italic and small caps formed an enlarged tribal alliance at that time, and most text families continue to include them.

Bold and condensed faces became a fashion in the nineteenth century, partially displacing italics and small caps. Bold weights and sets of titling figures have been added retroactively to many earlier faces, though they lack any historical justification. Older text faces, converted from metal to digital form, are usually available in two fundamentally different versions. The better digital foundries supply authentic reconstructions; others supply the fonts without small caps, text figures and other essential components, but usually bearing the burden of an inauthentic bold.

Among recent text faces, two basic family structures are now common. The simplified model consists only of roman, italic and titling figures, in a range of weights – light, medium, bold and black, for example. The more elaborate family structure includes small caps and text figures, though these are sometimes present only in the lighter weights.

A family with all these elements forms a hierarchical series, based not on historical seniority but on general adaptability and frequency of use. And the series works the way it does not so much from force of custom as from the force of physiology. The monumentality of the capitals, the loudness of the bold face, the calligraphic flow and slope of italic, stand out effectively against a peaceful roman ground. Reverse the order and the text not only looks peculiar, it causes the reader physical strain.

Fonts in each of these categories are called into use, through a surprisingly complex grammar of editorial and typographic rules, by fonts in the category above. The typographer can intervene in this process at will, and alter it to any degree. But good type is good because it has natural strength and beauty. The best results come, as a rule, from finding the best type for the work and then guiding it with the gentlest possible hand.

The standard North American reference on the editorial tradition is *The Chicago Manual of Style*.

| | | | |
|---|---|---|---|
| | Primary: | roman lower case | 1.1 |
| | Secondary: | Roman Upper Case | 2.1 |
| | | ROMAN SMALL CAPS | 2.2 |
| | | roman text figures | 2.3 |
| | | *italic lower case* | 2.4 |
| *Tribal* | Tertiary: | *True Italic (Cursive) Upper Case* | 3.1 |
| *Alliances* | | *italic text figures* | 3.2 |
| *and* | | *SLOPED SMALL CAPS* | 3.3 |
| *Families* | | Roman Titling Figures | 3.4 |
| | | **bold lower case** | 3.5 |
| | Quaternary: | *False Italic (Sloped Roman) Upper Case* | 4.1 |
| | | **Bold Upper Case** | 4.2 |
| | | **BOLD SMALL CAPS** | 4.3 |
| | | **bold text figures** | 4.4 |
| | | ***bold italic lower case*** | 4.5 |
| | Quintary: | *Italic Titling Figures* | 5.1 |
| | | ***Bold Italic (Sloped Roman) Upper Case*** | 5.2 |
| | | ***bold italic text figures*** | 5.3 |
| | | **Bold Titling Figures** | 5.4 |
| | Sextary: | ***Bold Italic Titling Figures*** | 6.1 |

3.4.2 *Don't use a font you don't need.*

The marriage of type and text requires courtesy to the in-laws, but it does not mean that all of them ought to move in, nor even that all must come to visit.

Boldface roman type did not exist until the nineteenth century, and bold italic is even more recent. Generations of good typographers were quite content without such variations. Font manufacturers nevertheless now often sell these extra weights as part of a basic package, thereby encouraging typographers – beginners especially – to use bold roman and italic whether they need them or not.

Bold and semibold faces do have their value. They can be used, for instance, to flag items in a list; to set titles and sub-heads u&lc in small sizes; to mark the opening of the text on a complex page; to thicken the texture of lines that will be printed in pale ink or as dropouts (negative images) in a colored field. Sparingly used, they can effectively emphasize numbers or

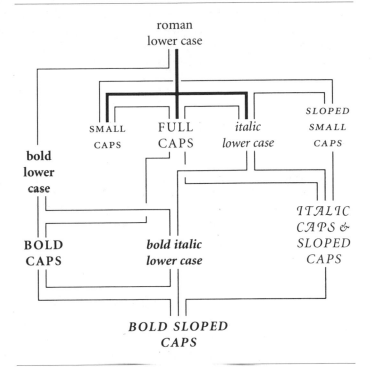

words, such as the headwords, keywords and definition numbers in a dictionary. They can also be used (as they often are) to
shout at readers, putting them on edge and driving them away;
or to destroy the historical integrity of a typeface designed
before boldface roman was born; or to create unintentional
anachronisms, something like adding a steam engine or a fax
machine to the stage set for *King Lear*.

3.4.3 *Use sloped romans sparingly and artificially sloped romans
more sparingly still.*

It is true that most romans are upright and most italics slope to
the right – but flow, not slope, is what really differentiates the
two. Italics have a more cursive structure than romans, which is
to say that italic is closer to longhand or continuous script.
Italic serifs are usually *transitive;* they are direct entry and exit
strokes, depicting the pen's arrival from the previous letter and
its departure for the next. Roman serifs, by contrast, are gener-

53

ally *reflexive:* they show the pen doubling back onto itself, emphasizing the end of the stroke. Italic serifs also tend to slope at a natural writing angle, tracing the path from one letter to another. Roman serifs, especially at the baseline, tend to be level, tying the letters not to each other but to an invisible common line.

e *e* l *l* m *m* u *u*

Baskerville roman and italic. Baskerville has less calligraphic flow than most earlier typefaces, but the italic serifs are, like their predecessors, transitive and oblique, showing the path of the pen from letter to letter. The roman serifs are reflexive and level, tying letters to a common line.

Some italics are more cursive than others; so are some romans. But any given italic is routinely more cursive than the roman with which it is paired.

Early italic fonts had only modest slope and were designed to be used with upright roman capitals. There are some beautiful fifteenth-century manuscript italics with no slope whatsoever, and some excellent typographic versions, old and new, that slope as little as 2° or 3°. Yet others slope as much as 20°.

Italic and roman lived quite separate lives until the middle of the sixteenth century. Before that date, books were set in either roman *or* italic, but not in both. In the late Renaissance, typographers began to use the two for different features in the same book. Typically, roman was used for the main text and italic for the preface, headnotes, sidenotes and for verse or block quotations. The custom of combining italic and roman *in the same line,* using italic to emphasize individual words and mark classes of information, developed late in the sixteenth century and flowered in the seventeenth. Baroque typographers liked the extra activity this mixing of fonts gave to the page, and the convention proved so useful that no subsequent change of taste has ever driven it entirely away. Modulation between roman and italic is now a basic and routine typographical technique, much the same as modulation in music between major and minor keys. (The system of linked major and minor keys in music is, of course, also a Baroque invention.)

Since the seventeenth century, many attempts have been made to curb the cursive, fluid nature of italic and to refashion it on the roman model. Many so-called italics designed in the last two hundred years are actually not italics at all, but sloped romans. And many are hybrids between the two.

₁ adefmpru *adefmpru*

₂ adefmpru *adefmpru*

₃ adefmpru *adefmpru*

₄ adefmpru *adefmpru*

₅ adefmpru *adefmpru*

**1** Adrian Frutiger's Méridien roman and italic; **2** Lucida Sans roman and italic, by Kris Holmes & Charles Bigelow; **3** Perpetua roman and its italic, which is a hybridized sloped roman, by Eric Gill; **4** Univers roman and oblique (a pure sloped roman), by Adrian Frutiger; **5** Romulus roman and oblique (again a pure sloped roman), designed by Jan van Krimpen.

As lowercase italic letterforms mutated toward sloped roman, their proportions changed as well. Most italics (though not all) are 5% to 10% narrower than their roman counterparts. But most sloped romans (unless designed by Eric Gill) are as wide or wider than their upright roman companions.

Renaissance italics were designed for continuous reading, and modern italics based on similar principles tend to have similar virtues. Baroque and Neoclassical italics were designed to serve as secondary faces only, and are best left in that role. Sloped romans, as a general rule, are even more devotedly subsidiary faces. Their slope makes sense only as a temporary perturbation of the upright roman.

Typesetting software is capable of distorting letters in many different ways: condensing, expanding, outlining, shadowing, sloping, and so on. If the only difference between a roman and its companion font were slope, the roman font alone would be enough for the computer. Sloped versions could be generated at will. But italic is not sloped roman, and even a good sloped roman is more than simply roman with a slope.

Direct electronic sloping of letterforms changes the weight of vertical and sloped strokes, while the weight of the horizontal strokes remains the same. Strokes that run northwest-southeast in the parent form – like the right leg of the A or the upper right and lower left corners of the O – are rotated toward the vertical when the letter is given a slope. Rotation toward the vertical causes these strokes to thicken. But strokes running northeast-southwest, like the left leg of the A, and the other corners of the O, are rotated farther away from the vertical. Rotation away from the vertical thins them down. Stroke curvature is altered in this translation process as well. The natural inclinations of a calligrapher drawing a sloped roman are likely to differ from what is convenient for the machine.

More sophisticated character-design and character-editing programs (such as the Ikarus and Metafont systems widely used by type designers themselves) are considerably more responsive to artistic demands – and the more sophisticated they become, the more closely they mimic those primitive and subtle instruments that lie at the root of all typography: the stick, the brush, the chisel and the broad-nib pen.

Even 'italic' capitals – which nowadays are rarely anything other than sloped roman – require individual shaping and editing to reach a durable form.

# A A A O O O

Caslon roman, the same roman sloped electronically, and the 'italic' capitals as drawn. The latter have a slope of 20°.

# a a a o o o

Palatino roman, the same roman sloped electronically, and the true italic, whose average slope is 9°.

# A C E M R S T Y

True italic capitals: the swash forms from Robert Slimbach's Minion italic. It is the structure, not the slope, of the letters that marks them as italic.

Once in a while, nevertheless, a typographer will pine for a sloped version of a font such as Haas Clarendon or André Gürtler's Egyptian 505, for which no italic, nor even a sloped roman, has been drawn. On such occasions, a computer-generated sloped roman will often suffice as a temporary solution. But the slope should be modest (perhaps 10° maximum), because less slope yields less distortion.

*Harmony and Counterpoint*

3.4.4 *If you wish to avoid text figures and small caps, choose faces actually designed to be without them.*

Orphaned text fonts, sold without the small caps and text fig ures they were originally designed to have, are the typographic equivalent of fast food, perhaps suitable for emergencies but never for a steady diet.

There are better alternatives. Most unserifed faces, and in recent years, many fine serifed faces as well, have been designed without small caps and text figures. All of them are faces with large x-height, minimizing the size differential between lower and upper case. Hermann Zapf's Optima, Gerard Unger's Hollander and Swift, Adrian Frutiger's Méridien, and Gudrun Zapf-von Hesse's Carmina are all faces designed to function well without small caps and text figures. Another example is Hans Eduard Meier's Syntax, the font used for captions in this book. The options are further explored in Chapter 10.

3.5 CONTRAST

3.5.1 *Change one parameter at a time.*

When your text is set in a 12 pt medium roman, it should not be necessary to set the heads or titles in 24 pt bold italic capitals. If boldface appeals to you, begin by trying the bold weight of the text face, u&lc, *in the text size.* As alternatives, try u&lc italic, or letterspaced small caps, or letterspaced full caps in the text weight and size. If you want a larger size, experiment first with a larger size of the text face, u&lc in the text weight. For a balanced page, the weight should *decrease* slightly, not increase, as the size increases.

### 3.5.2 *Don't clutter the foreground.*

When boldface is used to emphasize words, it is usually best to leave the punctuation in the background, which is to say, in the basic text font. It is the words, not the punctuation, that merit emphasis in a sequence such as the following:

*Contrast*

> ... on the islands of **Lombok, Bali, Flores,**
> **Timor** and **Sulawesi,** the same textiles ...

But if the same names are emphasized by setting them in italic rather than bold, there is no advantage in leaving the punctuation in roman. With italic text, italic punctuation normally gives better letterfit and thus looks less obtrusive:

> ... on the islands of *Lombok, Bali, Flores,*
> *Timor* and *Sulawesi,* the same textiles ...

If spaced small caps are used for emphasis – changing the stature and form of the letters instead of their weight or slope, and thereby minimizing the surface disturbance on the page – the question of punctuation does not arise. The punctuation used with small caps is (except for question and exclamation marks) the same as roman punctuation; it is only necessary to check it for accurate spacing:

> ... on the islands of LOMBOK, BALI, FLORES,
> TIMOR and SULAWESI, the same textiles ...

## 4.1 OPENINGS

4.1.1 *Make the title page a symbol of the dignity and presence of the text.*

If the text has immense reserve and dignity, the title page should have these properties as well – and if the text is devoid of dignity, the title page should in honesty be the same.

Think of the blank page as alpine meadow, or as the purity of undifferentiated being. The typographer enters this space and must change it. The reader will enter it later, to see what the typographer has done. The underlying truth of the blank page must be infringed, but it must never altogether disappear – and whatever displaces it might well aim to be as lively and peaceful as it is. It is not enough, when building a title page, merely to unload some big, prefabricated letters into the center of the space, nor to dig a few holes in the silence with typographic heavy machinery and then move on. Big type, even huge type, can be beautiful and useful. But poise is usually far more important than size – and poise consists primarily of emptiness. Typographically, poise is made of white space. Many fine title pages consist of a modest line or two near the top, and a line or two near the bottom, with little or nothing more than taut, balanced white space in between.

4.1.2 *Don't permit the titles to oppress the text.*

In books, spaced capitals of the text size and weight are often perfectly adequate for titles. At the other extreme, there is a fine magazine design by Bradbury Thompson, in which the title, the single word *boom,* is set in gigantic bold condensed caps that fill the entire two-page spread. The text is set in a tall narrow column *inside the stem* of the big B. The title has swallowed the text – yet the text has been reborn, alive and talkative, like Jonah from the whale.

For reproductions of this and other examples of Thompson's work, see Philip B. Meggs, *A History of Graphic Design,* p 405.

Most unsuccessful attempts at titling fall between these two extremes, and their problem is often that the title throws its weight around, unbalancing and discoloring the page. If the title is set in a larger size than the text, it is often best to set it u&lc in a light titling font or a lightened version of the text font. Inline capitals (like the Castellar initial on p 62) are another device that typographers have used since the fifteenth century to get large size without excessive weight.

*Openings*

  There are other ways of creating large letters of light weight, but some only arise at the film-making and printing stage. The designer can, for instance, *screen* the type (that is, to break up the solid image with an optical filter) or instruct the printer to print it in a second ink of a paler color.

## 10 20 30 40 50

## 60 70 80 90 100

Screened text. The numbers indicate the percentage of ink coverage permitted by the screen.

4.1.3 *Set titles and openings in a form that contributes to the overall design.*

Renaissance books, with their long titles and ample margins, generally left no extra space at the heads of chapters. In modern books, where the titles are shorter and the margins have been eaten by inflationary pressure, a third of a page sometimes lies vacant just to celebrate the fact that the chapter begins. But space alone is not enough to achieve the sense of richness and celebration, nor is absence of space necessarily a sign of typographic poverty.

  Narrow row houses flush with the street are found not only in urban slums but in the loveliest of the old Italian hill towns and Mediterranean villages. A page full of letters presents the same possibilities. It can lapse into a typographical slum, or grow into a model of architectural grace, skilled engineering and simple economy. Broad suburban lawns and wide typographical front yards can also be uninspiringly empty or welcoming and graceful. They can display real treasure, including the treasure of empty space, or they can be filled with souvenirs of wishful thinking. Neoclassical birdbaths, effigies of liveried

slaves or stable boys, and faded pink flamingoes all have counterparts in the typographical world.

4.1.4  *Mark each beginning and resumption of the text.*

The simplest way of beginning any block of prose is to start
from the margin, flush left, as this paragraph does. On a peaceful page, where the text is announced by a head or subhead, this
is enough. But if the text, or a new section of text, begins at the
top of a page with no heading to mark it, a little fanfare will
probably be required. The same is true if the opening page is
busy. If there is a chapter title, an epigraph, a sidenote, and a
photograph and caption, the opening of the text will need a
banner, a ten-gallon hat or a bright red dress to draw the eye.

*Fleurons* (typographical ornaments) are often used to flag
text openings, and are often printed in red, the typographer's
habitual second color. The opening phrase, or entire first line,
can also be set in small caps or in bold u&lc. But the most
traditional method of marking the start of the text, inherited
from ancient scribal practice, is a large initial capital or *versal.*
Versals can be treated in many ways. Indented or centered, they
can stick up from the text. Flush left, they can be nested into the
text (typographers call these *drop caps,* as opposed to *elevated* or
*stick-up caps*). Or they can hang in the left margin. They can be
set in the same face as the text or in something outlandishly
different. In scribal and typographic tradition alike, where the
budget permits, versals too are generally red or another color in
preference to black.

Elevated caps are easier to set well from a keyboard, but
drop caps have closer links with the scribal and letterpress tradition. And the tooling and fitting of drop caps is something
typographers do for fun, to test their skill and visual intuition.
It is common practice to set the first word or phrase after the
versal in caps, small caps or boldface, as a bridge between versal
and normal text. Examples are shown on the following page.

In English, if the initial letter is A, I or O, a question can
arise: is the initial letter itself a word? The answer to this question must come in the spacing of the text in relation to the
versal. If the first word of the text is *Ahead,* for example, excessive space betwen the initial A and the rest of the word is bound
to cause confusion.

OSCULETUR me osculo oris sui; quia meliora sunt ubera tua vino, ¶ fragantia unguentis optimis. Oleum effusum nomen tuum; ideo adolescentulae dilexerunt te.

TRAHE ME, post te curremus in odorem unguentorum tuorum. Introduxit me rex in cellaria sua; exsultabimus et laetabimur in te, memores uberum tuorum super vinum. Recti diligunt te.

«

NIGRA SUM, sed formosa, filiae Ierusalem, sicut tabernacula Cedar, sicut pelles Salomonis. Nolite me considerare quod fusca sim, quia decoloravit me sol. Filii matris meae pugnaverunt contra me.... »

"ADIURO VOS, filiae Ierusalem, per capreas cervosque camporum, ne suscitetis, neque evigilare faciatis

dilectam, quoadusque ipsa velit."

VOX DILECTI MEI; ecce iste venit, saliens in montibus, transiliens colles. ¶ Similis est dilectus meus capreae, hinnuloque cervorum. En ipse stat post parietem nostrum, respiciens per fenestras, prospiciens per cancellos. En dilectus meus loquitur mihi.

SURGE, propera, amica mea, columba mea, formosa mea, et veni. ¶ Iam enim hiems transiit; imber abiit, et recessit. ¶ Flores apparuerunt in terra nostra....

LAVI PEDES MEOS, quomodo inquinabo illos? ¶ Dilectus meus misit manum suam per foramen, et venter meus intremuit ad tactum eius. ¶ Surrexit ut aperirem dilecto meo; manus meae stillaverunt myrrham, et digiti mei pleni myrrha probatissima. Pessulum ostii mei....

Passages from the Song of Songs, set in Aldus 10/12 × 10 RR. Elevated cap: Castellar 54 pt. Drop caps: Aldus 42 pt, mortised line by line.

4.1.5 *If the text begins with a quotation, include the initial quotation mark.*

It is an old typographic custom to omit the initial quotation mark in any text beginning with a versal. This habit saved the compositor the labor of mortising a quotation mark into the margin, and it saved the designer the trouble of deciding just how large the initial quotation mark should be and exactly where it should be located. For the reader, however, this old habit can only cause confusion. Digital typography makes it simple to control the exact size and position of the opening quotation mark. Since it is possible to make the mark look good, there is no reason to hide it from the reader.

## 4.2  HEADINGS & SUBHEADS

4.2.1  *Set headings in a form that contributes to the style of the whole.*

Headings can take many forms, but one of the first choices to make is whether they will be symmetrical or asymmetrical. Symmetrical heads, which are centered on the measure, are known to typographers as *crossheads.* Asymmetrical heads usually take the form of *left sideheads,* which is to say they are set flush left, or modestly indented or outdented from the left. *Right sideheads* work well in certain contexts, but more often as main heads than as subheads. A short, one-line head set flush right needs substantial size or weight to prevent the reader from missing it altogether.

One way to make heads prominent without making them large is to set them entirely in the margin, like the running heads in this book.

4.2.2  *Use as many levels of headings as you need: no more and no fewer.*

As a rule it is best to choose a predominantly symmetrical or asymmetrical form for subheads. Mixing the two haphazardly leads to stylistic as well as logical confusion. But the number of levels available can be slightly increased, if necessary, by judicious combinations. If symmetrical heads are added to a basically asymmetrical series, or vice versa, it is usually better to put the visiting foreigners at the top or bottom of the hierarchical pile. Two six-level series of subheads are shown, by way of example, on the following pages.

In marking copy for typesetting, the various levels of subheads are generally given letters rather than names: A-heads, B-heads, C-heads, and so on. Using this terminology, the heads on the following pages run from A through F.

# ❧ Main Section Title ❧

I F A MAN walk in the woods for love of them half of each day, he is in danger of being regarded as a loafer; but if he spends his whole day as a speculator, shearing off those woods and making earth bald before her time, he is esteemed an industrious and enterprising citizen.

## MAIN CROSSHEAD

The ways by which you may get money almost without exception lead downward. To have done anything by which you earned money *merely* is to have been truly idle or worse.... If you would get money as a writer or lecturer, you must be popular, which is to go down perpendicularly....

### Heavy Crosshead

In proportion as our inward life fails, we go more constantly and desperately to the post office. You may depend on it, that the poor fellow who walks away with the greatest number of letters ... has not heard from himself this long while.

#### MEDIUM CROSSHEAD

I do not know but it is too much to read one newspaper a week. I have tried it recently, and for so long it seems to me that I have not dwelt in my native region. The sun, the clouds, the snow, the trees say not so much to me....

##### *Light Crosshead*

You cannot serve two masters. It requires more than a day's devotion to know and to possess the wealth of a day.... Really to see the sun rise or go down every day, so to relate ourselves to a universal fact, would preserve us sane forever.

*hypethral:*
*from Greek*
ἐν ὑπαίθρωι,
*"in the open air"*

RUN-IN SIDEHEAD Shall the mind be a public arena...? Or shall it be a quarter of heaven itself, an hypethral temple, consecrated to the service of the gods?

# Main Section
# *Title*

❀ IF I AM TO BE a thoroughfare, I prefer that it be of the mountain brooks, the Parnassian streams, and not the town sewers.... I believe that the mind can be permanently profaned by attending to trivial things, so that all our thoughts shall be tinged with triviality.

*Structural Forms and Devices*

The texts on this and the facing page are excerpts from HENRY DAVID THOREAU'S "Life Without Principle," *c.* 1854, first published in 1863. The type on the facing page is Adobe Caslon 10/12 × 21, and on this page, Monotype Centaur & *Arrighi* 11/12 × 21.

## MAIN CROSSHEAD

Our very intellect shall be macadamized, as it were: its foundation broken into fragments for the wheels of travel to roll over; and if you would know what will make the most durable pavement, surpassing rolled stones, spruce blocks, and asphaltum, you have only to look into some of our minds....

### ❦ ORNAMENTED CROSSHEAD ❦

Read not the Times. Read the Eternities.... Even the facts of science may dust the mind by their dryness, unless they are in a sense effaced each morning, or rather rendered fertile by the dews of fresh and living truth.

### MEDIUM SIDEHEAD

Knowledge does not come to us by details, but in flashes of light from heaven. Yes, every thought that passes through the mind helps to wear and tear it, and to deepen the ruts, which, as in the streets of Pompeii, evince how much it has been used.

### *Light Sidehead*

When we want culture more than potatoes, and illumination more than sugar-plums, then the great resources of a world are taxed and drawn out, and the result, or staple production, is not slaves, nor operatives, but ... saints, poets, philosophers....

*Run-in Sidehead*   In short, as a snowdrift is formed where there is a lull in the wind, so, one would say, where there is a lull of truth, an *institution* springs up....

65

### 4.3.1 *If the text includes notes, choose the optimum form.*

If notes are used for subordinate details, it is right that they be set in a smaller size than the main text. But the academic habit of relegating notes to the foot of the page or the end of the book is a mirror of Victorian social and domestic practice, in which the kitchen was kept out of sight and the servants were kept below stairs. If the notes are permitted to move around in the margins – as they were in Renaissance books – they can be present where needed and at the same time enrich the life of the page.

*Notes*

Footnotes are the very emblem of fussiness, but they have their uses. If they are short and infrequent, they can be made economical of space, easy to find when wanted and, when not wanted, easy to ignore. Long footnotes are inevitably a distraction: tedious to read and wearying to look at. Footnotes that extend to a second page (as some long footnotes are bound to do) are an abject failure of design.

Endnotes can be just as economical of space, less trouble to design and therefore less expensive to set, and they can comfortably run to any length. They also leave the text page clean except for a peppering of superscripts. They do, however, require the serious reader to use two bookmarks and to read with both hands as well as both eyes, swapping back and forth between the popular and the persnickety parts of the text.

Sidenotes give more life and variety to the page and are the easiest of all to find and read. If carefully designed, they need not enlarge either the page or the cost of printing it.

Footnotes rarely need to be larger than 8 or 9 pt. Endnotes are typically set in small text sizes: 9 or 10 pt. Sidenotes can be set in anything up to the same size as the main text, depending on their frequency and importance, and on the overall format of the page.

### 4.3.2 *Check the weight and spacing of superscripts.*

If they are not too frequent, sidenotes can be set with no superscripts at all (as in this book), or with the same symbol (normally an asterisk) constantly reused, even when several notes appear on a single page. For endnotes, superscript numbers are standard. For footnotes, symbols can be used if the notes are few. (The traditional order is * † ‡ § ‖ ¶. But beyond the asterisk, dagger and double dagger, this order is not familiar to most readers, and never was.) Numbers are more transparent, and their order is much less easy to confuse.

Many fonts include sets of superscript numbers, but these are not always of satisfactory size and design. Text numerals set at a reduced size and elevated baseline are sometimes the best or only choice. Establishing the best size, weight and spacing for superscripts will, however, require some care. In many faces, smaller numbers in semibold look better than larger numbers of regular weight. And the smaller the superscripts are, the more likely they are to need increased character space.

Superscripts frequently come at the ends of phrases or sentences. If they are high above the line, they can be kerned over a comma or period, but this may endanger readability, especially if the text is set in a modest size.

4.3.3 *Use superscripts in the text but full-size numbers in the notes themselves.*

In the main text, superscript numbers are used to indicate notes because superscript numbers minimize interruption. They are typographical asides: small because that is an expression of their relative importance, and raised for two reasons: to keep them out of the flow of the main text, and to make them easier to find. In the note itself, the number is not an aside but a target. Therefore the number in the note should be full size.[1]

To make them easy to find, the numbers of footnotes or endnotes can be hung to the left (like the numbers 1–6 on the following two pages, and the footnote number below). Punctuation, apart from some empty space, is not normally needed between the number and text of the note.

4.3.4 *Avoid ambiguity in the numbering and placement of end-notes.*

Readers should never be forced to hunt for the endnotes. As a rule, this means the endnotes should not appear in small

---

1  This footnote is flagged by a superscript in the text, but the note itself is introduced by an outdented figure of the same size used for the text of the note. The main text on this page is set 10/12 × 21, and the note is 8/9.

clumps at the end of each chapter. It is better to place them together at the end of the book. Wherever possible, they should also be numbered sequentially from the beginning to end of the book, and the notes themselves should be designed so the numbers are readily visible. If the notes are numbered anew for each section or chapter or essay, running heads will be needed along with the notes to point the way. If the running heads accompanying the notes say, for instance, "Notes to pages 44–62," readers will know their way. But if the running heads say something like "Notes to Chapter 5," then Chapter 5 must be identified as such by running heads of its own.

*Notes*

## 4.4 TABLES & LISTS

*4.4.1 Edit tables with the same attention given to text, and set them as text to be read.*

For graphic alternatives to typographic tables, see Edward R. Tufte, *The Visual Display of Quantitative Information* and *Envisioning Information.*

Tables are notoriously time-consuming to typeset, but the problems posed are often editorial as much as typographic. If the table is not planned in a readable form to begin with, the typographer can render it readable only by redesigning it from scratch.

Tables, like text, go awry when approached on a purely technical basis. Good typographical answers are not elicited by asking questions such as "How can I cram this number of characters into that amount of space?"

If the table is approached as merely one more form of text, which must be made both good to read and good to look at, several principles will be clear:

1  All text should be horizontal, or in rare cases oblique. Setting column heads vertically as a space-saving measure is quite feasible if the text is in Japanese or Chinese, but not if it is written in the roman alphabet.

2  Letterforms too small or too condensed for comfortable reading are not part of the solution.

3  There should be a minimum amount of furniture (rules, boxes, dots and other guiderails for travelling through typographic space) and a maximum amount of information.

4  Rules, tint blocks or other guides and dividers, where they are necessary at all, should run in the predominant reading direction: vertically in the case of lists, indices and some numerical tables, and horizontally otherwise.

5  A rule located at the edge of a table, separating the first or final line or row from the adjacent empty space, ordinarily serves no function.

6  A table, like any other text in multiple columns, must contain within itself an adequate amount of white space.

### 4.4.2 *Avoid overpunctuating lists.*

A list is an inherently spatial and numerical arrangement. Speakers reciting lists often enumerate on their fingers, and lists set in type often call for equivalent typographical gestures. This means that the list should be clarified as much as possible through spatial *positioning* and *pointing,* usually done with bullets, dashes or numerals. (Examples occur throughout this book.) If the numbers are made visible either through position (e.g., by hanging them in the margin) or through prominence (e.g., by setting them in a contrasting face), additional punctuation – extra periods, parentheses or the like – should rarely be required.

Dot leaders (lines of dots leading the eye from one word or number to another) are rarely beneficial in tables.

### 4.4.3 *Set lists and columns of figures to align flush right or on the decimal.*

The numerals in most fonts are all of equal width, though there is often an alternative, narrower form of the numeral one. This *fitted one* is generally used when setting figures in the midst of text, while the *unfitted one* (of standard numeral width) is often used when setting figures in columns. Most fonts also include a *figure space* – a fixed blank space corresponding to the width of a standard, unkerned numeral. This makes it a simple matter to compose lists and columns of figures in rigorous mechanical alignment.

If you alter the set-widths of numerals, kern numeral combinations, or use the fitted one when setting columns or lists, the individual digits will not align, but *columns* of figures can still be aligned. For much tabular matter (as for the first table on the following page) this is sufficient. If notes are required in a table with flush-right columns, the superscripts should be hung to the right (as in column 3, line 2 of the example overleaf) so they will not disrupt the alignment.

| | | | |
|---|---|---|---|
| 8 | 98 | 998 | 9.75 |
| 9 | 99 | 999* | 10 |
| 10 | 100 | 1000 | 10.25 |
| 11 | 101 | 1001 | 10.5 |

4.4.4 *For text and other matter, choose harmonious and legible tabular alignments.*

Simple tables and lists of paired items, such as the sample lists of contents on page 34, are often best aligned against each other, the left column flush right and the right column flush left. Financial statements and other numerical tables usually follow the opposite pattern: a column of words, on the left, is aligned flush left, and the subsequent columns of numbers align flush right or on the decimal.

Any repeating character – a dimension sign or equal sign, for instance – is potentially of use in tabular alignment. But many columns with many different alignments can generate overall visual chaos. Occasionally it is better, in such cases, to set all columns or most columns either flush right or flush left, for the sake of general clarity.

| | | | | |
|---|---|---|---|---|
| *Aster* | 2 : 3 | 24 × 36 | 0.667 | $a = 2b$ |
| *Valerian* | 271 : 20 | 813 × 60 | 13.550 | $6a = c$ |

Columns in multiple alignment

## 4.5 FRONT & BACK MATTER

4.5.1 *Leave adequate space at the beginning and end of every publication.*

A brief research paper may look its best with no more space at beginning and end than is provided by the standard page margins. The same is rarely true of a book, whose text should generally be, and should seem to be, a living and breathing entity, not aged and shrink-wrapped meat. A short, staple-bound booklet can begin directly with the title page. Otherwise, a half-title is customary, preceding the title page. It is equally customary to leave a blank leaf, or at least a blank page, at the end of a book. These blanks provide a place for inscriptions and notes and allow the text to relax in its binding.

### 4.5.2 *Give adequate space to the prelims.*

A text preceded by an interminable chain of forewords, prefaces, introductions and prologues is unlikely to be read. But a dedication stuffed onto the copyright page is no dedication at all. And a list of contents which is incomplete (or missing altogether), and which does not have the page to itself, is a sign of typographic desperation and disregard for the reader.

### 4.5.3 *Balance the front and back matter.*

Books are normally built up from *gatherings* or *signatures* – printed and folded sheets – with each signature forming a unit of 8, 12, 16, 24 or 32 pages. The 16-page signature is by far the most common. Typographers therefore work to make most of their books seem divinely ordained and conceived to be some multiple of 16 pages in length. Seasoned book typographers recite in their meditations not only the mantra of points and picas – 12, 24, 36, 48, 60, 72... – but also the mantra of octavo signatures: 16, 32, 48, 64, 80, 96, 128, 144, 160, 176, 192, 208, 224, 240, 256, 272, 288, 304, 320, 336, 352, 368, 384, 400....

In a work of continuous prose, the illusion of divine love for the number sixteen is obtained by straightforward copyfitting. If the length of the text is accurately measured, the page can be designed to yield a book of appropriate length. More complicated books are often surrounded by paraphernalia – not only the standard half-title, title page, copyright page, dedication page and some blanks, but also perhaps a detailed table of contents, a list of charts, illustrations and maps, a table of abbreviations, a page or two of acknowledgements, and a preface, counterbalanced by appendices, endnotes, bibliography, index and a colophon. Copyfitting the main text for a volume of this kind may be highly complex, and room may be taken up or conserved in the large aura of front and back matter. But for complex books and simple books alike, it is up to the typographer to balance the front matter, back matter and text. A wad of blank leaves at the end of a book is a sign of carelessness, not of kindliness toward readers who like to take notes.

ABCDEFGHIKL

MNOPQ RSTV

XYZabcdefghil

mnopqrsſtuvxyz

1234567890,. ʼ!?;:-⁹ ᷉

Æ æ ɹ ff fi fl œ ſſ ſi ſt ſl ℞

&ãáàâçééèêëẹ̃ĩíìîïị̃p

*Iuris præcepta ſunt hæc, Honeſté viuere, alterum
non lædere, ſuum cuíq̃; tribuere. Huius ſtudij duæ
ſunt poſitiones, Publicum & priuatum. Publicum
ius eſt, quod ad ſtatum rei Romanæ ſpectat. Priua
tum, quod ad ſingulorum vtilitatem pertinet.
Dicendum eſt igitur de iure priuato, quòd triperti-
tum eſt: collectum eſt enim ex naturalibus præcep-
tis, aut g̃etium aut ciuilibus. Ius naturale eſt quòd*

A roman titling font (cut *c.* 1520, revised *c.* 1550) and a large italic text
font (*c.* 1539). Both were cut by Claude Garamond, Paris. The italic is
shown actual size and the roman reduced by about one fifth. Matrices for
the roman font survive at the Plantin-Moretus Museum, Antwerp.

72

# ANALPHABETIC SYMBOLS

---

## 5.1 ANALPHABETIC STYLE

It falls to the typographer to deal with an increasing herd of flicks, squiggles, dashes, dots and ideographs that travel with the alphabet yet never quite belong. The most essential of these marks – period, comma, parenthesis, and the like – are signs of logical pause and intonation, much like the slurs and rests in a musical score. Some, like the dollar and per cent signs, are stylized abbreviations. Others, like the asterisk and the dagger, are silent typographical cross-references. And a few that are normally unspoken have tried to sneak their way into the oral tradition. Speakers who say *quote unquote* or *who slash what* or *That's it, period!* are, of course, proving their debt to these para-literary signs.

Approached through the scribal and typographic tradition, the palette of analphabetic symbols is much more supple and expressive than it appears through the narrow grill of the typewriter keyboard. A typographer will not necessarily use more analphabetic symbols per page than a typist. In fact, many good typographers use fewer. But even the most laconic typographer learns to speak this sign language with an eloquence that conventional word processors and typewriters preclude.

### 5.1.1 *To invoke the inscriptional tradition, use the midpoint.*

The earliest alphabetic inscriptions have no analphabetic furniture at all, not even spaces between the words. As writing spread through Greece and Italy, spaces appeared between the words, and a further sign was added: the centered dot, for marking phrases or abbreviations. That dot, the *midpoint* or small bullet, remains one of the simplest, most effective forms of typographic punctuation – useful today in lists and letterheads and signage just as it was on engraved marble twenty centuries ago.

Suite 6 · 325 Central Park South

Roman calligraphers lettered their inscriptions with a flat brush held in the right hand. The flat brush – thick in one direction, thin in the other, like a broad-nib pen – produces a *modulated* stroke. That is to say, the weight of the stroke varies predictably with direction. The letter O is an example. Because the brush is held in the scribe's right hand, the strokes are thickest in the northwest/southeast direction, at the natural inclination of the forearm and the hand. Using the same brush, Roman calligraphers also developed the subtle choreography of twists and turns at the stroke-ends that produces the imperial Roman serif. Roman capital letters have retained these forms for 2000 years.

In Asian and European scripts alike, modulated strokes are usually serifed and unmodulated strokes are usually not. Transitive brush serifs are evident in the *mincho* typeface above, designed by Takaichi Hori. The same *kanji* and *kana* are shown below in an unserifed face designed by Yasubumi Miyake. *Mincho katsuji* or 'Ming Dynasty script' is, roughly, the Japanese counterpart of serifed roman – but its serif structure is more cursive, like that of italic.

# O · I · M

When the centered dot or midpoint is made in the same way with the same tool, it becomes a small, curved wedge: a clockwise twist of the brush, with a short tail. Falling to the baseline, this tailed dot became our comma. The same calligraphic tradition has left us other useful marks, such as the double dot or colon (:), the slash or virgule (/), the hyphen (-), and the long dash (–).

5.1.2 *Use analphabetic symbols and diacritics that are in tune with the basic font.*

A normal type font now includes about two dozen mutant forms of the few ancient signs of punctuation (period, comma, colon, quotation marks, brackets, parentheses, dashes, and so on). It also includes about a dozen diacritics (acute and grave accents, the circumflex, tilde, ogonek, umlaut, and others), some legal and commercial logograms (@ # $ % ‰ etc) and a few arithmetical symbols. On the ISO Latin fonts (a series of nine standard roman character sets defined by the International Organization for Standardization and now routinely issued by digital foundries in Europe and North America), analphabetic symbols outnumber the basic roman alphabet three to one.

On some fonts, these analphabetic characters are beautifully designed; on others they are not designed at all. Often they are simply borrowed from another font, which may have been drawn in a different weight and style. Some digital foundries also confine most of their diacritics and symbols to a ghetto called the *pi font,* where style of any kind is wrongly presumed to be an unnecessary luxury.

Several analphabetic characters are notorious for poor design and should always be inspected when assessing a new font. These problem characters include *square brackets* [ ], which are often too dark; *parentheses* ( ), which are often too symmetrical and skinny; the *asterisk* \*, the *pilcrow* ¶ and the *section sign* §, which are often stiff and bland; and the *octothorp* or numeral sign #, which is frequently too large to be used for anything other than downscale commercial advertising. Fonts equipped with good versions of these characters must often lend them to those without. But not just any good version will do.

Neoclassical analphabetics, after John Baskerville, above
Neohumanist, drawn by Hermann Zapf, below

a \* & & § ; ! ?
1 2 3 4 5 6 ?

Baskerville, which is an eighteenth-century Neoclassical typeface, requires a Neoclassical asterisk. That means the lobes of the asterisk will be symmetrical teardrops with rounded ends. But a twentieth-century neohumanist face like Palatino requires an asterisk with more calligraphic character – sharper, slightly asymmetrical lobes showing the trace of the broad-nib pen. Well-made fonts are distinguished by similar differences in the question and exclamation marks, quotation marks and commas. Not even simple periods are freely interchangeable. Some are elliptical, diamond-shaped or square instead of round. Their weight and fitting varies as well. The *visible invisibility* of the marks of punctuation, which is essential to their function, depends on these details. So, therefore, does the visible invisibility of the typeface as a whole.

*Use the best available ampersand.*

The ampersand is a symbol evolved from the Latin *et,* meaning *and.* It is one of the oldest alphabetic abbreviations, and it has assumed over the centuries a wonderful variety of forms. Contemporary offerings are for the most part uninspired, stolid pretzels: unmusical imitations of the treble clef. Often the italic font is equipped with an ampersand less repressed than its roman counterpart. Since the ampersand is more often used in display work than in ordinary text, the more creative versions are often the more useful. There is rarely any reason not to borrow the italic ampersand for use with roman text.

*Analphabetic*
*Style*

## *Shakespeare & Co.*
## Brown & Son
## Smith & Daughter

Trump Mediäval italic (above), designed by Georg Trump; Pontifex roman (center), by Friedrich Poppl; Pontifex roman with italic ampersand (below)

5.1.4   *Consider even the lowly hyphen.*

It is worth taking a close look at hyphens, which were once more subtle and various than they tend to be today. The hyphen was originally a simple pen stroke, often the thinnest stroke the broad-nib pen could make, at an angle of 20° to 45°. To distinguish the hyphen from the comma (which could also be written as a simple, canted stroke), the hyphen was often doubled, like an equal sign heading uphill.

Many Renaissance typographers preferred the canted hyphen with italic and the level hyphen with roman. Others mixed the two at random – one of several techniques once used to give a touch of scribal variety to the typeset page. But after the death of the Parisian typographer Claude Garamond, in 1561, the level hyphen was the norm.

Most hyphens currently offered are short, blunt, thick, and perfectly level, like refugees from a font of Helvetica. This has sometimes been the choice of the designer, sometimes not. The double hyphen designed by Hermann Zapf in 1953 for his typeface Aldus, as an example, was omitted when the face was commercially issued in 1954. Foundry Centaur, designed by Bruce Rogers, had a hyphen inclined at 48°, but Monotype replaced it with a level bar when the face was adapted for machine composition in 1929. And the original Linotype issue of W.A. Dwiggins's Electra had a subtly tapered hyphen inclined at 7° from the horizontal; later copies of the face have substituted a bland, anonymous form.

If you are tempted to redesign an existing font, using a digital font editor, the hyphen is a good character to start on. It is a comparatively simple character, and you may be able to restore instead of subvert the designer's original intentions.

A few alternatives to the blunt and level hyphen are also still in circulation, and these are worth stealing on occasion for use with another face. The hyphen in Monotype Poliphilus is canted (as in the original design) at 42°. The hyphen in Monotype Blado (the companion italic to Poliphilus) is canted at 35° and tapered as well. The hyphens in most of Frederic Goudy's text faces are canted at angles ranging from 15° to 50°. Some digital versions preserve this feature; others are more homogenized. Canted and tapered hyphens are also to be found in many of the faces of Oldřich Menhart. (In Menhart's Figural, for example, the roman hyphen is tapered one way and the italic hyphen the other.) Frederic Warde's Arrighi, José Mendoza's Photina italic, and Warren Chappell's Trajanus all have hyphens that are level but asymmetrically serifed, which gives them a slight angular movement. The hyphen in Bram de Does's Trinité, a model of subtlety, is level and unserifed but has a slight calligraphic lift at one end.

*fine-tuned* / eagle-eye

Arrighi, left, and Trajanus, right

Hyphens also once varied considerably in width, but most now are standardized to a quarter of an em. Sometimes a shorter hyphen is better. Some of Gerard Unger's economical Dutch hyphens (in faces such as Swift and Flora) measure no more than a fifth of an em.

Line-end hyphens are often best hung in the right margin, like the line-end hyphens on this and the facing page. This was easy to do for the scribes, who made it a common practice, but it is tedious to emulate in metal. Digital typography makes it potentially easy once again – though not all typesetting software is equally eager to oblige.

## 5.2 DASHES, SLASHES & DOTS

**5.2.1** *Use spaced en dashes – rather than em dashes or hyphens – to set off phrases.*

Standard computer keyboards and typewriters include only one dash, but a normal font of roman or italic type includes at least three. These are the hyphen and two sizes of long dash: the *en dash* – which is one en (half an em, M/2) in width – and the *em dash*—which is one em (two ens) wide. Many fonts also include a subtraction sign, which may or may not be the same length and weight as the en dash. And some include a *figure dash* (equal to the width of a standard numeral); a *three-quarter em* dash; and a *three-to-em* dash, which is one third of an em (M/3) in length.

In typescript, a double hyphen (--) is often used for a long dash. Double hyphens in a typeset document are a sure sign that the type was set by a typist, not a typographer. A typographer will use an em dash, three-quarter em, or en dash, depending on context or personal style. The em dash is the nineteenth-century standard, still prescribed in many editorial style books, but the em dash is too long for use with the best text faces. Like the oversized space between sentences, it belongs to the padded and corseted aesthetic of Victorian typography.

Used as a phrase marker – thus – the en dash is set with a normal word space on either side.

**5.2.2** *Use close-set en dashes or three-to-em dashes between digits to indicate a range.*

Thus: 3–6 November; 4:30–5:00 PM; 25–30 mm. Set close in this way (and with careful attention to character spacing), the dash stands for the word *to.* The hyphen is too short to serve this function, and in some faces the en dash (which is traditionally prescribed) appears too long. A *three-to-em* (M/3) dash is often the best choice. Three-to-em dashes are missing from many type fonts, but they are easily made on digital equipment, by condensing or shortening an en dash.

When compound terms are linked with a dash in the midst of running prose, subtle clues of size and spacing can be crucial, and confusion can easily arise. A sentence such as *The office will be closed 25 December – 3 January* is a linguistic and typographical trap. Standing alone in a schedule or list, the phrase *25 December – 3 January* will be clear, but in running prose it is better both editorially and typographically to omit the dash and insert an honest preposition: *25 December to 3 January*.

5.2.3  *Use the em dash to introduce speakers in narrative dialogue.*

The em dash, followed by a thin space (M/5) or word space, is the normal European method of marking dialogue, and it is much less fussy than quotation marks:

— So this is a French novel? she said.
— No, he said, it's Manitoban.

5.2.4  *In lists and bibliographies, use a three-em rule when required as a sign of repetition.*

Set without spaces, a line of true em dashes forms a continuous midline rule. A three-em rule (three consecutive em dashes) is the old standard bibliographical sign for the repetition of a name. For example:

Boas, Franz. *Primitive Art.* Oslo: Aschehoug, 1927. Reissued Cambridge, MA: Harvard University Press, 1928; New York: Dover, 1955.
———. *Tsimshian Mythology.* BAE Ann. Rep. 31. Washington, DC: Bureau of American Ethnology, 1916.

In recent years, most professional scholars have abandoned this style of bibliography, but the three-em rule still has many nonacademic uses.

5.2.5  *Use the virgule with words and dates, the solidus with fractions.*

The slash, like the dash, is more various in real life than it is on the typewriter keyboard. A normal font of type includes a vertical bar and two slashes of differing inclinations. The steeper slash is the virgule (/), an alternative form of the comma. It is useful in dates (6/6/92 = 6.VI.92 = 6 June 92) and in text where a comma or parenthesis might otherwise have been used.

Wednesday / August 3 / 1977<br>
Tibetan Guest House / Thamel / Kathmandu<br>
Victoria University, Toronto / Ontario<br>
he/she hit him/her

*Dashes,*
*Slashes*
*and Dots*

The other slash mark on the font is a solidus or fraction bar, used to construct fractions such as $\frac{3}{32}$. The solidus generally slopes at close to 45° and kerns on both sides. The virgule, not the solidus, is used to construct *level* fractions, such as $2\pi/3$. (Notice, for instance, the difference in slope and kerning between the two slash marks in the type specification $8/9\frac{1}{2}$.)

5.2.6 *Use a dimension sign instead of a serifed x when dimensions are given.*

A picture is 26 × 42 cm; studs are 2 × 4 and shelving is 2 × 10 inches; North American letter paper is $8\frac{1}{2}$ × 11.

5.2.7 *Use ellipses that fit the font.*

Most digital fonts now include, among other things, a prefabricated *ellipsis* (a row of three baseline dots). Many typographers nevertheless prefer to make their own. Some prefer to set the three dots flush ... with a normal word space before and after. Others prefer ... to add *thin* spaces between the dots. Thick spaces (M/3) are prescribed by the Chicago Style Manual, but these are another Victorian eccentricity. In most contexts, the Chicago ellipsis is much too wide.

Flush-set ellipses work well with some fonts and faces but not with all. At small text sizes – in 8 pt footnotes, for example – it is generally better to add space (as much as M/5) between the dots. Extra space may also look best in the midst of light, open letterforms, such as Baskerville, and less space in the company of a dark font, such as Trajanus, or when setting in bold face. (The ellipsis generally used in this book is part of the font and sets as a single character.)

In English (but usually not in French), when the ellipsis occurs at the end of a sentence, a fourth dot, the period, is added and the space at the beginning of the ellipsis disappears.... When the ellipsis combines with a comma..., an exclamation mark, or question mark, the same typographical principle applies. Otherwise, a word space is required both fore and aft.

## 5.3 PARENTHESES

5.3.1 *Use the best available brackets and parentheses, and set them with adequate space.*

The parentheses of the Renaissance and early Baroque were pure line, like the virgule (/) and the long dash (–). They were curved rules, with no variation in weight – and they were loosely fitted, with plenty of space between them and the text they enclosed. Centaur is one of the few twentieth-century faces that have reasserted this Renaissance style, and Monotype Van Dijck is one of the few historical recuttings that are faithful on this important point of detail.

A few other recent faces, such as Trump Mediäval, have been designed with parentheses based on pen-drawn Renaissance forms. Others still, such as Hermann Zapf's Melior and Karl-Erik Forsberg's Berling, have parentheses distinctively their own, that are clearly evolved from these particular letterforms. But on many twentieth-century text fonts, the parentheses are stock eighteenth-century swelled rules. In company with a neoclassical alphabet, such as Baskerville, these parentheses look fine. With letters of most other kinds, they are out of place.

In older German typeface classifications, *Antiqua* means roman and *Mediäval* means Renaissance – because Italian Renaissance architects and scribes revived and updated the romanesque and Carolingian forms of the Middle Ages. *Trump Mediäval Antiqua*, or Trump Mediäval roman, in spite of its name, grows out of late Renaissance forms.

$$(abc)\ (abc)$$

Centaur and Trump, above. Baskerville and Melior, below.

$$(abc)\ (abc)$$

81

If you find yourself setting a face equipped with substandard parentheses, borrow a better pair from elsewhere. And whatever parentheses you use, check that they are not too tightly fitted.

5.3.2 *Use upright (i.e., "roman" ) rather than sloped parentheses, square brackets and braces, even if the context is italic.*

Parentheses and brackets are not letters, and it makes little sense to speak of them as roman or italic. There are vertical parentheses and sloped ones, and the parentheses on italic fonts are almost always sloped, but vertical parentheses are generally to be preferred. That means they must come from the roman font, and may need extra spacing when used with italic letterforms.

$$(\text{efg}) \ (\textit{efg})$$

The sloped square brackets usually found on italic fonts are, if anything, even less useful than sloped parentheses. If, perish the thought, there were a book or film entitled *The View from My [sic] Bed*, sloped brackets might be useful as a way of indicating that the brackets and their contents are actually part of the title. Otherwise, vertical brackets should be used, no matter whether the text is roman or italic: "The View from My [*sic*] Bed" and "*the view from my* [*sic*] *bed.*"

5.4  QUOTATION MARKS & OTHER INTRUSIONS

5.4.1 *Minimize the use of quotation marks, especially with Renaissance faces.*

Editors and typographers got by quite well for centuries without quotation marks. In the earliest printed books, quotation was marked merely by naming the speaker – as it still is in most editions of the Vulgate and King James Bibles. In the High Renaissance, quotation was generally marked by a change of font: from roman to italic or the other way around. Quotation marks evolved in the middle of the sixteenth century, and by the seventeenth, some printers liked to use them profusely. In books from the Baroque and Romantic periods, quotation marks are sometimes repeated at the beginning of every line of a long quotation. When these distractions were finally omitted, the space they had occupied was frequently retained. This is the origin of the indented block quotation. Renaissance block quotations were set in a contrasting face at full size and full measure.

Three forms of quotation mark are still in common use. Inverted and raised commas – "quote" and 'quote' – are generally favored in Britain and North America. But baseline and inverted commas – „quote" – are more widely used in Germany, and many typographers prefer them to take the shape of sloped primes („–") instead of tailed commas („–"). *Guillemets,* otherwise known as *duck foot quotation marks,* chevrons, or angle quotes – « quote » and ‹ quote › – are the normal form in France and Italy, and are widely used in the rest of Europe. French and Italian typographers set their guillemets with the points out, « thus », while German and Swiss typographers often set them » the opposite way «. In either case, thin spaces are customary between the guillemets and the text they enclose.

Quotation marks are sufficiently ingrained in modern editorial sign language that it is difficult, in many kinds of texts, to do entirely without them. But many nonprofessional writers overuse quotation marks. Good editors and typographers will reduce their appearance to a minimum, retaining only those that contribute real information.

When quotation marks (including guillemets) are used, the question remains, how many should there be? The usual British practice is to use single quotes first, and doubles within singles. 'So does "analphabetic" mean what I think it means?' she said suspiciously. When this convention is followed, most quotation marks will be singles and therefore less obtrusive.

Common American practice is the reverse. "So," she said, "does 'analphabetic' mean…?" This convention, using singles within doubles instead of doubles within singles, ensures that quotation flags will stand out. But some faces – Matthew Carter's Galliard, for example – have prominent quotation marks, while others have forms that are more discreet. Consider the face as well as the text when deciding which convention to follow in marking quotations.

*Position quotation marks consistently in relation to punctuation.*

*Quotation Marks and Other Intrusions*

Punctuation is normally placed inside a closing single or double guillemet if it belongs to the quotation, and outside otherwise. With other quotation marks, usage is less consistent. Most North American editors like their commas and periods inside the raised commas, "like this," but their colons and semicolons outside. Many British editors prefer to put all punctuation outside, with the milk and the cat. The kerning capabilities of digital typesetters, especially in the hands of advertising typographers, have evolved an intermediate third style, in which closing quotation marks are kerned over the top of commas and periods. Typographically, this is a good idea with some faces in large sizes, but a bad idea with many faces at text sizes, where a kerned quotation mark or apostrophe may look much like a question or exclamation mark.

# "kern, 'kerning,' kerned."

When quotation marks are not kerned, it makes no *typographical* difference whether they follow commas and periods or precede them. The difference is one of editorial rather than visual discretion. But typographers, like editors, should be consistent, whichever route they choose.

5.4.3 *Omit the apostrophe from numerical plurals.*

Houses are built with 2 × 4s; children and parents live through the terrible twos, and fewer people were killed in the 1800s than in the 1930s.

5.4.4 *Eliminate other unnecessary punctuation.*

Omit the period after metric units and other self-evident abbreviations. Set 5.2 m and 520 cm but 36 in. or 36", and in bibliographical references, p 36f, or pp 306–314.

North American editors and typesetters tend to put periods after all abbreviations or (more rarely) after none. The former practice produces a text full of birdshot and wormholes; the latter can cause confusion. As a form of compromise, the Oxford house style, which is widely followed in Britain, has much to commend it. This rule is: use a period only when the word stops prematurely. The period is omitted if the abbreviation begins with the first letter of the word and ends with the last. Thus: Mrs Bodoni, Mr John Adams Jr and Ms Lucy Chong-Adams, Dr McBain, St Thomas Aquinas, Msgr Kuruwezi and Fr O'Malley; but Prof. C.S. Miłosz and Capt. James Cook.

Periods are equally unnecessary in acronyms and other abbreviations commonly written with small or large capitals. Thus: 3:00 AM and 450 BC; Washington, DC, and Mexico, DF; Vancouver, BC, and Darwin, NT.

*Analphabetic Symbols*

In the interests of typographical hygiene, unnecessary hyphens should likewise be omitted. Thus: avant garde, bleeding heart, halfhearted, postmodern, prewar, silkscreen and typeface, in preference to the hyphenated alternatives. (It is good editorial practice, however, to hyphenate compound adjectives unless they can be fused into single words or will stand out as proper nouns. Thus, one finds twentieth-century typefaces in limited-edition books but publishes a limited edition at the end of the twentieth century and rides the New York Subway in New York. But one finds lowercase letters in the lower case.)

Apostrophes are needed for some plurals, but not for others, and inconsistency is better than a profusion of unnecessary marks. Thus: do's and don'ts; the ayes have it but the I's don't; the ewes are coming but the you's are staying home.

## 5.5 DIACRITICS

5.5.1 *Use the accents and alternate sorts that proper names and imported words and phrases require.*

Simplicity is good, but so is plurality. Typography's principal function (not its only function) is communication, and the greatest threat to communication is not difference but sameness. Communication ceases when one being is no different from another: when there is nothing strange to wonder at and no new information to exchange. For that reason among others, typography and typographers must honor the variety and complexity of human language, thought and identity, instead of homogenizing or hiding it.

Typography was once a fluently multilingual and multicultural calling. The great typographers of the fifteenth and sixteenth centuries worked willingly with Italian whiteletter, German blackletter, French script, Ashkenazi and Sephardic Hebrew, and two or three versions of Greek. The best typographers of the twentieth century have followed their lead. But typographic ethnocentricity and racism also have thrived in the last hundred years, and much of that narrow-mindedness is institutionalized in the workings of machines. Unregenerate, uneducated fonts and keyboards, defiantly incapable of setting anything beyond the most rudimentary Anglo-American alphabet, are still not difficult to find.

*Diacritics*

Recent digital technology has made it possible for any typeshop or publisher to create special characters on demand – a luxury most typographers have been without since the seventeenth century. Prepackaged fonts of impeccable design, with character sets sufficient to set any word in any European language, and the software to compose and kern these characters, are also now available even to the smallest home and desktop operations. Yet there are large-circulation newspapers in North America still incapable of typesetting even the names of major cities and statesmen, for want of letters like ñ and é.

Neither typographers nor their tools should labor under the sad misapprehension that no one will ever mention crêpes flambées or aïoli, no one will have a name like Antonín Dvořák, Søren Kierkegaard, Stéphane Mallarmé or Chloë Jones, and no one will live in Óbidos or Århus, København or Øster Vrå, Průhonice or Nagykőrös, Trois Rivières, Kırkağaç or Köln.

5.5.2 *Remap the font driver and keyboard to suit your own requirements.*

The conventional computer keyboard includes a number of characters – @ # ^ + = { } | \ ~ < > – rarely required by most typesetters, while frequently needed characters, such as the en dash, em dash, acute accent, midpoint and ellipsis, are nowhere to be seen. Unless your keyboard fits your needs as is, remap it. It should give you ready access to whatever accented and analphabetic characters you regularly use.

You may also want to edit your roman and italic fonts so that text figures, upright parentheses and upright brackets set automatically, in place of the more rarely needed lining and sloping forms.

Unless your composition software places ligatures automatically, you may find it easiest to insert them through a substitution routine after the text is fully set. Open and close quotes can be inserted at the same time in the same way, but many typesetters like to assign them specific keys.

Compositors who seldom use accented characters often prefer to set them as overstrikes, using an accent key or composite-character key that momentarily redefines the keyboard. Software that operates in this way may produce ó from the combination o/, ř from rv, Ů from UO and so on. But if you use accented characters with any frequency, you may find it worth your while to map them directly to the keyboard.

A typical customized keyboard for the roman font is shown on the following page. The purpose of this particular layout is general multilingual text work. This could mean something as complex as polylingual manuals and packaging for technical products sold on the global market, or something as simple as addressing an envelope to Poland, or spelling the names correctly in the program for a symphony performance in Detroit.

The keyboard layout shown is missing two characters (the tailed N and the barred T) required for Lapp and one (the barred H) required for Maltese. With those exceptions, it will accommodate all European and North Asian languages that use the Latin alphabet: Albanian, Basque, Breton, Catalan, Croatian, Czech, Danish, Dutch, Estonian, Faroese, Finnish, Flemish, French, Frisian, Gaelic, German, Greenlandic, Hungarian, Icelandic, Italian, Latvian, Lithuanian, Norwegian, Polish, Portuguese, Romansch, Romany, Rumanian, Slovak, Slovenian, Sorbian, Spanish, Swedish, Turkish and Welsh. In addition, it will accommodate the major Pacific languages written in Latin script (Bihasa Indonesia, Bikol, Cebuano, Hiligaynon, Ilocano, Malay, Maori, Pilipino and Tahitian); the major indigenous Latin American languages; upwards of twenty common African languages; and the standard romanized forms of Arabic, Chinese, Greek, Hebrew, Hindi, Japanese, Pali, Persian and Sanskrit, as well as Russian and the other Slavic languages.

This particular layout assumes the primary languages to be English, Spanish and French, but it is equally fast for German, Italian, Portuguese and the Scandinavian languages. If the primary languages were, for instance, English and Turkish, or English, Polish and Czech, several minor rearrangements might be made.

The individual characters are identified and discussed in Appendix A, p 215.

*Analphabetic Symbols*

Pilipino – the modern version of Tagalog – is the official language of the Philippines. Bikol, Cebuano, Hiligaynon and Ilocano are other Philippine languages with several million speakers each.

*Sample*
*Layout*
*for an*
*Expanded*
*Keyboard*

| Cntrl | ¡ | ´ | ˝ | £ | ‰ | ª | & | ° | † | ‡ | ... | × |
|---|---|---|---|---|---|---|---|---|---|---|---|---|
| Shift | ! | ´ | ˝ | $ | % | º | & | * | ( | ) | – | + |
| Plain | 1 | 2 | 3 | 4 | 5 | 6 | 7 | 8 | 9 | 0 | - | = |
| Alt | 1 | 2 | 3 | 4 | 5 | 6 | 7 | 8 | 9 | 0 | – | — |

| Cntrl | Ø | Ů | é | Å | Þ | Ÿ | ú | í | ó | ¶ | â | ê |
|---|---|---|---|---|---|---|---|---|---|---|---|---|
| Shift | Q | W | E | R | T | Y | U | I | O | P | ~ | ~ |
| Plain | q | w | e | r | t | y | u | i | o | p | [ | ] |
| Alt | ø | ů | è | å | þ | ÿ | ù | ì | ò | î | ô | û |

| Cntrl | á | § | Ð | Ä | Ë | Ï | Ö | Ü | Ł | ı | " | |
|---|---|---|---|---|---|---|---|---|---|---|---|---|
| Shift | A | S | D | F | G | H | J | K | L | : | " | |
| Plain | a | s | d | f | g | h | j | k | l | ; | ' | |
| Alt | à | ß | ð | ä | ë | ï | ö | ü | ł | đ | ' | |

| Cntrl | Ā | Õ | Ç | ˇ | ˘ | Ñ | ¯ | « | » | ¿ | · | | Æ |
|---|---|---|---|---|---|---|---|---|---|---|---|---|---|
| Shift | Z | X | C | V | B | N | M | ‹ | › | ? | . | | Œ |
| Plain | z | x | c | v | b | n | m | , | . | / | \ | | œ |
| Alt | ã | õ | ç | ˇ | ˘ | ñ | ¯ | , | · | ˛ | ˌ | ¥ | æ |

Ambiguous characters are as follows. **Row 1**: Shift-2 and Cntrl-2 are the lowercase and uppercase floating acute. Shift-3 and Cntrl-3 are the lowercase and uppercase double acute. Shift-hyphen is a subtraction sign. Alt-hyphen is an en dash, and Alt-equal is an em dash. **Row 2**: The two Shift-bracket keys are the uppercase and lowercase floating tilde. **Row 3**: Cntrl-colon is a dotless i. The double-quote key is a double close-quote. Cntrl-double-quote is the double open-quote. Alt-apostrophe is the single open-quote (inverted comma). **Row 4**: Cntrl-V and Alt-v are the uppercase and lowercase floating caron. Cntrl-B and Alt-b are upper- and lowercase breve. Cntrl-M and Alt-m are upper- and lowercase macron. Shift-comma and Shift-period are single guillemets rather than angle brackets. Alt-comma is a cedilla. Alt-period is a midpoint. The slash key is a virgule. Alt-slash is an ogonek (nasal hook).

The two extra keys shown to the right in the bottom row are placed in different positions by different manufacturers. On a standard keyboard, one of these keys carries the backslash and pipe; the other carries the swung dash or tilde and the open quote. Here, Shift-backslash is the underdot; Cntrl-backslash is the overdot.

CHOOSING & COMBINING TYPE

---

6.1 TECHNICAL CONSIDERATIONS

6.1.1 *Consider the medium for which the typeface was originally designed.*

Typographic purists like to see every typeface used with the technology for which it was designed. Taken literally, this means that virtually all faces designed before 1950 must be set in metal and printed letterpress, and the majority must be set by hand. Most typographers apply this principle in a more relaxed and complex way, and settle for preserving something rather than everything of a type's original character.

On the technical side, several things can be done to increase the chance that a letterpress typeface will survive translation to digital composition and offset printing.

6.1.2 *When using digital adaptations of letterpress faces, choose fonts that are faithful to the spirit as well as the letter of the old designs.*

Letterpress printing places the letterform *into* the paper, while offset printing lays it on the surface. Many subtle differences result from these two approaches to printing. The letterpress adds a little bulk and definition to the letter, especially in the thin strokes, and increases the prominence of the ends of thin serifs. Metal typefaces are designed to take advantage of these features of letterpress printing.

On the offset press – and in the photographic procedures by which camera-ready art and offset printing plates are prepared – thin strokes tend to get thinner and the ends of delicate serifs are eaten away. In a face like Bembo, for instance, offset printing tends to make features like the feet of i and l, and the heads and feet of H and I, slightly convex, while letterpress printing tends to make them slightly concave.

Ili

Faces designed for photographic manipulation and offset printing are therefore weighted and finished differently from letterpress designs. And adapting a letterpress face for digital composition is a far from simple task.

Digital fonts poorly translated from metal originals are sometimes too dark or light or blunt throughout, or uneven in stroke weight, or faithless in their proportions. They sometimes lack text figures or other essential components of the original design. But digital translations can also be *too faithful* to the original. They sometimes neglect the subtle adjustments that the shift from three-dimensional letterpress to two-dimensional offset printing requires.

*Technical Considerations*

6.1.3 *Check the weight and conformation of the letterforms at every proofing stage.*

Proofing the *type* is just as important as proofing the *text*. It is the only way to ensure that robust forms do not become anemic, or sharp forms bland, through crude resolution or sloppy exposure, even with the best digital fonts you can buy.

6.1.4 *Choose faces that will survive, and if possible prosper, under the final printing conditions.*

Bembo and Centaur, Spectrum and Palatino, are subtle and beautiful alphabets, but if you are setting 8 pt text with a laser printer on plain paper at 300 dpi, the refined forms of these faces will be rubbed into the coarse digital mud of the imaging process. If the final output will be 14 pt text set directly to film at 3000 dpi, then printed by good offset lithography on the best coated paper, every nuance may be crystal clear, but the result will still lack the character and texture of the letterpress medium for which these faces were designed.

Some of the most innocent looking faces are actually the most difficult to render by digital means. Optima and Formata, for example – both unserifed and apparently uncomplicated faces – are constructed of subtle tapers and curves that can be adequately rendered only at the highest resolutions.

Faces with blunt and substantial serifs, open counters, gentle modelling and minimal pretensions to aristocratic grace stand the best chance of surviving the indignities of low resolution. Amasis, Caecilia, Lucida, Photina, Stone and Utopia, for example, while they prosper at high resolutions, will also survive under cruder conditions that are lethal to faces like Centaur, Spectrum and Van Dijck.

And on the principle that a good hamburger is better than a

bad soufflé, even monospace typewriter fonts – such as IBM Courier and Prestige, which are models of their kind – remain well worth considering for routine work on laser printers.

6.1.5  *Choose faces that suit the paper you intend to print on, or paper that suits the faces you wish to use.*

Avoid, for example, printing Renaissance or Baroque faces on glossy and hard-surfaced paper, which is an eighteenth-century invention.

## 6.2  PRACTICAL TYPOGRAPHY

6.2.1  *Choose faces that suit the task as well as the subject.*

You are designing, let us say, a book about bicycle racing. You have found in the specimen books a typeface called Bicycle, which has spokes in the O, an A in the shape of a racing seat, a T that resembles a set of racing handlebars, and tiny cleated shoes perched on the long, one-sided serifs of ascenders and descenders, like pumping feet on the pedals. Surely this is the perfect face for your book?

Actually, typefaces and racing bikes are very much alike. Both are ideas as well as machines, and neither should be burdened with excess drag or baggage. Pictures of pumping feet will not make the type go faster, any more than smoke trails, pictures of rocket ships and lightning bolts tied to the frame will improve the speed of the bike.

The best type for a book about bicycle racing will be, first of all, an inherently good type. Second, it will be a good type for books, which is to say, a good type for comfortable long-distance reading. Third, it will be a type sympathetic to the theme. It will probably be lean, strong and swift; perhaps it will also be Italian. But it is unlikely to be carrying excess ornament or freight, and unlikely to be indulging in a masquerade.

6.2.2  *Choose faces that can furnish whatever special effects you require.*

If your text includes an abundance of numerals, you may want a face whose numerals are especially well designed. Palatino, Pontifex, Trump Mediäval and Zapf International, for example, all recommend themselves. But if you prefer three-quarter height lining numerals, your options include Bell, Trajanus and Weiss.

If you need small caps, faces that lack them (such as Frutiger, Méridien and Syntax) are out of the running. But if you need a range of weights, faces such as Centaur and Spectrum are disqualified instead.

If you need a matching phonetic face, your choices include Stone and Times Roman. If you need a matching Cyrillic, you might choose Minion, Lazurski, Trajanus or Baskerville. And for the sake of a matching sanserif, you might choose Lucida, Demos or Stone. These matters are explored in more detail in Chapter 10, which discusses individual typefaces.

Special effects can also be obtained through more unorthodox combinations, which are the subject of §6.5.

6.2.3 *Use what there is to the best advantage.*

If there is nothing for dinner but beans, one may hunt for an onion, some pepper, salt, cilantro and sour cream to enliven the dish, but it is generally no help to pretend that the beans are really shrimp or chanterelles.

When the only font available is Cheltenham or Times Roman, the typographer must make the most of its virtues, limited though they may be. An italic, small caps and hanging figures will help immensely if they can be added, but there is nothing to be gained by pretending that Times Roman is Bembo or Aldus in disguise.

As a rule, a face of modest merits should be handled with great discretion, formality and care. It should be set in modest sizes (better yet, in one size only) with the caps well-spaced, the lines well-leaded, and the lower case well fitted and modestly kerned. The line length should be optimal and the page impeccably proportioned. In short, the typography should be richly and superbly *ordinary*, so that attention is drawn to the quality of the composition, not to the individual letterforms. Only a face that warrants close scrutiny should be set in a form that invites it.

Using what there is to best advantage almost always means using *less* than what is available. Baskerville, Helvetica, Palatino and Times Roman, for example – which are four of the most widely available typefaces – are four faces with nothing to offer

# Baskerville roman
## *and its italic*

# Helvetica roman
## *and its oblique*

# Palatino roman
## *and its italic*

# Times New Roman
## *and its italic*

Baskerville is an English Neoclassical face designed in Birmingham in the 1750s by John Baskerville. It has a rationalist axis, thoroughgoing symmetry and delicate finish.

Helvetica is a twentieth-century Swiss revision of a late nineteenth-century German Realist face. The first weights were drawn in 1956 by Max Miedinger, based on the Berthold Foundry's old Odd-job Sanserif, or Akzidenz Grotesk, as it is called in German. The heavy, unmodulated line and tiny aperture evoke an image of uncultivated strength, force and persistence. The very light weights issued in recent years have done much to reduce Helvetica's coarseness but little to increase its readability.

Palatino is a lyrical modernist face with a neohumanist architecture, which is to say that it is written, not drawn, and it is based on Renaissance forms. It was created in 1948 by Hermann Zapf.

Times Roman – properly Times *New* Roman – is an historical pastiche drawn by Victor Lardent for Stanley Morison in London in 1931. The roman has a humanist axis but Mannerist proportions, Baroque weight, and a sharp, Neoclassical finish. The italic has a rationalist axis, but in other respects it matches point for point the eclecticism of the roman.

each other except public disagreement. None makes a good companion face for any of the others, because each of them is rooted in a different concept of what constitutes a letterform. If the available palette is limited to these faces, the first thing to do is choose *one* for the task at hand and ignore the other three.

## 6.3 HISTORICAL CONSIDERATIONS

Typography, like other arts, preys on its own past. It can do so with the callousness of a grave robber, or with the piety of unquestioning ancestor worship. It can also do so in thoughtful, enlightened and deeply creative ways.

Roman type has been with us for more than five centuries. Its root components – the roman upper and lower case, basic analphabetic symbols, and the arabic numerals – have been with us for much longer yet. There are typographers who resolutely avoid using any typeface designed in an earlier era, but even they must learn something of how the older letterforms functioned, because the ancient forms are living in the new. Typographers who willingly use the old faces, and who wish to use them intelligently, need to know all they can learn about the heritage they enjoy.

6.3.1 *Choose a face whose historical echoes and associations are in harmony with the text.*

Any contemporary North American library will furnish examples of typographical anachronism. There are books on contemporary Italy and on seventeenth-century France set in typefaces such as Baskerville and Caslon, cut in eighteenth-century England. There are books about the Renaissance set in faces that belong to the Baroque, and books about the Baroque set in faces from the Renaissance. To a good typographer it is not enough merely to avoid these kinds of humorous contradictions. The typographer seeks to *shed light* on the text, to generate insight and energy, by setting every text in a face and form in which it actually belongs.

It is not that good typographers object to mixing centuries and cultures. Many take delight in doing so – especially when they have no other choice. A text from ancient Athens, for example, cannot be set in an ancient Athenian version of roman type. A face designed in North America in the 1990s is likely to

94

be used instead. Texts from seventeenth-century France or eighteenth-century England also might be set perfectly well in faces of recent design. But a face that truly suits an historical text is likely to have some fairly clear historical content of its own. There is no typeface *equally suited* to texts from Greek antiquity, the French Baroque and the English Neoclassical period – though faces equally *unsuited* to each of them abound.

The historical affiliations of individual typefaces are examined in chapters 7 and 10.

6.3.2   *Allow the face to speak in its natural idiom.*

Books that leap historical boundaries and mix historical subjects can pose complex and exciting typographical problems. But often, if a text calls for a Renaissance type, it calls for Renaissance typography as well. This usually means Renaissance page proportions and margins, and an absence of bold face. It may also mean large Renaissance versals, Renaissance style in the handling of quotations, and the segregation of roman and italic. If the text calls for a Neoclassical type, it likewise often calls for Neoclassical page design. When you undertake to use an historical typeface, take the trouble to learn the typographical idiom for which it was intended. Works of reference that may be useful in solving particular problems are listed in Appendix C.

6.4   CULTURAL & PERSONAL CONSIDERATIONS

6.4.1   *Choose faces whose individual spirit and character is in keeping with the text.*

Accidental associations are rarely a good basis for choosing a typeface. Books of poems by the twentieth-century Jewish American poet Marvin Bell, for example, have sometimes been set in Bell type – which is eighteenth-century, English and Presbyterian – solely because of the name. Puns of this kind are a private amusement for typographers. But a typographic page so well designed that it attains a life of its own must be based on more than an inside joke.

Letterforms have character, spirit and personality. Typographers learn to discern these features through years of working first-hand with the forms, and through studying and compar-

95

ing the work of other designers, present and past. On close inspection, typefaces reveal many hints of their designers' times and temperaments, and even their nationalities and religious faiths. Faces chosen on these grounds are likely to give more interesting results than faces chosen through mere convenience of availability or coincidence of name.

If, for example, you are setting a text by a woman, you might prefer a face designed by a woman. Such faces were rare or nonexistent in earlier centuries, but there are now a number to choose from. They include Gudrun Zapf-von Hesse's Carmina, Diotima, Nofret and Christiana; Elizabeth Friedländer's Elizabeth; Kris Holmes's Lucida, Sierra, Leviathan and Kolibri; Kris Holmes's and Janice Prescott Fishman's Shannon; Carol Twombly's Charlemagne, Lithos and Trajan; Cynthia Hollandsworth's Hiroshige and Tiepolo; and Ilse Schüle's Rhapsodie. For some purposes, one might also go back to the work of Elizabeth Colwell, whose Colwell Handletter, issued by ATF in 1916, was the first American typeface designed by a woman.

But perhaps a text by a French author, or a text dealing with France, might best be set in a French typeface, without regard to the gender of author or designer. The choices include Garamond, Jannon, Mendoza, Méridien, Vendôme and many others – but even this abbreviated list covers considerable range. Garamond – of which there are many recent revivals – was designed in sixteenth-century Paris. It owes much to Italian forms and belongs to the world of Renaissance Catholicism. Jannon is equally elegant but nonconformist. It belongs to the Reformation rather than the Renaissance, and its designer, Jean Jannon, was a French Protestant who suffered all his life from religious persecution. Vendôme, designed by François Ganeau, is a witty twentieth-century face much indebted to Jannon. Mendoza, designed in Paris in 1990, goes back to the tough humanist roots from which Garamond sprang. Méridien, from the 1950s, is more in touch with the secular spirit of twentieth-century Swiss/French industrial design, yet it includes a regal, even imperious, upper case and a crisp, graceful italic. These five different faces invite additional differences in page design, paper, and binding as well as different texts, just as different musical instruments invite different phrasings, different tempi, different musical modes or keys.

Even nations like Greece and Thailand, which have alphabets of their own, share in a multinational tradition of type

# Garamond roman
## *and its italic*

# Jannon roman
## *and its italic*

# Mendoza roman
## *and its italic*

# Méridien roman
## *and its italic*

# Vendôme roman
## *and its oblique*

Adobe Garamond is a family created by Robert Slimbach, based on the designs of Claude Garamond (c. 1490–1561). (Compare the reproductions of some of Garamond's actual type, on p 72.)

Monotype 'Garamond' 156 is a revival of a type designed by Jean Jannon (1580–1658), the greatest typecutter of the French Baroque. Jannon's type was long misidentified as Garamond's and is still often sold under his name.

Mendoza is a recent design by José Mendoza y Almeida. Méridien, by Adrian Frutiger, and Vendôme, by François Ganeau, are both products of the 1950s. Ganeau – who worked as a painter, sculptor and set designer more than as a graphic artist – based Vendôme on Jannon's letters, but moved them playfully in the direction of French Neoclassicism.

design. Nevertheless, some typefaces seem more redolent of national character than others. Frederic Goudy, for example, is widely regarded as the most ebulliently American of all American type designers. The sensitive typographer would not choose one of Goudy's faces to set, let us say, the text of the Canadian or Mexican constitution.

*Cultural and Personal Considerations*

This subject is a lifelong study, and for serious typographers it is a lifelong source of discovery and delight. It is pursued at greater length in Chapter 10, which includes a cross-indexed list of type designs and designers.

6.5 THE MULTICULTURAL PAGE

Consistency is one of the forms of beauty. Contrast is another. A fine page, even a fine book, can be set from beginning to end in one type in one size. It can also teem with variety, like an equatorial forest or a modern city.

6.5.1 *Start with a single typographic family.*

Most pages, and most entire documents, can be set perfectly well with only one family of type. But perhaps the page confronting you requires a chapter title, two or three levels of subheads, an epigraph, a text in two languages, block quotations within the text, a couple of mathematical equations, a bar graph, several explanatory sidenotes, and captions for photographs and a map. An extended type family, such as Lucida or Stone, may provide sufficient resources even for this task. Another possibility is Gerard Unger's comprehensive series known as Demos, Praxis and Flora – which is a family with no surname to unite it. Each of these series includes both roman and italic in a range of weights, matching serifed and unserifed forms, and other variations. If you restrict yourself to faces within the family, you can have variety and homogeneity at the same time: many shapes and sizes but a single typographic culture. Such a form is well suited to some texts, but it is poorly suited to others.

You can also, of course, mix faces at random, by drawing them out of a hat.

Between these two extremes is the wide arena of thoughtful mixing and matching, in which the typographic intelligence often does its most creative work and play.

### 6.5.2 Respect the integrity of roman, italic & small caps.

It has been the normal practice of type designers since the middle of the sixteenth century to offer text faces in the form of a matched triad, consisting of roman, italic and small caps. Because some of these marriages are more successful than others, it is wise to examine the roman and the italic both separately and together when choosing a text face.

There are several celebrated instances in which an italic designed by one artist has been happily and permanently married to another designer's roman. These matches always involve some redrawing (and the face that is most heavily redrawn is almost always the italic, which is the subsidiary and "feminine" font in post-Renaissance typography). There are also instances in which a roman and its italic have been designed by the same artist many years apart. But casual liaisons, in which the roman of one family is paired momentarily with the italic of another, have little hope of success. Mixing small caps from one face with full caps from another is even less likely to succeed.

If you use type strictly in the Renaissance manner, treating the roman and italic as separate but equal, not mixing them on the line, you may find that greater latitude is possible. Jan van Krimpen's Lutetia italic mixes well with his Romanée roman, for example, if the two are not too intimately combined. One is visibly more mature than the other, but they are close in color and structure, and they are patently the work of the same designer.

### 6.5.3 Consider bold faces on their own merits.

The original boldface printing types are the blackletters used by Gutenberg in the 1440s. For the next two centuries, blackletter fonts were widely used not only in Germany but in France, the Netherlands and England. (That is why blackletter fonts are sometimes now sold as "Olde English.")

Boldface romans, however, are a nineteenth-century invention. Bold italic is even more recent, and it is hard to find a successful version designed before 1950. Bold romans and italics have been added retroactively to many earlier faces, but they are often simply parodies of the original designs.

Before using a bold weight, especially a bold italic, ask yourself whether you really need it at all. If the answer is yes, you may want to avoid type families such as Bembo, Garamond or Baskerville, to which bold weights have been retroactively added. You might, instead, choose a twentieth-century family such as Méridien, Nofret or Utopia, in which a range of weights is part of the original design.

If your text face lacks a bold weight, you may also find an appropriate bold close by. Hermann Zapf's Aldus, for example, is a twentieth-century family on the Renaissance model, limited to roman, italic and small caps. But Aldus is a close cousin of the same designer's Palatino family, which does include a bold, and Palatino bold sits well with Aldus text.

## **a** aardvark; **b** balloon; **3** thruppence

Palatino bold with Aldus roman

Equally interesting results can often be obtained by reaching much farther afield. The normal function of boldface type is, after all, to contrast with the roman text. If the bold is used in small amounts, and bold and roman are not too intimately combined, a difference in structure as well as weight may be an asset. Under these conditions, a typographer is free to choose both roman and bold on their own merits, seeking basic compatibility rather than close genetic connection.

A text might be set in Sabon, for example, with Zapf International as a titling face and Zapf International bold for subheads and flags. Structurally, these are very different faces, with very different pedigrees. But Sabon has the calm and steady flow required for setting text, while Zapf International's vitality makes it a good face for titling – and this vitality persists even in the boldest weights. Most of the bold fonts structurally closer to Sabon, on the other hand, look splayed and deformed.

## **c** coelacanth; **d** daffodil; **4** Franciscan

Zapf International bold with Sabon roman

Claude Garamond, one of the master typographers of the sixteenth century, liked roman for text, large roman for titling, and italic for secondary matter such as prefaces and sidenotes. Other than that, he avoided mixing faces and fonts. If, nevertheless, you were setting text in a face derived from his, and wanted to set the heads in bold, you might consider using the sort of bold face which Garamond *could* have used if he had wanted to: namely, a sixteenth-century blackletter.

**𝔈lève elephant; fool filibuster; 543 phytogenic**

A late humanist roman paired with a late neohumanist rotunda: Karlgeorg Hoefer's San Marco paired with Adobe Garamond roman

6.5.4  *Choose titling and display faces that reinforce the structure of the text face.*

Titling faces, display faces and scripts can be chosen on much the same principles as bold faces. Incestuous similarity is rarely a necessity, but empathy and compatibility usually are. A geometrically constructed, high-contrast face such as Bauer Bodoni, for example, beautiful though it may be, has marginal promise as a titling face for a text set in Garamond or Bembo, whose contrast is low and whose structure is fundamentally calligraphic. (Bodoni mixes far more happily with Baskerville.)

6.5.5  *Pair serifed and unserifed faces on the basis of their inner structure.*

When the basic text is set in a serifed face, a related sanserif is frequently useful for other elements, such as tables, captions or notes. In complicated texts, such as dictionary entries, it may also be necessary to mix unserifed and serifed fonts on the same line. If you've chosen a family that includes a matched sanserif, your problems may be solved. But many successful marriages between serifed and unserifed faces from different families are waiting to be made.

Suppose your main text is set in Méridien – a serifed roman and italic designed by Adrian Frutiger. It would be reasonable to look first of all among Frutiger's other creations for a related sanserif. Frutiger is a prolific designer of types, both serifed and unserifed, so there are several from which to choose. Univers, for example, is his most widely used and best-known sanserif. But another of his unserifed faces – the one to which he gave his own name – is structurally much closer to Méridien and works handsomely as a companion.

# Frutiger Méridien Univers

Hans Eduard Meier's Syntax is a sanserif much different in structure from either Frutiger or Univers. It is based on serifed Renaissance forms such as Garamond. It works well with such faces as Stempel or Adobe Garamond, or with Sabon, another descendant of Garamond, designed by Meier's contemporary and countryman, Jan Tschichold.

If your choice falls on a more geometric sanserif, such as Futura, a Renaissance roman will hardly suffice as a serifed companion. Many romans based on the work of Bodoni, however, breathe much the same spirit as Futura. They aspire not to calligraphic motion but to geometric purity.

Gabocse escobaG

**Gabocse** escobaG

Gabocse escobaG

Syntax and Minion, above; Futura and Berthold Bodoni, center; Helvetica and Haas Clarendon, below

## 6.6 MIXING ALPHABETS

### 6.6.1 *Choose non-Latin faces as carefully as Latin ones.*

Mixing Latin letters with Hebrew or Arabic is, in principle, scarcely different from mixing roman with blackletter or serif with sans. Different though they look, and even though they read in different directions, all these alphabets spring from the same source, and all are written with similar tools. Many structural similarities underlie the obvious differences. A book involving more than one alphabet therefore poses some of the same questions posed by a bilingual or polylingual book set entirely in Latin letters. The typographer must decide in each case – after studying the text – whether to emphasize or minimize the differences. In general, the more closely different alphabets are mixed, the more important it becomes that they should be close in color and in size, no matter how superficially different in form.

The Latin, Greek and Cyrillic alphabets are as closely related in structure as roman, italic and small caps. (And most Cyrillic fonts have much the same color and shape as Latin small caps.) Random marriages of Latin and Greek, or Latin and Cyrillic, look just as ungainly and haphazard as random combinations of roman, italic and small caps – but excellent sets of related faces, and a few homogeneous polyglot families, have been designed. Several are discussed in Chapter 10.

6.6.2 *Avoid using faces that attempt to regiment other alphabets into Latin forms.*

Coordinating differences is one thing; denying or eradicating differences is another. Attempts to remodel the Greek and Hebrew alphabets into servile and compliant variants of Latin – like the attempt to turn italic into sloped roman – have produced only disheartening results.

νομω τον λογον τονδον επι τοις εκ

σούμενα λυθήσεται, καὶ γῆ καὶ τὰ

θεοῦ ἐπεφέρετο ἐπάνω τοῦ ὕδατος

Eric Gill's Perpetua Greek (above) was an attempt to bring the Greek alphabet to heel using serifed roman letters as a model. Jan van Krimpen's Antigone (center) and Herman Zapf's Heraklit (below) maintain the Greek tradition: inscriptional upper case and cursive lower case, like italic.

6.7 NEW ORTHOGRAPHIES

No writing system is fixed. Even our ways of writing classical Latin and Greek continue to change, along with our ways of writing and spelling such rapidly mutating languages as English. But many languages old to speech are new to writing, and many have not yet decided their literate form.

In North America, for example, Navajo, Hopi, Tlingit, Cree, Ojibwa, Inuktitut and Cherokee, among others, have evolved quite stable writing systems, in which a substantial printed literature has accrued. But many Native American languages are still being written in different ways by every scholar and student who happens by. Some, like Tsimshian and Kwakwala, already possess a considerable written literature, but in cumbersome scripts that even scholars have ceased to use.

Typographers must generally confront these problems piecemeal. Alphabets are often created by fiat, but it is usually in tiny increments that real typographic style evolves.

6.7.1 *Add no unnecessary characters.*

Colonial expansion has carried the Arabic alphabet across Africa, the Cyrillic alphabet across Asia, and the Latin alphabet around the earth. For better or for worse, most of those learning to read and write in newly literate languages are exposed to writing in a colonial language first. For readers and typographers alike, the basic roman alphabet is therefore often the easiest place to start, and the fewer additional symbols required the better. The dream of a common language, imposed upon many minority cultures, has proven for most to be a nightmare. But in a world where there are hundreds of ancestral and classical languages and literatures instead of one or two, prayers for renewed diversification often entail the dream of a common script.

Wa′giên sq!ê′ñgua lā′na hîn sā′wan, "K!wa la t!āla′ñ ł gia′ḷ ītc!în."

Wagyan sqqinggwa laana hin saawan, "Kkwa la ttaalang hl gyadliittsin."

A sentence in the Haida language, in the earliest (1901) orthography and a more recent, simplified version. In the first, glottalized consonants are marked by exclamations and long vowels by macrons. In the second, both are notated by doubling. (Translation: *Then the one in the bow said, 'Let us take it aboard.'*)

6.7.2 *Add only characters that are visually distinct.*

The texture of the typographic page depends not only on how the type is designed, set and printed, but also on the frequency of different letters. Latin looks smoother than English (and much smoother than German) because it uses fewer ascending

104

and descending letters, no accented characters, and (in the hands of most editors) very few caps. Polynesian languages – Maori and Hawaiian, for example – which are long on vowels and short on consonants, compose into a texture even creamier than Latin, and require a smaller alphabet.

Most languages need more, not fewer, consonants than the basic Latin alphabet provides. There may be (as in the Athapaskan languages of Alaska and northern Canada) four forms of *k*, or (as in the San languages of southwest Africa) 36 different clicks – and if each is lexically significant, each needs a distinctive typographic form.

Vowels are fairly easy to elaborate when need be; except for the *y*, they have no extenders. Navajo, for example, involves twelve forms of *a* – a, aa, ą, ąą, á, áá, áa, aá, ą́, ą́ą́, ą́ą, ąą́ – all easily distinguished. Typographically, it would be no problem to add another dozen forms.

Consonants are not quite so easy to ramify, precisely because so many of them have extenders. Typographically deficient forms therefore often crop up. Lakota, for example – the most widely spoken language of the Sioux – requires two forms of *h*. Stephen Riggs, who published the first Lakota dictionary and grammar, in 1852, chose to mark the second form with an overdot: *ḣ*. This character, which is still used by some native speakers and scholars, is easily mistaken for *ḷi*. More recent Lakota spelling replaces the dotted *h* with an *x*. This is easier to set, but most importantly, it is easier to read.

In the Tlingit language, spoken and written in Alaska and the Yukon, underscores are used to mark uvular consonants, which is fine for k̲ and x̲, but not so fine for g̲. The underscore either intersects the lower bowl of the *g* and produces a blob, or it sits so low that it may blend with the subsequent line. A form like *ġ* or *ǧ*, though less consistent, is easier to read.

The desire for consistency was not the only factor that led earlier linguists to write g̲ instead of *ǧ*. The Tlingit alphabet was developed, like many early twentieth-century writing systems, using only the keyboard of a North American typewriter. Recent Tlingit publications are typeset in modified Palatino with up-to-date computer-driven systems, but the iron metaphor of the typewriter has not yet loosed its hold.

Elsewhere in the world, the mechanical typewriter and letterpress are still economically viable and socially prestigious tools – and this need not prevent new alphabet design. The font below was cut and cast commercially for hand composition in 1983. Mechanical typewriters using a monospaced version of the font entered production in 1985.

New
Orthographies

àbɓcddɗeəę́fghiîįjkƙl
ABƁCDDƊEƎÉFGHIIĮJKKꞰL
M N Ò Ọ P Ʀ S Ṣ Ṭ T Û Ụ̄ V W Y Z
mnòọprsṣṭûụ̄vwyz

Pan Nigerian alphabet designed in 1983 by Hermann Zapf, in collaboration with Victor Manfredi. This normalizes the missionary orthographies that have been used for Hausa, Igbo, Yoruba, Edo, Fulfulde and several other Nigerian languages.

6.7.3  *Avoid capricious redefinition of familiar characters.*

Mayan languages have been written in roman script since the 1550s, but more than one orthography remains in use. Perhaps the oldest, based on the manuscript tradition of the *Popol Vuh*, uses the numerals 3 and 4 and the digraphs 4h and 4, [*including* the comma] to write several glottalized consonants. The Quiché words for sun and moon, for example, can be written *k'ih* and *ic',* or *kkih* and *icc,* or *3ih* and *i4,* and the word for blood can be written *quit'z* or *quittz* or *qui4,.* In the final case – but not in any of the others – the comma is part of the word and not a mark of punctuation.

Though it is not as picturesque as Mayan hieroglyphs, this alphanumeric script appeals to some scholars and amateurs, perhaps because of its very strangeness. Typographically, it begs for clarification, either through the creation of unambiguous new symbols or through reversion to plain old roman letters (which is now a common practice).

ʔaƛ̓aqə́m is
Upper Chehalis,
meaning
*you will emerge;*
ɪntə-næʃənḷ
fənɛɾɪks
(*international
phonetics*) is
English.

6.7.4  *Don't mix faces haphazardly when specialized sorts are required.*

If a text involves setting occasional words such as ʔaƛ̓aqə́m or ɪntə-næʃənḷ fənɛɾɪks, it is best to plan for them from the beginning. International phonetic characters are available in only a

106

few faces. (Times Roman was the twentieth-century standard, but the more recent Stone phonetic is considerably more versatile.) The typographer therefore has two choices:

1 Set the entire text in a face for which matching phonetic characters are available, so that phonetic transcriptions can enter the text transparently and at will.

2 Set the main text in a suitably contrasting face, and switch to the phonetic font (along with its matching text font, if required) each time a phonetic transcription occurs.

If contrasting faces are used for phonetic transcriptions and main text, each entire phonetic word or passage, not just the individual phonetic characters, should be set in the chosen phonetic face. Patchwork typography, in which the letters of a single word come from different faces and fonts, is a sign of typographical failure.

## 6.8  BUILDING A TYPE LIBRARY

### 6.8.1  *Choose your library of faces slowly and well.*

Some of the best typographers who ever lived had no more than one roman font at a time, one blackletter and one Greek. Others had as many as five or six romans, two or three italics, three blackletters, three or four Greeks. Today, the typographer can buy fonts by the thousand on compact discs, and use the telephone to download thousands more: more fonts than any human could use, yet never a complete selection.

With type as with philosophy, music and food, it is better to have a little of the best than to be swamped with the derivative, the careless, the routine.

The stock fonts supplied with software packages and desktop printers are sometimes generous in number, but they are the wrong fonts for many tasks and people, and most of them are missing essential parts (small caps, text figures, ligatures, diacritics and important analphabetics).

Begin by buying one good face or family, or a few related faces, with all the components intact. And instead of skipping from face to face, attempting to try everything, stay with your first choices long enough to learn their virtues and limitations before you move on.

A I S C

H Y L O

M W G

R U I X

P T U K

Lithos, designed by Carol Twombly, is based on early Greek
inscriptional letterforms.

Printing from movable type was first invented not in Germany in the 1450s, as Europeans often claim, but in China in the 1040s. In preference to Gutenberg, we should honor a scholarly engineer by the name of Bí Sheng (畢昇). The earliest surviving works printed in Asia from movable type seem to date from the thirteenth century, but there is a clear account of the typesetting process, and Bí Sheng's role in its development, by the eleventh-century essayist Shěn Kuò.

The new technology reached Korea before the middle of the thirteenth century and Europe before the middle of the fifteenth. There it intersected the already long and fertile history of the roman letter. And there typesetting flourished as it had failed to do in China, because of the far smaller number of characters European scripts required. Even at the end of the nineteenth century, most printing in China was done by the same method used in the eighth century to make the first printed books: entire pages of text were carved by hand into wooden printing plates. Corrections were made by drilling out the error, installing a wooden plug, and cutting the new characters. It is the same technique used to make the woodcut illustrations that were often combined with printed text.

## 7.1 THE EARLY SCRIBAL FORMS

The earliest surviving European letterforms are Greek capitals scratched into stone. The strokes are bony and thin, almost ethereal – the opposite of the heavy substance they are carved in. The letters are made primarily from straight lines, and when curved forms appear, they have a very large *aperture*. This means that forms like S and C, which can be relatively open or relatively closed, are about as open as they can get. These early Greek letters were drawn freehand, not constructed with compasses and rule, and they have no serifs – neither the informal entry and exit strokes left by a relaxed and fluent writer, nor the symmetrical finishing strokes typically added to letters by a formal scribe.

In time, the strokes of these letters grew thicker, the aperture lessened, and serifs appeared. The new forms, used for

Shěn Kuò's account is contained in his *Mèngxi Bítán* (夢溪筆談), "Dream Creek Essays." For more information in English, see Denis Twitchett, *Printing and Publishing in Medieval China* (London, 1983), and Thomas F. Carter, *The Invention of Printing in China and Its Spread Westward*, 2nd ed., revised by L. Carrington Goodrich (New York, 1955).

inscriptions throughout the Greek empire, served as models for formal lettering in imperial Rome. And those Roman inscriptional letters – written with a flat brush, held at an angle like a broad-nib pen, then carved into the stone with mallet and chisel – have served in their turn as models for calligraphers and type designers for the past 2000 years. They have a modest aperture, a *modulated* stroke (a stroke whose thickness varies with direction), and they have lively but full and formal serifs.

# A B C O S P Q R

Trajan, designed by Carol Twombly in 1988, is based on the inscription at the base of Trajan's Column, Rome, carved in AD 113.

Between the Roman inscriptions and Gutenberg's time, there were many further changes in European letterforms. Narrow rustic capitals, wide uncials and other forms evolved. Writing spread to the farthest corners of Europe, and many regional scripts and alphabets arose. Monastic scribes – who were designers, copyists and archivists as well – kept many of the older letterforms alive. They used them for titles, subheads and initials, choosing newer and more compact scripts for running text. Out of this rich multiplicity of letters, a basic dichotomy evolved: *majuscules* and *minuscules:* large formal letters and smaller, more casual ones: the upper and lower case, as we call them now.

# CAROLUS MAGNUS

## Caroline or Carolingian means of the time of the Emperor Charlemagne, "Big Charles" ...

Carol Twombly's Charlemagne (above) and Gottfried Pott's Carolina (below). These typefaces are based on Carolingian majuscules and minuscules from ninth- and tenth-century European manuscripts.

Many of the old scribal conventions survive in typesetting today. Titles are still set in large, formal letters; large initials mark the beginnings of chapters or sections; small capitals mark an opening phrase. The well-made page is now what it was then: a window into history, language and the mind: a map of what is being said and a portrait of the voice that is silently speaking.

In the later Middle Ages and the early Renaissance, a well-trained European scribe might know eight or ten distinct styles of script. Each was defined as precisely as a typeface, stored like a font in the human memory, and each had certain uses. Sacred scriptures, legal documents, romance literature, business and personal letters all required different scripts, and particular forms evoked specific languages and regions.

*Historical Interlude*

When the technology of movable type arrived, Europe was rich with Gothic, Byzantine, Romanesque and humanistic hands, and with a wealth of older letters. They are all still with us in some way, but the humanistic hand, based on the Carolingian minuscule, has become the central form: the roman lower case, evolving into a thousand variations, sports and hybrids, like the willow or the rose.

7.2 THE TYPOGRAPHIC LATIN LETTER

Several systems are in use for classifying typefaces. Some of them use fabricated terms such as 'garalde' and 'didone.' Others rely on familiar but vague labels such as 'old style,' 'modern' and 'transitional.' But these systems leave much to be desired. They are neither good science nor good history.

Rigorously scientific descriptions and classifications of typefaces are certainly possible, and important research has been under way in this field for several years. Like the scientific study of plants and animals, the infant science of typology involves precise measurement, close analysis, and the careful use of technically descriptive terms.

But letterforms are not only objects of science. They also belong to the realm of art, and they participate in its history. They have changed over time just as music, painting and architecture have changed, and the same historical terms – Renaissance, Baroque, Neoclassical, Romantic, and so on – are useful in each of these fields.

This approach to the classification of letterforms has another important advantage. Typography never occurs in isolation. Good typography demands not only a knowledge of type itself, but an understanding of the relationship between letterforms and the other things that humans make and do.

Typographical history is just that: the study of the relationships between type designs and the rest of human activity – politics, philosophy, the arts, and the history of ideas. It is a lifelong pursuit, but one that is informative and rewarding from the beginning.

The
Typographic
Latin
Letter

### 7.2.1 The Renaissance Roman Letter

Renaissance roman letters developed among the scholars and scribes of northern Italy in the fourteenth and fifteenth centuries. Their translation from script to type began in Italy in 1465 and continued for more than a century. Like Renaissance painting and music, Renaissance letterforms are full of sensuous and unhurried light and space. They have served as a typographical benchmark for 500 years.

The earliest surviving roman punches or matrices are Garamond's, cut in Paris in the 1530s. For earlier type, we have no evidence beyond the printed books themselves. The basic structure and form of these early typefaces is clear beyond dispute,

abcefgnop

abcefgnop

abcefgnop

Three twentieth-century reconstructions of Renaissance roman typefaces. Centaur (above) was designed by Bruce Rogers, Boston, c. 1914, after Nicolas Jenson, Venice, 1469. Bembo (center) was cut by Monotype in 1929, based on the design of Francesco Griffo, Venice, 1499. Adobe Garamond (bottom) was designed by Robert Slimbach, San Francisco, 1988, after Claude Garamond, Paris, c. 1540.

but in their subtlest details, all the existing replicas of fifteenth-century Italian type are hypothetical reconstructions.

Like Roman inscriptional capitals, Renaissance roman lowercase letters have a modulated stroke (the width varies with direction) and a *humanist axis*. This means that the letters have the form produced by a broad-nib pen held in the right hand in a comfortable and relaxed writing position. The thick strokes run NW/SE, the axis of the writer's hand and forearm. The serifs are crisp, the stroke is light, and the contrast between thick strokes and thin strokes is generally modest.

In summary, the characteristics of the early Renaissance roman letter are these:

- *stems vertical*
- *bowls nearly circular*
- *modulated stroke*
- *humanist axis*
- *modest contrast*
- *modest x-height*
- *crisp, oblique head serifs (on letters such as* b *and* r)
- *abrupt, flat or slightly splayed bilateral foot serifs (on letters such as* r, l *and* p)
- *abrupt, pen formed terminals on* a, c, f *and* r
- *rising crossbar in* e, *perpendicular to the stroke axis*
- *the roman font is solitary (there is no italic or bold)*

In later Renaissance forms (from 1500 on), the letterforms grow softer and smoother in subtle ways:

- *head serifs become more wedge-shaped*
- *foot serifs become* adnate *(flowing smoothly into the stem) instead of abrupt*
- *terminals of* c, f *and* r *become less abrupt and more* lachrymal *(teardrop-shaped)*
- *crossbar of* e *becomes horizontal*

### 7.2.2   *The Renaissance Italic Letter*

Rome is located in the midst of Italy. Why is roman type a category separate from italic? It seems a question to which typographers might possess the answer. But the question has as much to do with politics and religion as with calligraphy and typography.

Roman type consists of two quite different basic parts. The upper case, which does indeed come from Rome, is based on Roman imperial inscriptions. The lower case was developed in northern Europe, chiefly in France, in the late Middle Ages, and given its final polish in Venice in the early Renaissance. Nevertheless, it too is Roman in the larger sense. While the roman upper case is a legacy of the Roman Empire, the lower case is a legacy of the Holy Roman Empire, the pagan empire's Christian successor. It acquired its fundamental form at the hands of Christian scribes, many of them employed as administrators and teachers by the Holy Roman Emperor Charlemagne.

Italic letterforms, on the other hand, are an Italian Renaissance invention. Some of them come from Rome, others from elsewhere in Italy, and when they were first converted to type, italics were still full of local flavor and freshness. But the earliest italic fonts, cut between 1500 and 1540, consist of lower case only. They were used with upright roman caps, but not in conjunction with the roman lower case.

The characteristics of the Renaissance italic letter can be summarized as follows:

- *stems vertical or of fairly even slope, not exceeding 10°*
- *bowls generally elliptical*
- *light, modulated stroke*
- *humanist axis*

*abcefgnopxyz*

*abcefgnopxyz*

Two revivals of Renaissance italic type. Monotype Arrighi (above), is one of several Arrighis designed by Frederic Warde, London and Paris, 1925–29, after Ludovico degli Arrighi, Rome, 1524. Monotype Bembo italic (below) was cut in London in 1929, based on the work of Giovanantonio Tagliente, Venice, 1524.

- *low contrast*
- *modest x-height*
- *cursive forms with crisp, oblique entry and exit serifs*
- *descenders serifed bilaterally or not at all*
- *terminals abrupt or lachrymal*
- *italic lower case paired with small, upright roman capitals, and with occasional swash capitals; italic otherwise fully independent of roman*

The last of these features has been ignored in almost all of the reconstructions. Sloped roman caps are usually supplied instead – but typographers have the option of replacing these sloped caps with more authentic upright forms, simply by borrowing them from a related roman font.

### 7.2.3 *The Mannerist Letter*

Mannerist art is Renaissance art to which subtle exaggerations – of length, angularity or tension, for example – have been added. Mannerist typographers, working chiefly in Italy and France in the middle of the sixteenth century, began the practice of using roman and italic in the same book, and even on the same page – though not on the same line. It was also during the Mannerist period that sloped roman capitals were first added to the italic lower case.

*equbdaffglopsßz*
abefop*abefop*

Two recent typefaces in the Mannerist tradition. Poetica (above) is a chancery italic based on sixteenth-century models. It was designed by Robert Slimbach and issued by Adobe in 1992. Galliard (below), designed by Matthew Carter, was issued by Linotype in 1978. It is closely based on letterforms cut in the sixteenth century by Robert Granjon.

There are many fine sixteenth-century examples of Mannerist typefaces, including roman titling fonts with long, delicate extenders; chancery italics with even longer and often ornamented extenders, and text faces with short extenders but increased tension in the forms. Yet twentieth-century revivals of Mannerist faces have been relatively scarce.

### 7.2.4  *The Baroque Letter*

Baroque typography, like Baroque painting and music, is rich with activity and takes delight in the restless and dramatic play of contradictory forms. One of the most obvious features of any Baroque typeface is the large *variation in axis* from one letter to the next. Baroque italics are *ambidextrous:* both right-and lefthanded. And it was during the Baroque that typographers first began mixing roman and italic *on the same line.*

In general, Baroque letterforms appear more modelled and less written than Renaissance forms. They give less evidence of the direct trace of the pen. Yet they take many different forms, and they thrived in Europe throughout the seventeenth century and endured through much of the eighteenth.

abefop*abefop*

abefop*abefop*

abefop*abefop*

Three revivals of Baroque typefaces. Monotype Garamond 156 (above) is based on fonts cut in France by Jean Jannon, about 1621. Linotype Janson (center) is based on fonts cut by Miklós Kis, Amsterdam, about 1685. Adobe Caslon (bottom), by Carol Twombly, is based on faces cut by William Caslon, London, in the 1730s.

Baroque letterforms generally differ from Renaissance forms in the following ways:

- *stroke axis of the roman lower case varies widely within a single alphabet*
- *slope of italic averages 15° to 20° and often varies considerably within a single alphabet*
- *contrast increased*
- *x-height increased*
- *aperture generally reduced*
- *further softening of terminals from abrupt to lachrymal*
- *roman head serifs become sharp wedges*
- *head serifs of italic ascenders become level and sharp*

### 7.2.5  The Rococo Letter

The historical periods listed here – Renaissance, Baroque and so on – belong to all the arts, and they are naturally not limited, in typography, to roman and italic letters. Blackletter and script types passed through the same phases as well. But the Rococo period, with its love of florid ornament, belongs almost entirely to blackletters and scripts. Roman and italic type was certainly used (chiefly in France) by Rococo typographers, who surrounded their texts with typographical ornaments, engraved medallions, and so on. They produced a good deal of Rococo *typography,* but no Rococo roman and italic *type.*

### 7.2.6  The Neoclassical Letter

Generally speaking, Neoclassical art is more static and restrained than either Renaissance or Baroque art, and far more interested in rigorous consistency. Neoclassical letterforms follow this pattern. In Neoclassical letters, the trace of the broadnib pen can still be seen, but it is rotated away from the natural writing angle to a strictly vertical or *rationalist axis.* The letters are moderate in contrast and aperture, but their axis is dictated by an idea, not by the truth of human anatomy. They are products of the Rationalist era: frequently beautiful, calm forms, but forms oblivious to the more complex beauty of organic fact. If Baroque letterforms are ambidextrous, Neoclassical letters are, in their quiet way, *neitherhanded.*

The first Neoclassical typeface was designed in France in

# abefop *abefop*

# abefop*abefop*

Two revivals of Neoclassical letterforms. Above, ITC Baskerville, based on the designs of John Baskerville, Birmingham, about 1754. Below, Monotype Fournier, based on the designs of Pierre Simon Fournier, Paris, about 1740.

the 1690s, not by a typographer but by a government committee consisting of two priests, an accountant and an engineer. Other Neoclassical faces were designed and cut in France, England, Italy and Spain during the eighteenth century, and some of them have remained in continuous use, throughout all subsequent changes of style and fashion.

The American printer and statesman Benjamin Franklin deeply admired the Neoclassical type of his English contemporary John Baskerville, and it is partly due to Franklin's support that Baskerville's type became more important in the United States and France than it ever was in Baskerville's native land. But the connection between Baskerville and America rests on more than Benjamin Franklin's personal taste. Baskerville's letters correspond very closely to the federal style in American architecture. They are as purely and unperturbably Neoclassical as the Capitol Building, the White House, and many another federal and state edifice. (The Houses of Parliament in London and in Ottawa, which are Neogothic instead of Neoclassical, call for typography of a different kind.)

In brief, Neoclassical letterforms differ from Baroque letters as follows:

- *uniformly vertical axis in both roman and italic*
- *slope of italic generally uniform, averaging 14° to 16°*
- *serifs adnate, but thinner, flatter, more level than in the Baroque*

118

# abefopabefop

# abefopabefop

Two revivals of Romantic letterforms. Berthold Bodoni (above) is based on faces cut by Giambattista Bodoni at Parma, about 1780, and Berthold Walbaum (below) is based on designs by Justus Erich Walbaum, Weimar, about 1805.

## 7.2.7  The Romantic Letter

Neoclassicism and Romanticism are not sequential movements in European history. They marched through the eighteenth century, and much of the nineteenth, side by side: vigorously opposed in some respects and closely united in others. Both Neoclassical and Romantic letterforms adhere to a rationalist axis, and both look more drawn than written, but it is possible to make some precise distinctions between the two. The most obvious difference is one of contrast.

Romantic letterforms are, as a rule, distinct from Neoclassical forms in the following ways:

· *artificial modulation of stroke*
· *vertical axis intensified through exaggerated contrast*
· *hardening of terminals from lachrymal to round*
· *serifs thinner and more abrupt*
· *aperture reduced*

This remarkable shift in type design – like *all* structural shifts in type design – is the record of an underlying change in handwriting. Romantic letters are forms from which the broad-nib pen has vanished. In its place is the pointed and flexible quill. The broad-nib pen produces a smoothly modulated stroke whose thickness varies with direction, but the pointed

119

quill performs quite differently. The stroke of a flexible quill shifts suddenly from thin to thick to thin again, in response to changes in pressure. Used with restraint, it produces a Neoclassical flourish. Used with greater force, it produces a more dramatic and Romantic one. Dramatic contrast, which is essential to much Romantic music and painting, is essential to Romantic type design as well.

Romantic letters can be extraordinarily beautiful, but they lack the flowing and steady rhythm of Renaissance forms. It is that rhythm which invites the reader to enter the text and read. The statuesque forms of Romantic letters invite the reader to stand outside and *look* at the letters instead.

### 7.2.8  The Realist Letter

The nineteenth and twentieth centuries have entertained a bewildering variety of artistic movements and schools – Realism, Naturalism, Impressionism, Expressionism, Art Nouveau, Art Deco, Constructivism, Cubism, Abstract Expressionism, Pop Art, Op Art, and many more. Virtually all of these movements have raised waves in the typographical world as well, though only a few are important enough to merit a place in this brief survey. One of these movements is typographical Realism.

The Realist painters of the second half of the nineteenth century turned their backs on the subjects and poses approved

# abcefgnop
# abcefgnop

Akzidenz Grotesk (above) is a Realist typeface issued by the Berthold Foundry, Berlin, in 1898. It is the immediate ancestor of Morris Benton's Franklin Gothic (1903) and of Helvetica. Haas Clarendon (below), designed in 1951 by Hermann Eidenbenz, is a revival of an earlier Realist face, the first Clarendon, designed by Robert Besley, London, 1845.

by the academy. They set out instead to paint ordinary people doing their ordinary tasks. Realist type designers worked in a similar spirit, producing blunt and simple letters, based on the script of people denied the opportunity to learn to read and write with ease. Realist letters usually have the same basic shape as Neoclassical and Romantic letters, but they have heavy, slab serifs or no serifs at all. The stroke is generally uniform in weight, and the aperture (often a gauge of grace or good fortune in typefaces) is tiny. Small caps, hanging figures and other signs of sophistication and elegance are always missing.

### 7.2.9  *Geometrical Modernism: The Distillation of Function*

Early modernism took many intriguing typographic forms, but the most obvious is geometric. The sparest, most rigorous architecture of the early twentieth century has its counterpart in the equally geometric typefaces designed at the same time, often by the same people. These typefaces, like their Realist predecessors, make no distinction between main stroke and serif. Their serifs are equal in weight with the main strokes, or they are missing altogether. But the Geometrical Modernist faces seek purity more than populism. Some show the study of archaic inscriptions, and some include text figures and other subtleties, but their shapes owe more to pure mathematical forms – the circle and the line – than to scribal letters.

# abcefgnop
# abcefgnop

Two examples of Geometrical Modernist typefaces. Futura (above) was designed in Germany in 1924–26 by Paul Renner. Memphis (below) was designed in 1929 by Rudolf Wolf. The original design for Futura included text figures and many, highly geometric, alternative characters which have never yet been issued.

The second major phase of modernism in type design is closely allied with abstract expressionist painting. Painters in the twentieth century rediscovered the physical and sensory pleasures of painting as an act, and the pleasures of making organic instead of mechanical forms. Designers of type during those years were equally busy rediscovering the pleasures of *writing* letterforms rather than drawing them. And in rediscovering calligraphy, they rediscovered the broad-nib pen, the humanist axis and humanist scale of Renaissance letters.

*The
Typographic
Latin
Letter*

abefop*abefop*

abefop*abefop*

Two neohumanist or Lyrical Modernist typefaces. Palatino (above) was designed by Hermann Zapf, Frankfurt, 1948. Pontifex (below) was designed by Friedrich Poppl, Wiesbaden, 1974.

7.2.11  *The Postmodern Letter*

Modernism in type design has its roots in the study of history, the facts of human anatomy, and in the pleasures of calligraphy. Like the Renaissance itself, modernism is not a rootless phase or fad that simply runs its course and expires. It remains very much alive in the arts generally and in type design in particular, though it no longer seems the last word. In the final decades of the twentieth century, critics of architecture, literature and music – along with others who study human affairs – have all perceived movements away from modernism. Lacking any proper name of their own, these movements have come to be called by the single term postmodernism. And postmodernism is as evident in the world of type design as it is in other fields.

Postmodern letterforms, like Postmodern buildings, habitually recycle and revise Neoclassical and Romantic forms. At their best, they do so with an engaging lightness of touch and a fine sense of humor. Postmodernist art is for the most part highly self-conscious, but devoutly unserious. Postmodernist designers – who frequently are or have been modernist designers as well – have proven that it is possible to infuse Neoclassical form, and the rationalist axis, with real calligraphic energy.

*Historical Interlude*

# abefop*abefop*

## abefop*abefop*

# abefop*abefop*

Three Postmodern typefaces. Zapf International (above), designed by Hermann Zapf, Darmstadt, 1976. Esprit (center), designed by Jovica Veljović, Beograd, 1985. Nofret (bottom), designed by Gudrun Zapf-von Hesse, Darmstadt, 1990.

## 7.3   MECHANICAL TYPESETTING

### 7.3.1   *The Linotype Machine*

The Linotype machine, invented in the 1880s by Ottmar Mergenthaler and much modified over the years, is a kind of cross between a casting machine, a typewriter, a vending machine and a backhoe. It consists of a series of slides, belts, wheels, lifts, vices, plungers and screws, controlled from a large mechanical keyboard. Its complex mechanism composes a line of matrices, justifies the line by sliding tapered wedges into the spaces between the words, then casts the entire line as a single metal slug for letterpress printing.

Typeface design for the Linotype was restricted by three

basic factors. First, kerning is impossible without special compound matrices. (The basic italic *f* in a Linotype font therefore always has a stunted head and tail.) Second, the em is divided into only 18 units, which discourages subtlety of proportion. Third, the italic and roman matrices are usually in one piece. In most faces, each italic letter must therefore have the same width as its counterpart in roman.

*Mechanical*
*Typesetting*

A number of typefaces designed for the Linotype were artistically successful in spite of these constraints. Hermann Zapf's Aldus and Optima, Rudolf Růžička's Fairfield, Sem Hartz's Juliana, and W. A. Dwiggins's Electra, Caledonia and Falcon were all designed for the Linotype machine. Linotype Janson, adapted by Zapf in 1952 from the seventeenth-century originals of Miklós Kis, is another eminent success. Many Linotype faces have nevertheless been modified in the course of digitization, to make use of the greater kerning capabilities of digital machines and restore the independent proportioning of roman and italic.

### 7.3.2 The Monotype Machine

In the 1890s, in competition with Mergenthaler, Tolbert Lanston created a machine that could cast individual letters in metal and assemble them into lines. The device that evolved is separated into a terminal and an output device, and in this respect it resembles most computer-driven typesetting machines. But the terminal in this case consists of a large mechanical keyboard, including seven full alphabets as well as analphabetics. The keyboard unit punches holes into a paper tape, like a narrow player-piano roll, by driving pins with compressed air. The output device is the caster, which reads the paper tape by whistling more compressed air through the punched holes, then casts and assembles the letters.

The Monotype em, like the Linotype em, is divided into only 18 units, but italic and roman are independent in width, kerning is possible, and because the type remains in the form of separate letters, typeset lines can be further adjusted by hand. Characters larger than 24 pt are cast individually and left for hand assembly. In fact, the Monotype machine is a portable typefoundry as much as it is a composing machine – and it is increasingly used as such, even though its unit system imposes restrictions on letterform design, and it is incapable of casting in hard metal. Computerized front ends have been fitted to many of the machines that are still in service.

### 7.3.3 Two-Dimensional Printing

From the middle of the fifteenth century to the middle of the twentieth, most roman letters were printed by a technique rooted in sculpture. In this process, each letter is carved at actual size on the end of a steel punch. The punch is then struck into a matrix of softer metal, the matrix is fitted into a mold, and three-dimensional metal type is cast from an alloy of lead, tin and antimony. The cast letters are locked in a frame and placed in a printing press, where they are inked. Their image is then imprinted *into* the paper, producing a tactile and visual image. The color and sheen of the ink join with the smooth texture of crushed paper, recessed into the whiter and rougher fibers surrounding the letters and lines. A book produced by this means is a folding inscription, a flexible sculpture in low relief. The black light of the text *shines out from within* a well-printed letterpress page.

*Historical Interlude*

Renaissance typographers reveled in the physical depth and texture they could achieve by this method of printing. Neoclassical and Romantic printers, like Baskerville, often took a different view. Baskerville printed his sheets by letterpress – since he had no other method – but then had them ironed like laundry to remove the sculptural tinge.

With the development of lithography, at the end of the eighteenth century, printing moved another step back toward the two-dimensional world of the medieval scribes. Since the middle of the twentieth century, most commercial printing has been by two-dimensional means. The normal method is photo-lithography, using the offset press, which converts a photographic image into ink and lays it flat on the surface of the page.

In the early days of commercial offset printing, type was still set with Linotype or Monotype machines. Proofs were pulled in a letterpress, then cut, pasted and photographed. Type designers, of course, saw their letterforms changed by this process. Most letters designed to be printed in three dimensions look weaker when printed in two. But other letters prospered: geometric letters, which evoked the world of the draftsman rather than the goldsmith, and flowing letters recalling the heritage of the scribe.

### 7.3.4 Phototype Machines

Light flashes through the image of a letter carried on glass or photographic film; the size of the letter is altered with a lens; its target location is fixed by a mirror, and it is exposed like any other photographic image onto photosensitive paper or film. Machines that operate on this principle are the natural children of the camera and the offset press. They were in use for setting titles and headlines as early as 1915, but it was not until the 1960s that they came to dominate the trade.

Just as the sophistication and subtlety of handset type seemed at first to be swept aside when composing machines appeared, so the sophistication slowly achieved with Linotype and Monotype machines seemed to be swept aside by this new technological wave. The photosetters were fast, but they knew nothing of subtle changes in proportion from size to size. Their fonts lacked ligatures, text figures and small caps. American-made fonts lacked even the simplest accented characters. The choice of faces was poor....

Phototypesetting machines had only begun to answer these complaints when digital equipment arrived to replace them. Some excellent faces were designed for phototype machines – from Adrian Frutiger's Apollo (1962) to Bram de Does's Trinité (1982) – but in retrospect, the era of phototype seems only a brief interregnum between hot metal and digital composition. The important innovation of the period was not, after all, the conversion of fonts from metal to film, but the introduction of microcomputers to edit, compose and correct the text and to drive the last generations of photosetting machines.

### 7.3.5 Historical Recutting & Twentieth-Century Design

New typefaces have been designed in vast numbers in the twentieth century, and many old ones have been resuscitated. From 1960 to 1980, most new types and revivals were designed for photosetting, and since 1980, almost all have been planned for digital composition. But most of the older faces now sold in digital form have already passed through another stylistic filter. They were recut in the early twentieth century, either as foundry type or as matrices for the Monotype or Linotype machines. Typography was radically reformed between 1920 and 1950, through the commercial reinvention of typographic history. It is worth looking back at this process to see something of what went on, because its legacy affects us still.

Two separate companies – one based in England, one in America – rose up around the Monotype machine and followed two quite separate development programs. The English company, advised during its heyday by a scholar named Stanley Morison, cut a series of facsimiles based on the work of Francesco Griffo, Giovanantonio Tagliente, Ludovico degli Arrighi and other early designers. It was Morison who conceived the idea of turning independent Renaissance faces into families by mating one designer's roman with another's formerly self-sufficient italic. The fruits of this enterprise included Poliphilus & Blado (one of Griffo's romans mated with one of Arrighi's italics), Bembo (another of Griffo's romans with one of Tagliente's italics), and the brilliantly successful shotgun marriage of Centaur roman (designed by Bruce Rogers) with the Arrighi italic (designed by Frederic Warde).

American Monotype made several historical recuttings of its own, and issued many new and historically based faces designed by its own typographical advisor, Frederic Goudy. The English company, meanwhile, supplemented its large historical program by commissioning new faces from living designers such as Eric Gill.

The larger surviving typefoundries – including ATF (American Type Founders) in the United States, Deberny & Peignot in France, Enschedé in the Netherlands, Stempel in Germany and Grafotechna in Czechoslovakia – continued ambitious programs of their own, lasting in some cases into the 1980s. Revivals of faces by Claude Garamond, Miklós Kis and other early designers came from these foundries during the twentieth century, along with important new faces by such designers as Hermann Zapf, Jan van Krimpen, Adrian Frutiger, Oldřich Menhart and Hans Eduard Meier. Zapf's Palatino, which is the most widely used (and most widely pirated) face of the twentieth century, was cut by hand in steel and cast as a foundry type in the ancient way, in 1949–50, while phototype machines and early computers were humming not far off.

The earlier history of type design is the history of forms made by individual artists and artisans who began their careers as apprentices and ended them as independent masters and small businessmen. The scale of the industry enlarged in the seventeenth and eighteenth centuries, and questions of fashion

127

increasingly superseded questions of artistry. By the end of the nineteenth century, commercial considerations had changed the methods as well as the taste of the trade. Punches and matrices were increasingly cut by machine from large pattern letters, and calligraphic models were all but unknown.

The twentieth-century rediscovery of the history and principles of typographic form was not associated with any particular technology. It occurred among scholars and artists who brought their discoveries to fruition wherever they found employment: in type foundries, typesetting-machine companies, art schools and their own small, independent studios.

*Mechanical Typesetting*

Despite commercial pressures, the best of the old metal foundries, like the best of the new digital ones, were more than merely market-driven machine shops. They were cultural institutions, on a par with fine publishing houses and the ateliers of printmakers, potters, weavers and instrument makers. What made them so was the stature of the type designers, living and dead, whose work they produced – for type designers are, at their best, the Stradivarii of literature: not merely makers of salable products, but artists who make the instruments that other artists use.

### 7.3.6 Digital Typography

It is much too soon to summarize the history of digital typography, but the evolution of computerized bitmapping, hinting and scaling techniques has proceeded very quickly since the development of the microchip at the beginning of the 1970s. At the same time, the old technologies, freed from commercial duties, have by no means died. Foundry type, Monotype and letterpress remain important artistic instruments, alongside brush and chisel, pencil, graver and pen.

Typographic style is founded not on any one technology of typesetting or printing, but on the primitive yet subtle craft of writing. Letters derive their form from the motions of the human hand, restrained and amplified by a tool. That tool may be as complex as a digitizing tablet or a specially programmed keyboard, or as simple as a sharpened stick. Meaning resides, in either case, in the firmness and grace of the gesture itself, not in the tool with which it is made.

SHAPING THE PAGE

A book is a flexible mirror of the mind and the body. Its overall
size and proportions, the color and texture of the paper, the
sound it makes as the pages turn, and the smell of the paper,
adhesive and ink, all blend with the size and form and placement of the type to reveal a little about the world in which it
was made. If the book appears to be only a paper machine,
produced at their own convenience by other machines, only
machines will want to read it.

8.1 ORGANIC & MECHANICAL PROPORTION

A page, like a building or a room, can be of any size and proportion, but some are distinctly more pleasant than others, and
some have quite specific connotations. A brochure that unfolds
and refolds in the hand is intrinsically different from a formal
letter that lies motionless and flat, or a handwritten note that
folds into quarters and comes in an envelope of a different
shape and size. All of these are different again from a book, in
which the pages flow sequentially in pairs.

Much typography is based, for the sake of convenience, on
standard industrial paper sizes, from 35 × 45 inch press sheets to
3½ × 2 inch conventional business cards. Some formats, such as
the booklets that accompany compact discs, are condemned to
especially rigid restrictions of size. But many typographic projects begin with the opportunity and necessity of selecting the
dimensions of the page.

There is rarely a free choice. A page size of 12 × 19 inches,
for example, is likely to be both inconvenient and expensive
because it is just in excess of 11 × 17, which is a standard industrial unit. And a brochure that is 5 × 9 inches, no matter how
handsome, might be unacceptable because it is too wide to fit
into a standard business envelope (4⅛ × 9½). But when the
realm of practicality has been established, and it is known that
the page must fall within certain limits, how is one to choose?
By taking whatever is easiest, or biggest, or whatever is the most
convenient standard size? By trusting to blind instinct?

Instinct, in matters such as these, is largely memory in disguise. It works quite well when it is trained, and poorly other-

wise. But in a craft like typography, no matter how perfectly honed one's instincts are, it is useful to be able to calculate answers exactly. History, natural science, geometry and mathematics are all relevant to typography in this regard – and can all be counted on for aid.

Scribes and typographers, like architects, have been shaping *Organic* visual spaces for thousands of years. Certain proportions keep *and* recurring in their work because they please the eye and the *Mechanical* mind, just as certain sizes keep recurring because they are com- *Proportion* fortable to the hand. Many of these proportions are inherent in simple geometric figures – equilateral triangle, square, regular pentagon, hexagon and octagon. And these proportions not only seem to please human beings in many different centuries and countries; they are also prominent in nature far beyond the human realm. They occur in the structures of molecules, mineral crystals, soap bubbles, flowers, as well as books and temples, manuscripts and mosques.

The tables on pp 132–133 list a number of page proportions derivable from simple geometric figures. These proportions occur repeatedly in nature, and pages that embody them recur in manuscripts and books from Renaissance Europe, Táng and Sòng dynasty China, early Egypt, precolumbian Mexico and ancient Rome. It seems that the beauty of these proportions is more than a matter of regional taste or immediate fashion. They are therefore useful for two purposes. Working and playing with them is a way of developing good typographical instincts, and they serve as useful references in analyzing old designs and calculating new ones.

For comparison, several other proportions are included in the tables. There are several simple numerical ratios, several standard industrial sizes, and several proportions involving three irrational numbers important in the analysis of natural processes and structures. These numbers are $\pi = 3.14159\ldots$, which is the circumference of a circle whose diameter is one; $e = 2.71828\ldots$, which is the base of the natural logarithms; and $\varphi = 1.61803\ldots$, a number discussed in greater detail on p 139. Certain of these proportions reappear in the structure of the human body; others appear in musical scales. The study of the interrelations between anatomy, music and typography reaches deeply into the elements of typographic style. But for the moment, some more general correspondences and differences may be useful to keep in mind.

Sizing and spacing type, like composing and performing music or applying paint to canvas, is largely concerned with intervals and differences. As the texture builds, precise relationships and very small discrepancies are easily perceived. Establishing the overall dimensions of the page is more a matter of limits and sums. In this realm, it is usually sufficient, and often it is better, if structural harmony is not so much enforced as implied. That is one of the reasons typographers tend to fall in love with books. The pages flex and turn; their proportions ebb and flow against the underlying form. But the harmony of that underlying form is no less important, and no less easy to perceive, than the harmony of the letterforms themselves.

Portions of this chapter are peppered with numbers. Some passages are also thick with the language of simple mathematics. Readers may well ask whether all this is necessary, merely in order to choose where some letters should sit on a piece of paper and where the paper itself should be trimmed. The answer, naturally, is no. It is not in the least necessary to understand the mathematics in order to perform the actions that the math describes. People walk and ride bicycles without mathematical analyses of these complex operations. The chambered nautilus and the snail construct perfect logarithmic spirals without any need of logarithmic tables, sliderules or the theory of infinite series. The typographer likewise can construct beautiful pages without knowing the meaning of symbols like $\pi$ or $\varphi$, and indeed without ever learning to add and subtract, if he has a well-educated eye and knows which buttons to push on the calculator and keyboard.

The mathematics are not here to impose drudgery upon anyone. On the contrary, they are here entirely for pleasure. They are here for the pleasure of those who like to examine what they are doing, or what they might do or have done, perhaps in the hope of doing it still better. Those who prefer to act directly at all times, and to leave the analysis to others, may be content in this chapter to study the pictures and skim the text.

*Organic and Mechanical Proportion*

| | | | | | |
|---|---|---|---|---|---|
| A | Double Square | 1 : 2 | 4.50 × 9 | 5.00 × 10 | 5.50 × 11 |
| B | Tall Octagon | 1 : 1.924 | 4.68 × 9 | 5.20 × 10 | 5.72 × 11 |
| C | Tall Hexagon | 1 : 1.866 | 4.82 × 9 | 5.36 × 10 | 5.89 × 11 |
| D | Octagon | 1 : 1.848 | 4.87 × 9 | 5.41 × 10 | 5.95 × 11 |
| | 5 : 9 | 1 : 1.8 | | 5.00 × 9 | |
| E | Hexagon | 1 : 1.732 | 4.91 × 8.5 | 5.20 × 9 | 6.36 × 11 |
| | $\pi : 2e$ | 1 : 1.731 | | | |
| F | Tall Pentagon | 1 : 1.701 | 5.00 × 8.5 | 5.29 × 9 | 6.47 × 11 |
| | 3 : 5 | 1 : 1.667 | | | |
| | Legal Sheet | 1 : 1.647 | | | 8.50 × 14 |
| G | Golden Section | 1 : 1.618 | 5.25 × 8.5 | 5.56 × 9 | 6.80 × 11 |
| | 5 : 8 | 1 : 1.6 | 5.00 × 8 | | |
| | 2 : $\pi$ | 1 : 1.571 | | | |
| H | Pentagon | 1 : 1.539 | 5.52 × 8.5 | 5.85 × 9 | 7.15 × 11 |
| | 2 : 3 | 1 : 1.5 | | 6.00 × 9 | |
| | | | | | |
| I | ISO = 1 : $\sqrt{2}$ | 1 : 1.414 | 6.36 × 9 | 7.07 × 10 | 7.75 × 11 |
| | 5 : 7 | 1 : 1.4 | | | |
| J | Short Pentagon | 1 : 1.376 | 6.54 × 9 | 7.27 × 10 | 8.00 × 11 |
| | 3 : 4 | 1 : 1.333 | 6.75 × 9 | 7.50 × 10 | 9.00 × 12 |
| K | Tall Half Octagon | 1 : 1.307 | 6.89 × 9 | 7.65 × 10 | 8.42 × 11 |
| | Letter Sheet | 1 : 1.294 | | | 8.50 × 11 |
| | 4 : 5 | 1 : 1.25 | | 8.00 × 10 | |
| L | Half Octagon | 1 : 1.207 | 7.46 × 9 | 8.29 × 10 | 9.11 × 11 |
| | 5 : 6 | 1 : 1.2 | | | |
| M | Truncated Pentagon | 1 : 1.176 | 7.65 × 9 | 8.50 × 10 | 9.36 × 11 |
| | 6 : 7 | 1 : 1.167 | | | |
| | $e : \pi$ | 1 : 1.156 | | | |
| N | Turned Hexagon | 1 : 1.155 | 7.79 × 9 | 8.67 × 10 | 9.53 × 11 |
| O | Tall Cross Octagon | 1 : 1.082 | 8.32 × 9 | 9.24 × 10 | 10.2 × 11 |
| P | Turned Pentagon | 1 : 1.051 | 8.56 × 9 | 9.51 × 10 | 10.5 × 11 |
| | | | | | |
| Q | Square | 1 : 1 | | | |
| R | Broad Pentagon | 1 : 0.951 | 9 × 8.56 | 10 × 9.51 | 11 × 10.5 |
| S | Broad Cross Octagon | 1 : 0.924 | 9 × 8.32 | 10 × 9.24 | 11 × 10.2 |
| T | Broad Hexagon | 1 : 0.866 | 9 × 7.79 | 10 × 8.67 | 11 × 9.53 |
| | $\pi : e$ | 1 : 0.865 | | | |
| U | Full Cross Octagon | 1 : 0.829 | 9 × 7.46 | 10 × 8.29 | 11 × 9.11 |
| | Landscape Letter | 1 : 0.773 | 9 × 6.96 | 10 × 7.73 | 11 × 8.50 |
| | $\varphi : 1$ | 1 : 0.618 | | | |

| | Column/Page Proportions | | | Sample sizes in inches | | |
|---|---|---|---|---|---|---|
| a | Quad Square | 1 : 4 | | 2.25 × 9 | 2.50 × 10 | 2.75 × 11 |
| | 1 : √15 | 1 : 3.873 | | | | |
| | 5 : 18 | 1 : 3.6 | | | | |
| b | Octagon Wing | 1 : 3.414 | | 2.64 × 9 | 2.93 × 10 | 3.22 × 11 |
| | 1 : 2φ | 1 : 3.236 | | | | |
| | 5 : 16 | 1 : 3.2 | | | | |
| c | 1 : √10 | 1 : 3.162 | | 2.85 × 9 | 3.16 × 10 | 3.48 × 11 |
| d | 1 : π | 1 : 3.142 | | 2.86 × 9 | 3.18 × 10 | 3.50 × 11 |
| e | Double Pentagon | 1 : 3.078 | | 2.92 × 9 | 3.25 × 10 | 3.57 × 11 |

| | | 1 : 3 | 1 : 3 | | | |
|---|---|---|---|---|---|---|
| f | Wide Octagon Wing | 1 : 2.993 | | 3.01 × 9 | 3.34 × 10 | 3.68 × 11 |
| g | 1 : 2√2 | 1 : 2.828 | | 3.18 × 9 | 3.54 × 10 | 3.89 × 11 |
| | 5 : 14 | 1 : 2.8 | | | | |
| h | Pentagon Wing | 1 : 2.753 | | 3.27 × 9 | 3.63 × 10 | 4.00 × 11 |
| i | 1 : e | 1 : 2.718 | | 3.31 × 9 | 3.68 × 10 | 4.05 × 11 |
| | 3 : 8 | 1 : 2.667 | | | | |
| j | 1 : √7 | 1 : 2.646 | | 3.40 × 9 | 3.78 × 10 | 4.16 × 11 |
| k | Extended Section | 1 : 2.618 | | 3.44 × 9 | 3.82 × 10 | 4.20 × 11 |
| l | Tall Octagon Column | 1 : 2.613 | | 3.44 × 9 | 3.83 × 10 | 4.21 × 11 |
| | 5 : 13 | 1 : 2.6 | | | | |
| m | Mid Octagon | | | | | |
| | Column | 1 : 2.514 | | 3.56 × 9 | 3.98 × 10 | 4.38 × 11 |

| | | 2 : 5 | 1 : 2.5 | | | |
|---|---|---|---|---|---|---|
| n | Short Octagon | | | | | |
| | Column | 1 : 2.414 | | 3.73 × 9 | 4.14 × 10 | 4.56 × 11 |
| | 5 : 12 | 1 : 2.4 | | | | |
| | 3 : 7 | 1 : 2.333 | | | | |
| o | Hexagon Wing | 1 : 2.309 | | 3.90 × 9 | 4.33 × 10 | 4.76 × 11 |
| p | Double Truncated | | | | | |
| | Pentagon | 1 : 2.252 | | 4.00 × 9 | 4.44 × 10 | 4.88 × 11 |
| | 1 : √5 | 1 : 2.236 | | 4.03 × 9 | 4.47 × 10 | 4.92 × 11 |
| | 5 : 11 | 1 : 2.2 | | | | |
| A | Double Square | 1 : 2 | | 4.50 × 9 | 5.00 × 10 | 5.50 × 11 |

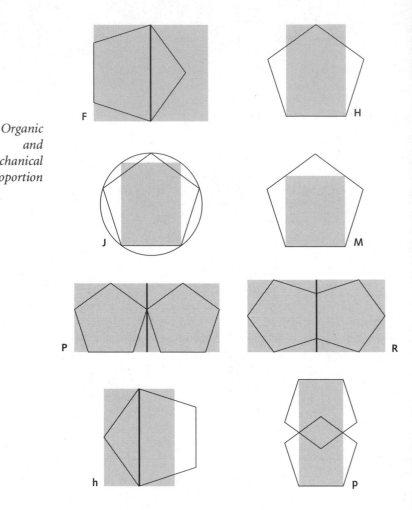

F, P, R and h are
shown here as
two-page spreads.
H, J, M and p are
shown as single
pages.

Pages derived from the pentagon: **F** the Tall Pentagon page, 1 : 1.701; **H** Pentagon page, 1 : 1.539; **J** Short Pentagon page, 1 : 1.376; **M** the Truncated Pentagon page, 1 : 1.176; **P** Turned Pentagon page, 1 : 1.051; **R** the Broad Pentagon page, 1 : 0.951; **h** Pentagon Wing, 1 : 2.753; **p** the Double Truncated Pentagon, 1 : 2.252. The pentagon page differs by 2% from the North American standard small trade book size, which is half the size of a letter sheet: 5½ × 8½ inches. A more eminent page proportion, the golden section, is also present in the pentagon; see p 139. In nature, pentagonal symmetry is rare in inanimate forms. Packed soap bubbles strive for it but never quite succeed, and there are no mineral crystals with true pentagonal structures. But pentagonal geometry is basic to many living things, from roses and forget-me-nots to sea urchins and starfish.

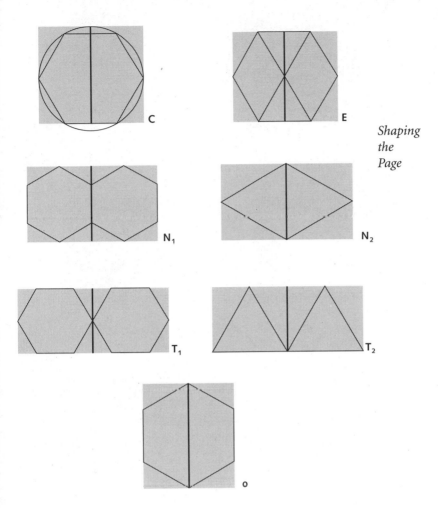

Pages derived from the hexagon: **C** the Tall Hexagon page, 1 : 1.866; **E** Hexagon page, 1 : √3 = 1 : 1.732; **N** Turned Hexagon page, 1 : 1.155; **T** Broad Hexagon page, 1 : 0.866; **o** Hexagon Wing, 1 : 2.309. The hexagon consists of six equilateral triangles, and each of these page shapes can be derived directly from the triangle instead. The hexagon merely clarifies their existence as mirror images, like the pages of a book. Hexagonal structures are present in both the organic and the inorganic world – in lilies and wasps' nests, for example, and in snowflakes, silica crystals and sunbaked mudflats. The proportions of the broad hexagon page are within one tenth of one per cent of the natural ratio $\pi/e$, while the turned hexagon page (which is the broad hexagon rotated 90°) approximates the ratio $e/\pi$. (The hexagon page used in this book is analyzed on p 6.)

All formats on this page are shown as two-page spreads.

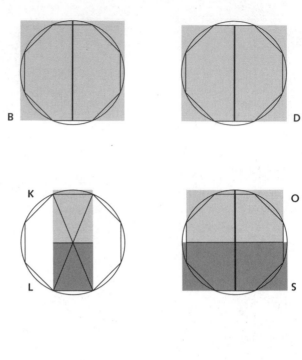

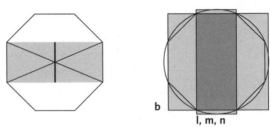

B, D, O, S and U
are shown as
two-page spreads.

Pages derived from the octagon: **B** the Tall Octagon page, 1 : 1.924; **D** Octagon page, 1 : 1.848; **K** Tall Half Octagon page, 1 : 1.307; **L** Half Octagon page, 1 : 1.207; **O** Tall Cross Octagon, 1 : 1.082; **S** Broad Cross Octagon page, 1 : 0.924; **U** the Full Cross Octagon page, 1 : 0.829; **b** Octagon Wing, 1 : 3.414; **f** Wide Octagon Wing, 1 : 2.993; **l, m, n** Tall, Middle and Short Octagon Columns, 1 : 2.613, 1 : 2.514 and 1 : 2.414. The tall half octagon page (K), used in Roman times, differs by a margin of 1% from the standard North American letter size. Are proportions derived from the hexagon and pentagon livelier and more pleasing than those derived from the octagon? Forms based on the hexagon and pentagon are, at any rate, more frequent in the structure of flowering plants and elsewhere in the living world.

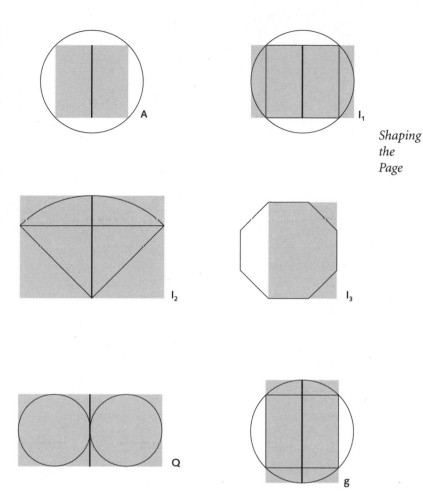

Pages derived from the circle and the square: **A** Double Square page, 1 : 2; **I** the Broad Square page, which is the ISO standard, 1 : $\sqrt{2}$ = 1 : 1.414; **Q** the Perfect Square; **g** Double ISO, 1 : 2$\sqrt{2}$ = 1 : 2.828. The proportion 1 : $\sqrt{2}$ is that of side to diagonal in a square. A rectangle of these proportions (and no others) can be halved or doubled indefinitely to produce new rectangles of the same proportion. The proportion was chosen for that reason as the basis for ISO (International Organization for Standardization) paper sizes. The A4 sheet, for example, is standard European letter size, 210 × 297 mm = 8¼″ × 11⅝″. An 8½″ × 12″ book page also embodies this proportion.

The ISO or broad square page is latent not only in the square but in the octagon.

Except for $I_3$, all formats on this page are shown as two-page spreads.

AO

A2

A1

A4

A3

A5

ISO sheet sizes    A0 = 841 × 1189 mm    A1 = 594 × 841 mm
                                      A2 =  420 × 594 mm    A3 = 297 × 420 mm
                                        A4 =  210 × 297 mm    A5 = 148 × 210 mm

The golden section is a symmetrical relation built from asymmetrical parts. Two numbers, shapes or elements embody the golden section when the smaller is to the larger as the larger is to the sum. That is, $a : b = b : (a + b)$. In the language of algebra, this ratio is $1 : \varphi = 1 : (1 + \sqrt{5})/2$, and in the language of trigonometry, it is $1 : (2 \sin 54°)$. Its approximate value in decimal terms is $1 : 1.61803$.

*Shaping the Page*

The second term of this ratio, $\varphi$ (the Greek letter *phi*), is a number with several unusual properties. If you *add* one to $\varphi$, you get its square ($\varphi \times \varphi$). If you *subtract* one from $\varphi$, you get its reciprocal ($1/\varphi$). And if you multiply $\varphi$ endlessly by itself, you get an infinite series embodying a single proportion. That pro portion is $1 : \varphi$. If we rewrite these facts in the typographical form mathematicians like to use, they look like this:

$$\varphi + 1 = \varphi^2$$

$$\varphi - 1 = 1/\varphi$$

$$\varphi^{-1} : 1 = 1 : \varphi = \varphi : \varphi^2 = \varphi^2 : \varphi^3 = \varphi^3 : \varphi^4 = \varphi^4 : \varphi^5 \ldots$$

If we look for a numerical approximation to this ratio, $1 : \varphi$, we will find it in something called the Fibonacci series, named for the thirteenth-century mathematician Leonardo Fibonacci. Though he died two centuries before Gutenberg, Fibonacci is important in the history of European typography as well as mathematics. He was born in Pisa but studied in North Africa. On his return, he introduced arabic numerals to the North Italian scribes.

As a mathematician, Fibonacci took an interest in many problems, including the problem of unchecked propagation. What happens, he asked, if everything breeds and nothing dies? The answer is a logarithmic spiral of increase. Expressed as a series of integers, such a spiral takes the following form:

0, 1, 1, 2, 3, 5, 8, 13, 21, 34, 55, 89, 144, 233, 377, 610, 987, 1597, 2584, 4181, 6765, 10 946, 17 711, 28 657 …

Here each term after the first two is *the sum of the two preceding*. And the farther we proceed along this series, the

The screened area represents a two-page spread in which each page embodies the golden section. The root of the spiral, which is the navel of the page, lies at the intersection of the diagonals. This is a Renaissance structure: precisely measured and formed, yet open-ended, unconfined. Like Thoreau's vision of the mind (p 64), it is *hypethral.* Compare the equally elegant but closed, medieval structure on p 157.

**G** Golden Section, $1 : \varphi = 1 : 1.618$. In the pentagon, the side $s$ and the chord $c$ embody the golden section. The smaller is to the larger as the larger is to the whole, or $s : c = c : (s + c)$. When two chords intersect, they divide each other in the same proportion: $a : b = b : c$, where $c = a + b$. Moreover, $b = s$. Thus, $a : s = s : c = c : (s + c) = 1 : \varphi$.

An evolving sequence of figures that embody the golden section also defines the path of a logarithmic spiral. And if the lengths of the sides of the figures are rounded off to the nearest whole numbers, the result is a Fibonacci series of integers.

closer we come to an accurate approximation of the number φ. Thus 5 : 8 = 1 : 1.6; 8 : 13 = 1 : 1.625; 13 : 21 = 1 : 1.615; 21 : 34 = 1 : 1.619, and so on.

In the world of pure mathematics, this spiral of increase, the Fibonacci series, proceeds without end. In the world of mortal living things, of course, the spiral quickly breaks off. It is repeatedly interrupted by death and other practical considerations – but it is visible nevertheless in the short term. Abbreviated versions of the Fibonacci series, and the proportion 1 : φ, can be seen in the structure of pineapples, pinecones, sunflowers, sea urchins, snails, the chambered nautilus, and in the proportions of the human body as well.

If we convert the ratio 1 : φ or 1 : 1.61803... to percentages, the smaller part is roughly 38.2% and the larger 61.8% of the whole. But we will find the *exact* proportions of the golden section in several simple geometrical figures. These include the pentagon, where they are relatively obvious, and the square, where they are somewhat more deeply concealed.

The golden section was much admired by classical Greek geometers and architects, and by Renaissance mathematicians, architects and scribes, who often used it in their work. It has also been much admired by artists and craftsmen, including typographers, in the modern age. Paperback books in the Penguin Classics series have been manufactured for more than half a century to the standard size of 111 × 180 mm, which embodies the golden section. The Modulor system of the Swiss architect Le Corbusier is based on the golden section as well.

If type sizes are chosen according to the golden section, the result is again a Fibonacci series:

(a)   5, 8, 13, 21, 34, 55, 89 ...

These sizes alone are adequate for many typographic tasks. But to create a more versatile scale of sizes, a second or third interlocking series can be added. The possibilities include:

(b)   6, 10, 16, 26, 42, 68, 110 ...
(c)   4, 7, 11, 18, 29, 47, 76 ...

All three of these series – a, b and c – obey the Fibonacci rule (each term is the sum of the two terms preceding). Series b is also related to series a by simple doubling. The combination of **a** and **b** is therefore a two-stranded Fibonacci series with incremental symmetry, forming a very versatile scale of type sizes:

(**d**)  6, 8, 10, 13, 16, 21, 26, 34, 42, 55, 68 …

A similar double-stranded Fibonacci series was used by Le Corbusier (with other units of measurement) in his architectural work:

(**e**)
| 4 | 6½ | 10½ | 17 | 27½ | 44½ | 72 | |
|---|---|---|---|---|---|---|---|
| | 5 | 8 | 13 | 21 | 34 | 55 | 89 | … |

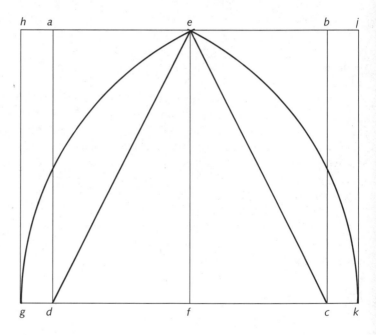

Finding the golden section in the square. Begin with the square *abcd*. Bisect the square (with the line *ef*) and draw diagonals (*ec* and *ed*) in each half. An isosceles triangle, *cde,* consisting of two right triangles, is formed. Extend the base of the square (draw the line *gk*) and project each of the diagonals (the hypoteneuse of each of the right triangles) onto the extended base. Now *ce* = *cg,* and *de* = *dk.* Draw the new rectangle, *efgh.* This and its mirror image, *ejkf,* each have the proportions of the golden section. That is to say, *eh* : *gh* = *gh* : (*gh* + *eh*) = *ej* : *jk* = *jk* : (*jk* + *ej*) = 1 : φ. (Compare this with figure I$_2$ on p 137.)

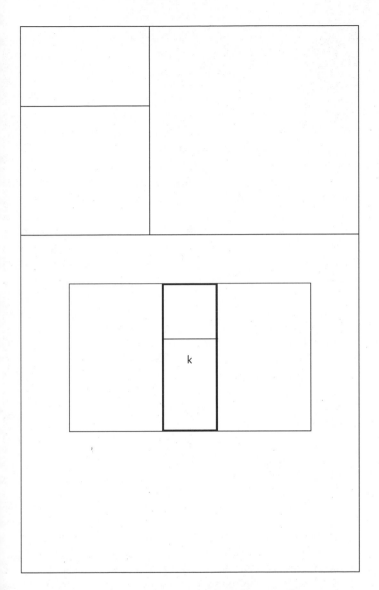

The relationship between the square and the golden section is perpetual. Each time a square is subtracted from a golden section, a new golden section remains. If two overlapping squares are formed within a golden-section rectangle, two smaller rectangles of golden-section proportions are created, along with a narrow column whose proportions are $1 : (\varphi + 1) = 1 : 2.618$. This is **k**, the Extended Section, from the table on p 133. If a square is subtracted from this, the golden section is restored.

T HIS PARAGRAPH, for example, is indented according to the golden section. The indent is to the remainder of the line as that remainder is to the full text measure. Here the measure is 21 picas, and the indent is 38.2% of that, which is 8 picas.

The amount of *sinkage* (extra white space allowed at the top of the page) is 7 lines (here equal to 7 picas). Add the extra pica of white space created by the indent itself, and you have an imaginary 8-pica square of empty space in the upper left corner of the typeblock.

The size of the elevated cap is related in turn to the size of the indent and the sinkage. Eight picas is 96 pt, and 61.8% of that is 59.3 pt. But the relationship between 59 or 60 pt type and an 8-pica indent would be difficult to perceive, because a 60 pt letter is not visibly 60 pt high. The initial used has an actual 60 pt cap height instead. Depending on the face, such a letter could be anywhere from 72 to 100 pt nominal size; here it is 84 pt.

8.3  PROPORTIONS OF THE EMPTY PAGE

8.3.1  *Choose inherently satisfying page proportions in preference to stock sizes or arbitrary shapes.*

The proportions of a page are like an interval in music. Some proportions are consonant, others are dissonant. And some are not only familiar but inescapable, because of their presence in the structures of the natural as well as the man-made world. Some proportions also seem particularly linked to living things. It is true that wastage is often increased when an 8½ × 11 inch page is trimmed to 7¾ × 11 or 6¾ × 11, or when a 6 × 9 book page is narrowed to 5⅝ × 9. But an organic page looks and feels different from a mechanical page, and the shape of the page itself will provoke certain responses and expectations in the reader, independently of whatever text it contains.

8.3.2 *Choose page proportions suited to the content, size and ambitions of the publication.*

There is no one ideal proportion, but some are clearly more ponderous, others more brittle. In general, a book page, like a human being, should not peer down its nose, nor should it sag.

The narrower page shapes require a soft or open spine so Shaping that the opened book lies flat, and at smaller sizes, narrower the pages are suitable only for text that can be set to a narrow Page measure. At larger sizes, the narrow page is more adaptable.

For ordinary books, consisting of simple text in a modest size, typographers and readers both gravitate to proportions ranging from the light, agile 5 : 9 [1 : 1.8] to the heavier and more stolid 4 : 5 [1 : 1.25]. Pages wider than 1 : $\sqrt{2}$ are useful primarily in books that need the extra width for maps, tables, sidenotes or illustrations, and for books in which a multiple-column page is preferred.

When important illustrations are involved, these generally decide the shape of the page. Typically, one would choose a page somewhat deeper than the average illustration, both to leave extra blank space at the foot of the page, and to permit the insertion of captions. The *e/π* or turned hexagon page, 1 : 1.16, for example, which is slightly deeper than a perfect square, is useful for square artwork, such as photographs taken with a square-format camera. The *π/e* or broad hexagon page, 1 : 0.87, is useful for landscape photographs in the 4 × 5 format, and the full cross octagon page, 1 : 0.83, for landscape photos in the wider format of 35 mm. (Uncropped 35 mm transparencies are of the proportion 2 : 3.)

8.3.3 *Choose page and column proportions whose historical associations suit your intended design.*

Early Egyptian scribes (when not writing vertically) tended to write a long line and a wide column. This long, Egyptian line reappears in other contexts over the centuries – on Roman imperial writing tablets, in medieval European charters and deeds, and in many poorly designed twentieth-century works of academic prose. It is a sign, generally speaking, that the emphasis is on the writing instead of the reading, and that writing is seen as an instrument of power, not an instrument of freedom.

Early Hebrew scribes generally favored a narrower column, and early Greek scribes a column narrower still. But they, like the Egyptians, were making scrolls instead of bound books. It is difficult, therefore, to compare their notions of the page. You can open a scroll as wide as you like, exposing one column, two columns, three.... This flexible approach to the concept of the page is also present in early codices (bound books). There are early books that are three times taller than wide, others that are close to square, and many shapes between.

*Proportions of the Empty Page*

In medieval Europe, most books, though certainly not all, settled down to proportions ranging from 1:1.5 to 1:1.25. Paper was commonly made in sheets whose proportions were 2:3 [1:1.5] or 3:4 [1:1.33], and these proportions reproduce one another with each fold. If a sheet is 40 × 60 cm [2:3] to start with, it folds to 30 × 40 [3:4], which folds to 20 × 30, and so on. The 25 × 38 inch [roughly 2:3] and 20 × 26 inch [roughly 3:4] press sheets used today in North America are survivors of this medieval tradition.

The page proportion 1:$\sqrt{2}$, which is now the European standard, was also known to the medieval scribes. And the tall half octagon page, 1:1.3 (the proportions of North American letter paper) has a similar pedigree. The British Museum has a Roman wax-tablet book of precisely this proportion, dated about AD 300.

Renaissance typographers continued to produce books in the proportions 1:1.5. They also developed an enthusiasm for narrower proportions. The proportions 1:1.87 (tall hexagon), 1:1.7 (tall pentagon), 1:1.67 [3:5], and of course 1:1.62, the golden section, were used by typographers in Venice before the end of the fifteenth century. The narrower page was preferred especially for works in the arts and sciences. Wider pages, better able to carry a double column, were preferred for legal and ecclesiastical texts. (Even now, a Bible, a volume of court reports or a manual on mortgages or wills is likely to be on a wider page than a book of poems or a novel.)

Renaissance page proportions (generally in the range of 1:1.4 to 1:2) survived through the Baroque, but Neoclassical books are often wider, returning to the heavier Roman proportion of 1:1.3.

8.4.1 *If the text is meant to invite continuous reading, set it in columns that are clearly taller than wide.*

Horizontal motion predominates in alphabetic writing, and for beginners, it predominates in reading. But vertical motion predominates in reading for those who have really acquired the skill. The tall column of type is a symbol of fluency, a sign that the typographer does not expect the reader to have to puzzle out the words.

*Shaping the Page*

The very long and very narrow columns of newspapers and magazines, however, have come to suggest disposable prose and quick, unthoughtful reading. A little more width not only gives the text more presence; it implies that it might be worth savoring, quoting and reading again.

8.4.2 *Shape the typeblock so that it balances and contrasts with the shape of the overall page.*

The proportions that are useful for the shapes of pages are equally useful in shaping the typeblock. This is not to say that the proportions of the typeblock and the page should be *the same.* They often were the same in medieval books. In the Renaissance, many typographers preferred a more polyphonic page, in which the proportions of page and typeblock differ. But it is pointless for them to differ unless, like intervals in music, they differ to a clear and purposeful degree.

For all the beauty of pure geometry, a perfectly square block of type on a perfectly square page with even margins all around is a form unlikely to encourage reading. Reading, like walking, involves navigation – and the square block of type on a square block of paper is short of basic landmarks and clues. To give the reader a sense of direction, and the page a sense of liveliness and poise, it is necessary to break this inexorable sameness and find a new balance of another kind. Some space must be narrow so that other space may be wide, and some space emptied so that other space may be filled.

In the simple format shown overleaf, a page whose proportions are 1 : 1.62 (the golden section) carries a typeblock whose proportions are 1 : 1.8 [5 : 9]. This difference constitutes a primary visual chord which generates both energy and harmony in the page. It is supplemented by secondary harmonies created by the proportions of the margins and the placement of the typeblock – not in the center of the page but high and toward the spine.

The typeblock itself, in this example, is symmetrical, but it is placed asymmetrically on the page. The lefthand page is a mirror image of the right, but no mirror image runs the other way. The two-page spread is *symmetrical horizontally* – the direction in which the pages turn, either backward or forward, as the reader consults the book – but it is *asymmetrical vertically* – the direction in which the page stays put while the reader's eye repeatedly works its way in one direction: down.

*The Typeblock*

This interlocking relationship of symmetry and asymmetry, and of balanced and contrasted shape and size, was not new when this example was designed (in Venice in 1501). The first European typographers inherited some 2000 years' worth of research into these principles from their predecessors, the scribes. Yet the principles are flexible enough that countless new typographic compositions wait to be designed.

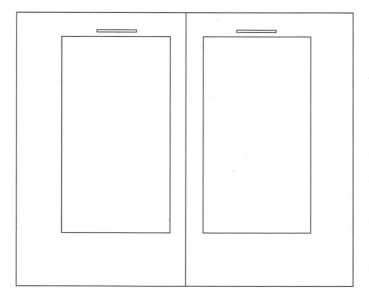

Page spread, probably by Francesco Griffo, Venice, 1501. The text is Virgil's *Aeneid*, set entirely in a crisp, simple italic, roughly 11/11.5 × 16, with roman small capitals, approximately 5 pt high. The original page size is 10.7 × 17.3 cm.

8.5.1  *Bring the margins into the design.*

In typography, margins must do three things. They must *lock the typeblock to the page* and *lock the facing pages to each other* through the force of their proportions. Second, they must *frame the typeblock* in a manner that suits its design. Third, they must *protect the typeblock,* leaving it easy for the reader to see and convenient to handle. (That is, they must leave room for the reader's thumbs.) The third of these is easy, and the second is not difficult. The first is like choosing type: it is an endless opportunity for typographical play and a serious test of skill.

*Shaping the Page*

Perhaps fifty per cent of the character and integrity of a printed page lies in its letterforms. Much of the other fifty per cent resides in its margins.

8.5.2  *Bring the design into the margins.*

The boundaries of the typeblock are rarely absolute. They are nibbled and punctured by paragraph indents, blank lines between sections, gutters between columns, and the sinkage of chapter openings. They are overrun by hanging numbers, out-dented paragraphs or heads, marginal bullets, folios (page numbers) and often running heads, marginal notes and other typographic satellites. These features – whether recurrent, like folios, or unpredictable, like marginal notes and numbers – should be designed to give vitality to the page and further bind the page and the typeblock.

8.5.3  *Mark the reader's way.*

Folios are useful in most documents longer than two pages. They can be anywhere on the page that is graphically pleasing and easy to find, but in practice this reduces to few possibilities:

1  at the head of the page, aligned with the outside edge of the textblock (a common place for folios accompanied by running heads);

2  at the foot of the page, aligned with or slightly indented from the outside edge of the text;

3  in the upper quarter of the outside margin, beyond the outside edge of the text;

at the foot of the page, horizontally centered beneath the text-block.

The fourth of these choices offers Neoclassical poise, but it hinders quick navigation. Folios near the upper or lower outside corner are the easiest to find by flipping pages in a small book. In large books and magazines, the bottom outside corner is generally more convenient for joint assaults by eye and thumb. Folios placed on the inner margin are invisible when needed, and all too visible otherwise.

It is usual to set folios in the text size and to position them near the textblock. Unless they are very black, brightly colored or large, the folios may drown if they get very far away from the text. Strengthened enough to stand on their own, they are likely to prove a distraction.

8.5.4 *Don't restate the obvious.*

In Bibles and other large works, running heads have been standard equipment for two thousand years. Photocopying machines, which can easily separate a chapter or a page from the rest of a book or journal, have also given running heads (and running feet, or footers) new importance.

Except as insurance against photocopying pirates, running heads are nevertheless pointless in many books and documents with a strong authorial voice or a unified subject. They remain essential in most anthologies and works of reference, large or small.

Like folios, running heads pose an interesting typographical problem. They are useless if the reader has to hunt for them, so they must somehow be distinguished from the text, yet they must not become a distraction. It has been a common typographical practice since 1501 to set them in spaced small caps of the text size, or if the budget permits, to print them in the text face in a second color.

8.6 PAGE GRIDS & MODULAR SCALES

8.6.1 *Use a modular scale if you need one to subdivide the page.*

Grids are often used in magazine design and in other situations where unpredictable graphic elements must be combined in a rapid and orderly way.

Standard grid for three-column magazine

Modular scales serve much the same purpose as grids, but they are more flexible. A modular scale, like a musical scale, is a prearranged set of harmonious proportions. In essence, it is a measuring stick whose units are indivisible and not of uniform size. The traditional sequence of type sizes shown on page 43, for example, is a modular scale. The single- and double-stranded Fibonacci series discussed on pp 141–142 are modular scales as well. These scales can, in fact, be put directly to use in page design by altering the units from points to picas.

It is perfectly feasible to create a new modular scale for any project requiring one, and the scale can be founded on any convenient single or multiple proportion – a given page size, for example, or the dimensions of a set of illustrations, or something implicit in the subject matter. A work on astronomy might use a modular scale based on star charts or Bode's law of interplanetary distances. A work on Greek art might be laid out using intervals from one or more of the Greek musical scales. A book of modernist literature might be designed using something deliberately arcane – perhaps a scale based on the proportions of the author's hand. Generally speaking, a scale based on two ratios (1 : φ and 1 : 2, for example) will give more flexible and interesting results than a scale founded on one.

The Half Pica Modular scale illustrated here is actually a miniaturized version of the architectural scale of Le Corbusier, which was based in turn on the proportions of the human body.

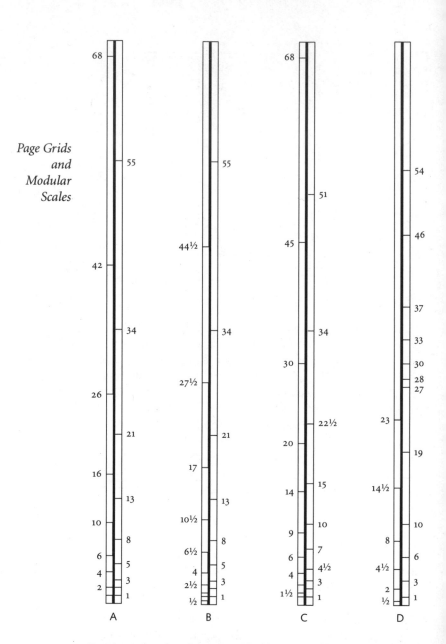

Four examples of modular pica sticks (shown at half actual size). **A** Whole Pica Modular scale. **B** Half Pica Modular scale. These are both two-stranded Fibonacci series, based on the ratios 1 : φ and 1 : 2. **C** Medieval Interval scale, based on the proportions 2 : 3 and 1 : 2. **D** Timaean Scale, a simplified version of the Pythagorean scale outlined in Plato's *Timaeus*.

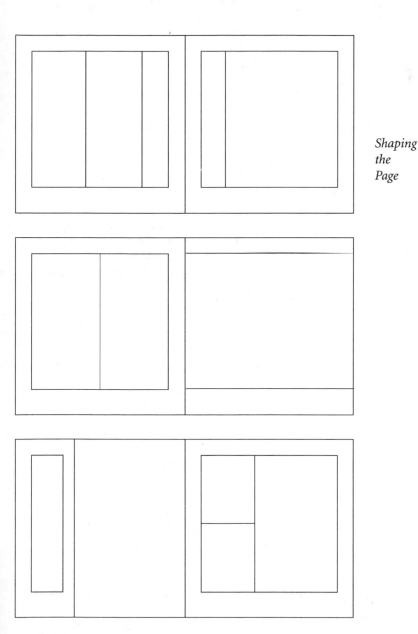

Use of the modular scale. These pages and typeblocks have been subdivided with the Half Pica Modular scale. The pages are 52 × 55 picas
(8⅝" × 9⅛"), with margins of 5, 5, 5 & 8 picas. The basic typeblock is 42
picas square. Thousands of different subdivisions are possible. For more
complex examples on similar principles, see Le Corbusier, *The Modulor*.

*Examples*

The formula for designing a perfect page is the same as the formula for writing one: start at the upper left hand corner and work your way across and down; then turn the page and try again. The examples on the following pages show only a few of the many kinds of typographic structures that might evolve along the way.

In fact, the weaving of the text and the tailoring of the page are thoroughly interdependent. We can discuss them one by one, and we can separate each in turn into a series of simple, unintimidating questions. But the answers to these questions must all, in the end, fold back into a single answer. The page, the pamphlet or the book must be seen as a whole if it is to look like one. If it appears to be only a series of individual solutions to separate typographical problems, who will believe that its message coheres?

In analyzing the examples on the following pages, these symbols are used:

| | |
|---|---|
| Proportions: | P = page proportion = $h/w$ |
| | T = typeblock proportion = $d/m$ |
| Page size: | $w$ = width of page (trim-size) |
| | $h$ = height of page (trim-size) |
| Typeblock: | $m$ = measure (width of primary type block) |
| | $d$ = depth of primary type block |
| | (excluding running heads, folios, etc) |
| | $n$ = secondary measure (width of secondary column) |
| | $c$ = column width, where there are even multiple columns |
| Margins: | $s$ = spine margin (back margin) |
| | $t$ = top margin (head margin) |
| | $e$ = fore-edge (front margin) |
| | $f$ = foot margin |
| | $i$ = internal gutter (on a multiple-column page) |

Page and typeblock proportions (P and T in the examples) are given here as single values (1.414, for example). To find the same values in the table on page 132, look up the corresponding *ratio* (1 : 1.414, for example).

P = variable; T = 1.75. Margins: $t = h/12$; $f = 1.5t$; $i = t/2$ or $t/3$. Text columns from Isaiah Scroll A, from Qumran Cave I, on the Dead Sea. The column depth is 29 lines and the measure is 28 picas, giving a line length of roughly 40 characters. Elsewhere in the scroll, column widths range from 21.5 to 39 picas, but the dimensions shown above are typical. Paragraphs begin on a new line but – in keeping with the crisp, square Hebrew characters – are not indented. (Palestine, perhaps first century BC.) Original size: $26 \times 725$ cm.

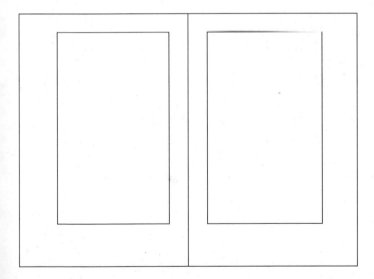

P = 1.5 [2 : 3]; T = 1.7 [tall pentagon]. Margins: $s = t = w/9$; $e = 2s$. The text is a fantasy novel, Francesco Colonna's *Hypnerotomachia Poliphili*, set in a roman font cut by Francesco Griffo. (Aldus Manutius, Venice, 1499.) Original size: $20.5 \times 31$ cm.

*Examples*

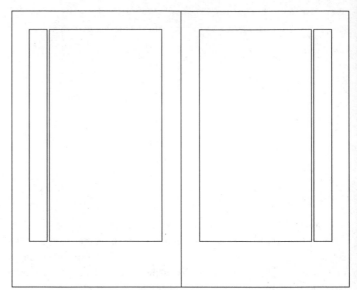

P = 1.62 [golden section]; T = 1.87 [tall hexagon]. Margins: *s = w*/9; *t = s;* *e* = 2*s*. Secondary column: *i = w*/75; *n = s*. The text is in roman, the sidenotes in italic at roughly 80% of text size. The gutter between main text and sidenotes is tiny – 6 or 7 pt against a main text measure of 33.5 picas – but the differences in size and face prevent any confusion. The text is a history, set in text and titling fonts cut by Claude Garamond. (Jean Froissart, *Histoire et chronique*, Jean de Tournes, Paris, 1559.) Original size: roughly 21 × 34 cm.

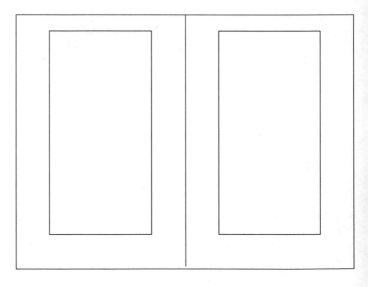

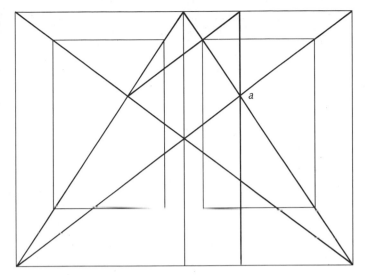

P = T = 1.5 [2 : 3]. Margins: $s = w/9$; $t = h/9$; $e = 2s$; $f = 2t$. The margins are thus in the proportion $s : t : e : f = 2 : 3 : 4 : 6$. A sound, elegant and basic medieval structure, which will work for any proportion of page and typeblock, so long as the two remain in unison. Spine and head margins may be ninths, tenths, twelfths or any other desired proportion of the page size. Twelfths, of course, give a fuller and more efficient page, with less white space. But if the page proportion is 1 : 1.5 and the spine and head margins are ninths, as shown here, the consonance of typeblock and page is considerably deepened, because $d = w$, which is to say, the *depth* of the typeblock matches the *width* of the page. Thus $m : w = d : h = w : h = m : d = s : t = e : f = 2 : 3$. Point *a*, where the half and full diagonals intersect, is one third of the way down and across the typeblock and the page. Jan Tschichold, 1955, after Villard de Honnecourt, France, c. 1280. See Tschichold's *The Form of the Book* (1991).

$<$ P = 1.5 [2 : 3]; T = 2 [double square]. Margins: $s = e = w/5$; $t = s/2$. The text is a book of poems, set throughout in a chancery italic with roman capitals. The designer and publisher of this book was a master calligrapher, certainly aware of the tradition that the inner margins should be smaller than the outer. He followed that tradition himself with books of prose, but in this book of poems he chose to center the textblock on the page. The text throughout is set in one size. Titles are set in the capitals of the text font, letterspaced about 30%. There are no running heads or other diversions. (Giangiorgio Trissino, *Canzone*, Ludovico degli Arrighi, Rome, c. 1523.) Original size: 12.5 × 18.75 cm.

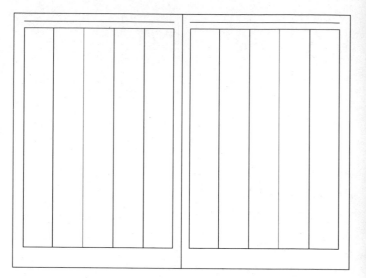

P = 1.5 [2 : 3]; T = 1.54 [pentagon typeblock]. Margins: $s = w/20$; $t = s = h/30$; $e = w/15 = 4s/3$; $f = 2t$. This is the format used for the index to the fifth edition of the *Times Atlas of the World* (London, 1975). The page is a standard medieval shape. The text is set in 5.5 pt Univers leaded 0.1 pt on a 12-pica measure, in five subdivided columns per page. Columns are separated by thin vertical rules. Key words and folios, at the top of the page, are in 16 pt Univers semibold. (Because of their prominence, these running heads are included here in calculating the size and shape of the typeblock.) The column-depth, not counting these headers, is 204 lines, yielding an average of 1000 names per page for 217 pages. This index is a masterpiece of its kind: a potent typographic symbol, an efficient work of reference, and a comfortable text to browse. Original size: 30 × 45 cm.

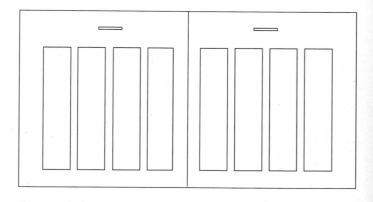

P = 1.414 [$\sqrt{2}$]; T = 1.62 [φ, the golden section]. Margins: $s = t = w/9$ and $e = f = 2s$. This is a simple format for placing a golden-section typeblock on an ISO page, locking the two together with margins in the proportions 1 : 2. Two possible locations for folios are shown, and there is room for sidenotes in the fore-edge if required.

If the spine and top margins on these pages are increased to $w/8$, while the typeblock and page are held at their original proportion, the relationship of the margins becomes $e = f = φs$, another golden section.

P = 1.1; T = 0.91; $c = w/6$. Margins: $s = w/14$; $e = 2s$; $t = 3s$; $f = 3s/2$; $i = m/20$. The proportions of the typeblock are the *reciprocal of the proportions of the page:* 0.91 = 1/1.1, which is to say that the typeblock is the same shape as the page, rotated 90°. But if the gutters are removed from the typeblock and the four columns closed up solid, the typeblock collapses to the same shape *in the same orientation* as the page. In other words, the typeblock has been expanded from the same shape to the reciprocal shape of the page *entirely by the addition of white space.* The text is the Greek Bible, lettered in uncials, about 13 characters per line. There are no spaces between the words, but there is some punctuation, and the text has a slight rag, with line breaks carefully chosen. This subtle piece of craftsmanship was produced in Egypt in the fourth century. It is the Codex Sinaiticus, Add. Ms. 43725, at the British Museum, London. Original size: 34.5 × 38 cm.

P = 1.414 [$\sqrt{2}$]; T = 2 [double square]. Margins: $s = w/12$; $f = 2t = h/9$; $e = w/3$. The wide fore-edge of this manuscript book had a purpose: it was deliberately left free for sidenotes to be added by the owner. The text is a sequence of Latin poems by the Roman poet Horace, written in Caroline minuscule. (Ms. Plut. 34.1, Laurentian Library, Florence; tenth century.)

P = 1.176 [truncated pentagon page]; T = 1.46. Margins: $s = h/11$; $t = 5s/6$; $e = 5s/2$; $f = 3s/2$. Columns: $c = 3w/10$; $i = s/4$. The text (set in Pontifex 11/13 × 17 RR) is a series of essays on contemporary art, with many full-page illustrations. Original size: 24 × 28 cm.

## 8.8 IMPROVISATIONS & ADJUSTMENTS

### 8.8.1 *Improvise, calculate, and improvise some more.*

Numerical values – used by all typographers in their daily work – give an impression of exactness. Careful measurement and accurate calculation are indeed important in typography, but they are not its final purpose, and moments arise in every project when exactness bumps its head against approximation. On the mechanical side, paper expands and contracts, and printing presses, folding machines and trimming knives – not to speak of typesetting hardware and software – all have their margins of error. The typographer can rarely profit from these variations, and cannot entirely prevent them. On the planning side, however, imprecision can often be put to better use.

*Shaping the Page*

Some typographers prefer to design by arithmetic from the outset, in a space composed of little invisible bricks called points and picas. Others prefer to work in the free two-dimensional space of a sketchpad, converting their layouts afterward to typographic measure. Most work involves a combination of these methods, with occasional collisions between the two. But the margins of inexactness that crop up in the rounding of units, in conflicts between optical and arithmetic spacing and centering, in combining proportions, and in translating from one form of measurement to another should be welcomed as opportunities, not as inconsistencies to be ignored, glossed over or begrudged. The equal temperament of the typesetting machine and the just intonation of the sketchpad should be used to test and refine one another until the final answer sings.

### 8.8.2 *Adjust the type and the spaces within the typeblock using typographic increments, but rely on free proportions to adjust the empty space.*

Proportions are more flexible than picas, and it is usually convenient and appealing to work in even units. A margin of 5.32 picas, for example, begs to be altered to 5 or 5¼ or 5½. But picas per se are less important than proportions, and the system of typographical sizes and units serves the interrelations of letterforms better than it serves the interrelations of empty space. As a general rule, it is better to make incremental jumps in the typeblock first and to readjust the margins thereafter – paying more attention in the latter case to absolute proportion than to convenient units of measurement. When space is measured purely in points, the temptation to rearrange it into even picas is miraculously lessened.

8.8.3 *Keep the page design supple enough to provide a livable home for the text.*

Architects build perfectly proportioned kitchens, living rooms, bedrooms in which their clients will make, among other things, a mess. So the typographer builds perfectly proportioned pages, then distorts them on demand. The text takes precedence over the purity of the design, and the typographic texture of the text takes precedence over the absolute proportions of the individual page.

If, for instance, three lines remain at the end of a chapter, looking forlorn on a page of their own, the design must flex to accommodate them. The obvious choices are:

1 running two of the previous spreads a line long (that is, adding one line to the depth of two pairs of facing pages), which will leave the final page one line short;
2 running half a dozen of the previous spreads a line short, thereby bumping a dozen lines along to the final page; or
3 reproportioning some non-textual element – perhaps an illustration or the sinkage, if any, at the head of the chapter.

Spacious chapter heads stand out in a book, as they are meant to. Reproportioning the sinkage is therefore a poor option unless *all* chapter heads can be reproportioned to match. And running six spreads short is, on the face of it, clearly a greater evil than running two spreads long.

If there are only a few pages to the document, the whole thing can, and probably should, be redesigned to fit the text. But in a book of many pages, widow lines, orphaned subheads, and the runt ends of chapters or sections are certain to require reproportioning some spreads. A rigid design that demands an invariant page depth is therefore inappropriate for a work of any length. Altering the leading on short pages to preserve a standard depth (vertical justification, as it is sometimes called) is not a solution. Neither is stuffing extra space between the paragraphs. These antics destroy the fabric of the text and thus strike at the heart of the book.

## 9.1 GALLEYS & PROOFS

### 9.1.1 Check the type at every stage.

Digital letterforms can be printed directly at low resolutions using devices such as a laser printer. They can also be set on photosensitive paper, negative film or positive film, from which printing plates or letterpress blocks are then made. Or they can be etched directly onto printing plates to be run on an offset press. Each of these electrostatic and photographic processes provides an opportunity for overexposing or underexposing the type.

Check for accurate color and sharpness in the final letterforms, and check for consistency throughout. Inconsistent exposure is often encountered when the work is set a section at a time, or when corrected pages are rerun. But even when all the work is run at once, on one machine, inconsistencies can occur. If, for instance, two shelf lots of film or photosensitive paper are inadvertently mixed, the same machine settings will give two different results.

Mechanical errors are also not unknown in the superficially sanitized, high-tech world of computerized type. Many a finely tooled page has been spoiled in the end by a loose roller or unlubricated ratchet. Check the output against a grid to make sure the leading is consistent, multiple columns align as they should, and the type block is not trapezoidal unless it is truly intended to be.

## 9.2 PAPER & INK

### 9.2.1 Follow the work to the printer.

Digital methods have helped to bring editing, typography and type design back to the close relationship they enjoyed in the golden age of letterpress. But everything the writer, type designer, editor and typographer do is still contingent on the skills and methods of the printer, and printing often remains a world apart.

All typographic decisions – the choice of the type, the choice of size and leading, the calculation of margins and the shaping of the page – involve assumptions about the printing. It is well to find out in advance whether these assumptions stand any chance of being correct. Good printers also have much to teach their clients, and the best typographer can always find

something to learn. But printing has not yet passed as fully as typography into the postindustrial world. Because printing remains for the most part a commercialized, standardized and highly industrial process, it will readily erase the typographer's personal touch.

The margins of books cannot be calculated correctly until the binding method is chosen, and they cannot be right in the end unless the chosen method is followed. The type cannot be chosen without coming to some decision about the kind of paper it will be printed on, and cannot look right in the end if that decision is later betrayed. A change of ⅛ inch in the folding pattern or trim size will ruin a precisely designed page.

Yet another way to undercut the type is to print it with the wrong ink. Color control is important whether or not color is used, for there are many hues of black, some veering toward red, some veering toward blue. Redder blacks are acceptable on ivory paper. If the paper is closer to gray or white, the black of the ink should move closer to blue. But it will be process black by default – and the density of the type will be at the mercy of the press foreman's final color adjustments – if type and process-color illustrations are printed in one go.

Ink gloss is rarely a problem on uncoated paper. On coated stock, the sheen of the ink is frequently out of control. For the sake of legibility in artificial light, the ink used to print type on a coated sheet should have *less* reflectivity than the paper, rather than more.

### 9.3 MAINTAINING THE SYSTEM

#### 9.3.1 *Consult the ancestors.*

Typography is an ancient craft and an old profession as well as a constant technological frontier. It is also in some sense a trust. The lexicon of the tribe and the letters of the alphabet – which are the chromosomes and genes of literate culture – are in the typographer's hands. Maintaining the system means more than merely buying the latest fonts from digital foundries and the latest updates for typesetting software.

The rate of change in typesetting methods has been steep – perhaps it has approximated the Fibonacci series – for more than a century. Yet, like poetry and painting, storytelling and weaving, typography itself *has not improved*. There is no greater proof that typography is more art than engineering. Like all the arts, it is basically immune to progress, though it is not immune to change. Typography at its best is sometimes as good, and at its worst is just as bad, as it ever was. The speed of certain processes has certainly increased; some old, hard tricks have come to seem easy, and some new ones have been learned. But the quality of typography and printing, their faithfulness to themselves, and the inherent grace and poise of the finished page, is not greater now than it was in 1465. In several respects, digital typography lags far behind the methods and resources of Renaissance compositors and medieval scribes.

Maintaining the system means openness to the surprises and gifts of the future; it also means keeping the future in touch with the past. Two examples will suffice.

Handcut letterpress faces vary in weight, proportion and detailing from size to size. The 7 pt font will have a larger torso, darker stroke and *looser dressing* (wider inherent character spacing) than the 12 pt font. The 24 pt font will be lighter in the stroke, smaller in x-height, more tightly fitted and more sharply detailed. Titles, text and footnotes set on the same page in the same face will therefore look balanced in color and form. Digital typography has only begun to meet the challenge posed on this front by the typecutters of old.

In manuscripts, letters vary even within one size, and their subtle, often subliminal variations give life to the manuscript page. The best of the Renaissance typographers answered this challenge by cutting multiple versions of common letters and of common analphabetics (especially hyphens). A hand compositor reaching into the typecase for an *e* might therefore come up with any of several forms. All might be of identical width, and all so nearly alike that few readers would consciously notice the difference, yet these slyly variant letters contributed their extra mote of unostentatious vitality to the page. The same deliberate and subtle irregularity is within the capabilities of digital composition, but this frontier – well known to Francesco Griffo in 1495 – has only begun to be re-explored.

bpfi
bpſi
bpfi

*Above:* 6 pt, 8 pt and 12 pt Monotype Centaur, enlarged to 24 pt size. *Below:* the actual 24 pt type.

bpfi

### 9.3.2  *Look after the low- as well as the high-technology end.*

A computer typesetting system is now likely to consist of three basic pieces of hardware: the computer itself (including processor, keyboard and monitor), a proofing device in the form of a low- or medium-resolution laser printer, and a high-resolution digital output device, which is often separately owned. Inside this hardware there are likely to be four interdependent pieces of software. These are the text editor or word processor; the composition and page make-up system; a library of digital fonts; and a font editor. There may also be a manipulation program for curving the baseline and for shadowing, texturing, warping and other effects designed to blur the ancient boundary between type and illustration. Outside the hardware, but no less essential to the system, more primitive tools are still required: a pica stick; a sketch pad; a drawing board and instruments; and a library of type specimens, reference works and examples of fine typography for discussion and inspiration. It is the latter, low-technology end of most typesetting systems that usually seems in most urgent need of upgrading.

Recommendations concerning specific hardware and software should be made case by case – and can only be made moment by moment, given the current rate of technological change. But at least two basic principles seem clear.

The first is the principle of versatility. Fonts intended for text work should include the full range of ISO characters and diacritics (itemized in Appendix A). Composition systems should permit ready access to this full range of characters, and to an open set of special characters, whether obtained from technical fonts or specially made. The composition system should also permit any diacritic or combination of diacritics to be easily superimposed, at any height, upon any letter. At the compositor's discretion, it should substitute any specified ligature for any keyed sequence of letters. And of course, it should permit any line or character to be conveniently placed in any position: right, left, indented, outdented, centered or justified. In short, a computerized typesetting system should not be more restrictive than hand composition.

The second principle is one of quality. One good typeface is better and more useful than an infinity of poor ones. The following chapter is devoted entirely to a discussion of the origins and merits of individual faces.

Type is idealized writing – yet there is no end of typefaces, as there is no end to visions of the ideal. The following selection includes a wide historical range – Renaissance, Baroque, Neoclassical and Romantic – as well as many twentieth-century faces. It also includes a wide stylistic variety – formal, informal, fluid, crisp, delicate and robust. The emphasis is on faces legible and fluid enough for setting text, and one thing unites them: all the faces listed seem to me among the finest of their kind. Each has its uses and limitations. Together, they represent no more than a small fraction of the faces currently available. I've included some very well-known faces like Baskerville and Palatino; some others, like Fairbank italic and Figural, that are undeservedly forgotten; and a few, like Martin Majoor's Scala, that have not yet had time to establish themselves. Some, like Photina and Vendôme, are well-known in Europe but scarce in North America; others, like Deepdene, have had just as unbalanced a reception the other way round.

I take for granted that most readers of this book will have access to typesetters' specimen books or font manufacturers' catalogues. This chapter is no substitute for them. On the contrary, I hope, by pointing out some prominent landmarks and interesting hidden features, to make it easier to navigate at will through the dense fog of conflicting advertisement that gathers on the sea of letters.

Most of the faces listed in this chapter are now available in digital form, and many of those that have not been digitized are likely to be issued soon. But some that were originally cut in metal are still missing essential components in digital form – small capitals and text figures, for example. With luck, these shortcomings will soon be remedied. Digital foundries nevertheless continue to issue faces and families of type in abbreviated, distorted or pirated form. The presence of a typeface here in this list is not an endorsement of every or any marketed version.

Buyers of type should be aware that they are always buying a copy of someone's original design. Licensed copies are preferable to unlicensed copies for two important reasons. First, if the designer is still alive, the license implies that the fonts are being

Notes on the current status of digital faces appear in Appendix D, p 245.

sold with the designer's permission and that royalties from the sale are being paid. Second, the license gives some hope – though rarely a guarantee – that the fonts are not being sold in truncated form.

*Prowling the Specimen Books*

Fonts from East European foundries such as Typoart in Dresden and Grafotechna in Prague have almost entirely escaped digitization. There are many treasures to come from these sources, and from younger designers in Eastern Europe, whose work has seldom been seen in the West. Because of the problems of availability, only a few of these faces are listed here.

At the beginning of each entry, the original form of the font is indicated by a simple code:

H = originally a metal type for hand composition
M = originally for machine composition in metal
F = originally designed for filmsetting
D = originally designed in digital form

## 10.1 SERIFED TEXT FACES

For a specimen of Aldus, see p 180.

*Aldus* M Roman and italic, designed in 1953 by Hermann Zapf as a Linotype companion to his new foundry face, Palatino. Aldus is narrower than Palatino and has a lower midline (smaller x-height). It is a crisply sculptured and compact text face, rooted in Renaissance scribal tradition. Small caps and text figures are essential to the spirit of the face, but it needs no ligatures. Palatino roman and italic are the customary titling faces used with Aldus, and Palatino bold is used when a bold companion is required. (See pp 50, 62, 100.)

*Baskerville* H Roman and italic, designed in several variants by John Baskerville in the 1750s. This is the epitome of neo-classicism and eighteenth-century rationalism in type, and the face was far more popular in Republican France and the American colonies than in eighteenth-century England, where it was made. On Baskerville's death, his roman and italic punches were taken to France. They have since been returned and are now in the University Library, Cambridge.

The digital faces sold under Baskerville's name are for the most part reasonably faithful to his designs, but small caps and text figures, often omitted, are essential to the spirit of the original, and to an even flow of text. The bold fonts routinely offered in their stead are inauthentic and unBaskervillian. The digital version below is ITC Baskerville. (See also pp 13, 54, 75, 81, 93, 118.)

abcefghijop 1 2 3 AO *abcefghijop*   *Baskerville*

abcefghijop 1 2 3 AO *abcefghijop*   *Bell*

*Bell* H   The original Bell type was cut in London in 1788 by Richard Austin for a publisher named John Bell. It lacks the refinement of Baskerville, but it was warmly greeted in the USA. It was widely used at Boston and Philadelphia in the 1790s, and it remains useful for period design work, as an alternative to Baskerville. Monotype cut a facsimile in 1931, and this version has been digitized. Bell is somewhat narrower and darker than Baskerville, but it too is an English Neoclassical face. The serifs are very sharp, but the overall spirit is nevertheless closer to brick than to granite, evoking Lincoln's Inn more than St Paul's, and Harvard Yard more than Pennsylvania Avenue.

Bell numerals are three-quarter height, neither hanging nor fully ranging. (See also p 45.)

*Bembo* H   Bembo was produced by Monotype in 1929, based on a roman cut at Venice by Francesco Griffo in 1495. The companion italic is based on a font designed in Venice in the 1520s by Giovanni Tagliente. Bembo roman and italic are somewhat quieter and less faithful to their sources than Centaur and Arrighi. They are nevertheless serene and versatile faces of genuine Renaissance structure, and they seem to have survived the transition to digital composition and offset printing. Text figures and small caps are essential to the design. The bold fonts are irrelevant to the spirit of the face. (See pp 49, 113, 114.)   For a specimen of Bembo, see p 182.

abcefghijop 123 AO *abcefghijop*   *Berkeley*

*Berkeley* M   ITC Berkeley is a revision of Frederic Goudy's University of California Oldstyle, designed in 1938 as a proprietary face for the University of California Press. The face was issued publicly by Lanston Monotype in 1956 as Californian. The original was one of Goudy's masterpieces. While the new version, drawn by Tony Stan and issued in 1983, retains many of its virtues, it also lacks much of its character. A more faithful   *   The asterisk in the margin means that a further note on this face will be found in Appendix D.

digital revival would be welcome, but the merits of this one should not be denied. The titling figures are very well formed, but small caps and text figures are implicit to the design. Goudy Sans is the obvious choice as a companion sanserif.

*Berling*  abcefghijop (y!) AO *abcefghijop*

*Berling* ʜ Designed by the Swedish typographer and calligrapher Karl-Erik Forsberg. This face was issued in 1951 by the foundry from which it takes its name, the Berling Foundry in Lund, Sweden. It is a neohumanist design, with vigorous modulation of the stroke. Ascenders and descenders are even more frequent in Swedish than in English, and Forsberg's extenders are designed to give minimal interruption to the flow of the text. They are also designed to require no ligatures. The face has a Scandinavian sharpness and clarity, with sharply hooked f, j, y and ! in the roman. The parentheses are among the best in any twentieth-century design. The titling figures are well designed, but the text figures (omitted from many digital cuts) are better.

*Berthold Bodoni*  abcefghijop 123 AO *abcefghijop*

*Bodoni* ʜ Giambattista Bodoni of Parma, the most prolific of all type designers, is also the nearest typographical counterpart to Byron and Liszt. He is typography's arch-romantic. His hundreds of faces, designed between about 1765 and his death in 1813, embrace considerable variety, and more than 25,000 of his punches are in the Bodoni Museum collection in Parma. The revivals issued in his name reflect only a tiny part of this legacy, and many are simply parodies of his ideas. The typical features of Bodoni revivals are abrupt hairline serifs, ball terminals, vertical axis, small aperture, high contrast, and exaggerated modulation. Many typographers prefer the version cut by Louis Hoell for the Bauer Foundry, Frankfurt, in 1924, and the Berthold Foundry version, produced in 1930. Both have now been issued in digital form. Small caps and text figures are available for both the Bauer and Berthold fonts, and they are essential to these designs. (See also pp 13, 119.)

*Caecilia* ᴅ Designed by Peter Matthias Noordzij of the Netherlands and issued by Linotype in 1991. This is a graceful and sturdy yet unpretentious slab-serif face, useful for general

170

printing. It is a neohumanist slab-serif, perhaps the first of its kind, with a slab-serifed true italic to match. The italic is built to Renaissance parameters, sloping at a modest 4°. Small caps and text figures are intrinsic to the design, and the face is issued in a range of weights. Licensed versions are sold under the trade name PMN Caecilia.

abcefghijop 1 2 3 AO *abcefghijop*    *Caecilia*

abcefghijop 123 AO *abcefghijop*    *Carmina*

*Carmina* D Designed by Gudrun Zapf-von Hesse and issued by Bitstream in 1987. The face has a humanist axis, strong contrast, large aperture, sharp serifs, and considerable energy and poise. The design includes a range of weights in roman and italic, but there are no small caps or text figures.

*Caslon* H William Caslon designed and cut a large number of romans, italics and non-Latin faces between 1720 and his death in 1766. His work is the typographical epitome of the English Baroque, and it is well preserved. He published thorough specimens, and many of his punches are now in the St Bride Printing Library, London. There have been countless copies of his types, but many of the Caslons now available bear virtually no resemblance to anything Caslon designed. The most accurate modern versions of the type are Adobe Caslon, drawn by Carol Twombly, and Lanston's Caslon 37. Small caps and text figures are available for both of these cuts and are essential to the design. Both the Adobe and Lanston versions also include Baroque ligatures, swash capitals, ornaments and other alternate sorts required for eighteenth-century period typography. (See pp 12, 48, 49, 64, 116.)

For a specimen of Caslon, see p 64.

abcefghijop (y!) 123 AO *abcefghijopz*    *Centaur & Arrighi*

*Centaur & Arrighi* H Centaur roman was designed by Bruce Rogers in 1912–14, based on the roman type cut at Venice by Nicolas Jenson in 1469. In 1928, the face was mildly sanitized in the course of transposition to the Monotype machine.

Frederic Warde drew the Arrighi italic in 1925, based on a chancery font designed at Rome and Venice in the 1520s by the calligrapher Ludovico degli Arrighi. In 1929, after several revisions, Rogers chose Warde's font as the companion italic for Centaur, provoking more revisions still. The fonts are used both separately and together.

Printed letterpress, Centaur and Arrighi are unrivalled in their power to evoke the typographic spirit of the Venetian Renaissance, but in the two-dimensional world of digital composition and offset printing, this power is easily lost. Small caps and text figures have been digitized from the Monotype originals, and these are essential. The titling figures – not Rogers's – are best forgotten. (See also pp 12, 65, 77, 81, 113.)

*Charter* abcefghijop 123 AO *abcefghijop*

*Charter* D Designed by Matthew Carter and issued by Bitstream in 1987. Charter is an economical and serviceable face for general printing, with large x-height, variable axis and low contrast. The serifs are blunt and abrupt. There is a range of weights. Text figures and small caps are also available to supplement the design.

*Haas Clarendon* AO abcdefghijklmnopqrstuvwxyz

*Clarendon* H Clarendon is the name of a whole genus of Victorian typefaces, spawned by a font cut by Benjamin Fox for Robert Besley at the Fann Street Foundry, London, in 1845. These faces reflect the hearty, stolid, bland, unstoppable aspects of the British Empire. They lack cultivation, but they also lack menace and guile. They squint, and stand their ground, but they do not glare. In other words, they consist of thick strokes melding into thick slab serifs, fat ball terminals, vertical axis, large x-height, low contrast and tiny aperture. There was, of course, no italic, as the face had nothing of the fluent hand or the sculpted nib left in its pedigree.

Hermann Eidenbenz drew a revival Clarendon for the Haas Foundry in Münchenstein, Switzerland, in 1951, and in 1962 the foundry finally added the light weight that transformed the series, paring it down from premodern ponderousness to postmodern insubstantiality. In this guise, as a kind of nostalgic steel frame from which all the Victorian murk has been removed, the face has many genuine uses.

Monotype Clarendon lacks the presence of the Haas Clarendon, but other useful variations on the theme exist. The most ubiquitous is Morris Fuller Benton's well-known claren-don, called Century Schoolbook, issued by ATF in 1924 and by Monotype in 1928. This too is now available in a light weight and in digital form. (See also pp 102, 120.)

abcefghijop 123 AO *abcefghijop*

*Dante* H Roman and italic. Designed by Giovanni Marder-steig and cut in 1954 by Charles Malin. Monotype adapted the face for machine setting in 1957 and has now produced a digitized version. Dante is an elegant and finely tooled neo-humanist face, a stately roman coupled with a mobile and lucid italic. It has more authority (and a somewhat larger x-height) than Bembo, more versatility than Centaur, and is useful as an alternative to its equally noble but much overworked and repeatedly pirated cousin, Hermann Zapf's Palatino. Small caps and text figures are essential to the design.

*

abcefghijop 1 2 3 A O *abcefghijop*

*Deepdene* M This may be the gentlest and most lyrical of Frederic Goudy's many book faces. The aperture is large (especially by Goudy's standards), the x height is modest, the axis is serenely neohumanist, and the drawing is graceful and even. The roman was designed in 1927. The italic – which is easily graceful and legible enough to serve as an independent text face – was drawn in the following year, when the face was first issued by Lanston Monotype. Small caps and text figures (available in the Lanston digital version) are requirements of the design.

abcefghijklmnop 123 *abcefghijop*

*Diotima* H Designed by Gudrun Zapf-von Hesse and cut by the Stempel Foundry, Frankfurt, in 1953. Diotima is considerably more delicate than the same designer's more recent Carmina, and it has a smaller x-height but no less energy and presence. The roman is wide and the italic markedly narrow. The original design includes text figures but no titling figures. The face is named, aptly, for the earliest woman philosopher on record: Diotima of Mantinea, whose metaphysic of love is recited in Plato's *Symposium* by her former student, Socrates.

*Electra* M    There are two eminent Early Modernist book faces distinguished by their clarity, readability and their debt to Neoclassical form. Both were designed in the USA for the Linotype machine, and both have remained staple faces of the American book trade since their initial release. One of these faces is Rudolf Růžička's Fairfield, issued in 1940. The other is W.A. Dwiggins's Electra, issued in 1935. Electra is the livelier of the two. It has a predominantly rationalist axis and modest aperture but considerable animation and subtle irregularity. Electra was originally issued with a sloped roman in lieu of an italic, but in 1940, Dwiggins himself replaced this sloped roman with the simple, crisp italic now normally used. Small caps and text figures are inherent in the design.

*Electra*  abcefghijop 123 AO *abcefghijop*

*Esprit*  abcefghijop 123 AO *abcefghijop*

*Esprit* F    Designed by Jovica Veljović in Beograd and issued by ITC, New York, in 1985. A sharply serifed roman and italic of variable axis, large x-height and small aperture. The strokes and bowls of the lower case are full of oblique lines and asymmetric curves which add further energy to the basically rowdy neo-baroque structure. A related but somewhat simpler face is the same designer's earlier Veljović. Small caps and text figures are implicit in the design. (See also p 123.)

*Fairbank Italic*  *AO abcdefghijklmnopqrstuvwxyz*

\*    *Fairbank Italic* M    English calligrapher Alfred Fairbank designed this face in 1928 as a companion for Monotype Bembo roman. It is narrow and has a slope of only 4°, but it is full of tensile strength, and in the estimation of Monotype's typographical advisor, Stanley Morison, it overpowered the dignified, soft-spoken roman to which it was betrothed. A new and milder italic – the present Bembo italic – was cut to replace it, and Fairbank has remained a distinguished typographic loner. It can in fact be used with Bembo roman in many contexts, but it functions happily alone. The italics from which it descends were used for setting extended texts, not as helpmeets to roman faces. Fairbank has the same potential – and Bembo roman caps and small caps can be used with the Fairbank lower case in the

Aldine manner. (The face is often misdescribed – against its designer's explicit wishes – as 'Bembo Condensed Italic.')

abcefghijop 123 A O *abcdefghijop*

*Figural* H  Designed by Oldřich Menhart in 1940 and finally     *
cut and cast by the Grafotechna Foundry, Prague, in 1949.
Menhart was the master of Expressionism in type design, and
Figural is among his finest creations: a rugged but graceful
roman and italic, deliberately preserving the expressive irregularity of pen-written forms. The same designer's Manuscript is
another face of similar character, and his Monument is a congenial titling face for use with either Manuscript or Figural.

abcefghijop 123 AO *abcefghijop*

*Fournier* H  The typefaces of Pierre-Simon Fournier come
from the same historical period – and much the same rationalist spirit – as Baskerville's designs, and Richard Austin's Bell. Yet
these types are by no means all alike. Fournier's faces are as
French as Bell and Baskerville are English, and Fournier's type is
Fournier's, speaking subtly of the man himself.

Fournier is also famous for his use of ornaments. Like
Mozart, he moves between pure Neoclassicism and airy Rococo.
His letters have more variation of axis than Baskerville's, his
romans are a little narrower, and his italics are sharper. Late in
his life, he cut some of the first condensed roman faces.

Monotype Fournier and Monotype Barbou, cut in 1925, are
both facsimiles of Fournier's faces. The Mergenthaler (Linotype) digital version is shown here. (See also p 118.)

abcefghijop 123 AO *abcefghijop*

*Galliard* D  Designed by Matthew Carter and issued by Mergenthaler and ITC in 1978. Galliard (once the name of a type
size as well as a dance and its musical form) is a crisp, formal
but energetic roman and italic, based on the designs of the
sixteenth-century Parisian typecutter Robert Granjon. This is
the preeminent example of a Mannerist revival typeface. Text
figures and small caps are implicit in the design. For period
typography, a set of Mannerist ligatures and swash capitals is
available as well. (See also p 115.)

*Garamond* ʜ Claude Garamond, who died in 1561, was one of several great typecutters at work in Paris during the early sixteenth century. His teacher, Antoine Augereau, and his gifted contemporaries are remembered now only by scholars, while Garamond suffers posthumous fame. Many of his punches and matrices survive in museum collections, and his style is not

hard to learn to recognize. This has not prevented people from crediting him with type he could not possibly have designed and would not, perhaps, have admired.

Garamond's romans are stately High Renaissance forms with humanist axis, moderate contrast and long extenders. He cut several beautiful italics as well, with some of the first sloped capitals, but he took no interest in the radical new idea of pairing italics with romans. Revivals of his roman faces are often mated instead with italics based on the work of his younger colleague Robert Granjon. The three Garamond/Granjon revivals worthy of serious consideration are:

1 Stempel Garamond, issued by the Stempel foundry in 1924 and later digitized by Mergenthaler (Linotype);
2 Granjon, designed by George W. Jones and issued by Linotype in 1928 – now also in the Linotype digital library – and
3 Adobe Garamond, drawn by Robert Slimbach, issued by Adobe in 1989.

Jan Tschichold's Sabon, which is listed separately on p 183, is also closely based on Garamond's originals. Small caps and text figures are available for all of these versions and are quintessential to the designs.

*Stempel Garamond*   abcefghijop 123 AO *abcefghijop*

*Linotype Granjon*   abcefghijop 123 AO *abcefghijop*

*Adobe Garamond*   abcefghijop 123 AO *abcefghijop*

Among the italics, Stempel Garamond may be structurally the closest of all the revivals to Garamond's style (it is based on Garamond's own 18 pt italic font, reproduced on p 72), but the overall proportions of the letters in the Stempel italic are considerably changed from the model.

An entirely separate strain of designs, based on the work of Jean Jannon, is also sold under the name Garamond. These are discussed in the following entry. (See also pp 97, 101, 113.)

*Jannon* H  Jean Jannon, born in 1580, was the earliest of the
great typographic artists of the European Baroque. (The others,
in chronological order, are Van Dijck, Kis and Caslon.) Jannon
was also a French Protestant, printing illegally in a Catholic
regime, and the type he cut and cast during the early seventeenth century was seized in 1641 by agents of the French
crown. After two centuries in storage, it was revived and misidentified as the work of Claude Garamond.

Jannon's punches are still at the Imprimerie Nationale,
Paris. His type is elegant and disorderly: of widely varying axis
and slope, sharply serifed and asymmetrical. The best revivals
of these lovely, and distinctly non-Garamondian, letters are:

1  ATF 'Garamond,' drawn by M.F. Benton and issued in 1918;
2  Lanston's 'Garamont,' which was drawn by Frederic Goudy and
   issued in 1921;
3  Monotype 'Garamond,' issued in 1922; and
4  Simoncini 'Garamond,' drawn by Francesco Simoncini and issued in metal by the Simoncini Foundry, Bologna, in 1958.

Monotype has been particularly thorough in Jannon's case,
issuing two different cuts of italic, both in metal and in digital
form. Monotype 156, in which the slope of the caps varies
rambunctiously, is closer to Jannon's originals. Monotype 176
was the corporate revision: an attempt to bring the unrepentant
French typecutter, or at least his italic upper case, back into line.
But irregularity lies at the heart of the Baroque, and at the heart
of Jannon's letters, just as it may lie at the heart of his refusal to
conform to the state religion of his day. I prefer Monotype 156
italic for that reason.

abcefghijop 1 2 3 AO *abcefghijop*

abcefghijop 123 AO *abcefghijop*

Yet another version of Jannon's type is known as 'Garamond 3.' This is the ATF 'Garamond' of 1918 as adapted in 1936
for the Linotype machine, now re-revised for digital composition. It is perfectly serviceable as a text face, but it lacks both the
slightly disheveled grace of Monotype Garamond and the more
carefully combed and erect grace of the Simoncini version.

The face called ITC Garamond, designed in the 1970s by
Tony Stan, has, once again, nothing to do with Garamond or his
type. It is, instead, a radically distorted form of Jannon's. What-

ever its merits for signage, it should not be mistaken for a text face in either the Baroque or the Renaissance mode. (See also pp 97, 116.)

*Janson*   See Kis.

Joanna   abcefghijop 123 AO abcefghijopmxyz

\*   *Joanna* H   Designed by the English artist Eric Gill and cut by the Caslon Foundry in 1930. The Monotype version was produced in 1937. This is a face of spartan simplicity, with flat serifs and very little contrast but considerable variation in stroke axis. The italic has a slope of only 3° and includes many roman forms, but it is sufficiently narrower than the roman to minimize confusion. Text figures are essential to Gill's design.

*Kennerley*   abcefghijop 123 AO *abcefghijop*

*Kennerley* H   This was Frederic Goudy's first successful typeface, designed in 1911. (Goudy was 46 at the time, but his career as a type designer was just beginning.) By his own account, the designer wanted a new type with some of the flavor of Caslon – and Kennerley has Caslon's homey unpretentiousness, though it has returned to Renaissance forms for its underlying architecture and many of its structural details. The italic was drawn seven years after the roman, but Goudy had found his style; the two mate well. Text figures and small caps are required by the design.

(The spelling 'Kennerly' appears frequently in type catalogues, but the face was commissioned by and named for a Chicago publisher whose name was Mitchell Kennerley.)

*Kis*   abcefghijop 123 AO *abcefghijnop*

*Kis* H   The Hungarian Miklós Kis is a major figure in Dutch typography, as well as that of his own country. He spent most of the 1680s in Amsterdam, where he learned the craft and cut some wonderfully toothy and compact Baroque type. But for many years Kis's work was incorrectly ascribed to the Dutch punchcutter Anton Janson. Commerce has no conscience, and to this day, Kis's type is often sold, even by people who know better, under Janson's name.

178

Many of Kis's original punches and matrices found their way to the Stempel Foundry in Frankfurt, and Stempel Janson is Kis's actual type, with a few lost letters replaced by other hands. Linotype Janson was produced in 1954, based on the Kis originals, under the supervision of Hermann Zapf. Monotype Erhardt is also adapted, less successfully, from Kis's designs. Digital fonts have been prepared based on the Linotype version and on the original punches. The bold weights included in digital versions are extraneous, while text figures and small caps are essential to the design. (See also p 116.)

abcefghijopz 123 AO *abcefghijop*  Manuscript

*Manuscript* H Designed by Oldřich Menhart in the midst of World War II and issued by Grafotechna, Prague, in 1951. Manuscript is even rougher than the same designer's Figural, but its rough forms are carefully chosen and juxtaposed. The roman and italic are perfectly balanced with each other and within themselves. The numerals are ranging, though their heights are uneven. There is a Cyrillic companion face by the same name.   *

abcefghijop 1 2 3 AO *abcefghijop*   Mendoza

*Mendoza* D Designed by José Mendoza y Almeida, Paris, and released by ITC in 1991. This is a forceful and resilient neo-humanist text face with low contrast and a spartan finish. It prospers under careful handling but is tough enough to survive printing conditions lethal to other text faces. Small caps and text figures, which are implicit in the design, are included in the ITC master artwork. There is also an extensive range of weights.

abcefghijop 123 AO *abcefghijop*   Méridien

*Méridien* H This was Adrian Frutiger's first text face, designed in 1954 and cut by Deberny & Peignot, Paris, for hand composition. The serifs are triangular and abrupt but subtly inflected. The eye of the face is large, but the italic has impeccable balance and flow. The roman caps, which have unusual authority and poise, make an excellent titling face in themselves. The same designer's Frutiger makes a useful sanserif companion. There is a range of weights, but there are no small caps or text figures. (See also pp 55, 97, 102.)

A *scaling* font is one whose color and proportions are optically adjusted from size to size. See pp 165 and 237.

*Minion* D Designed by Robert Slimbach, San Francisco, and issued by Adobe in 1989. As of 1991, it is available in both scaling and non-scaling forms. Minion is a fully developed neo-humanist text face with unobtrusive texture but substantial x-height. Small caps and text figures are available in roman, italic and bold weights. The family also now includes a font of typographic ornaments, swash characters, and a Cyrillic. Slimbach's chancery italic, Poetica, is another useful companion face. (Minion is the face in which this book is set.)

*Nofret*

# abcefghijop 123 AO *abcefghijop*

*Nofret* D Designed by Gudrun Zapf-von Hesse and issued by Berthold in 1987. This is a text face related to, but more versatile than, the same designer's Diotima and Carmina. Nofret is substantially narrower than Diotima in the roman lower case, but of similar width in the italic. There is a range of weights, and even the heaviest of these retain their grace.

In the nineteenth century, dark, abruptly serifed (and distinctly unfeminine) faces were commonly called egyptians. Twentieth-century faces with similar structure have been given names like Memphis, Cairo and Karnak. Nofret, which is named for Nefertiti, can lay claim to be the queen of typographical egyptians. Small caps and text figures are included in the design. (See also p 123.)

*48 pt Foundry Palatino, reduced*

*Linotype digital Palatino*

*Linotype digital Aldus*

abcefghijop 123 AO *abcefghijop*

abcefghijop 123 AO *abcefghijop*

abcefghijop 123 AO *abcefghijop*

*Palatino* H/M Designed in 1948 by Hermann Zapf. Palatino roman was first cut by hand and cast in metal at the Stempel Foundry, then adapted by its designer for the Linotype machine. In photo and digital form, it is the most widely used of all neohumanist faces, among typographic professionals and amateurs alike. As the most universally admired of Zapf's designs, it is also the most heavily pirated. Phototype imitations abound under names such as Malibu, Palladium, Patina and Pontiac: all to be avoided. In its authentic incarnations, Palatino is a superbly balanced, powerful and graceful contribution to typography – but its close relative, Aldus, which was designed expressly for text setting, is often a better choice for that purpose, in company with Palatino as a display face. There is a bold weight, designed in 1950. A bold italic was added, evidently to combat existing forgeries, nearly thirty years later. The extended Palatino family includes two sets of display capitals (Michelangelo and Sistina), a text Greek (Heraklit) and Greek capitals (Phidias). Small caps and text figures are essential to Palatino. Because it was first designed as a display face for handsetting in metal, then adapted for use in text sizes on the Linotype machine, there are two fundamentally different yet authentic versions of Palatino italic. There is a wide version, originally matching the roman letter-for-letter in set-width, as required by the Linotype system, and a narrower, more elegant version intended for hand composition. The Linotype italic (actually the first to be issued) has better readability in sizes of 10 pt and below, but the best digital fonts for larger sizes – in both roman and italic – are based on the large foundry designs.

(See also pp 15, 56, 75, 93, 100, 122, and the title page.)

abcefghijop 1 2 3 AO *abcefghijop*

*Photina*

*Photina* F A text face with predominantly rationalist axis, small aperture and narrow set width but unmistakable calligraphic energy. It was designed by José Mendoza y Almeida, on commission from Monotype as their first face for photocomposition, and issued in 1972. It has been used often and well by British typographers but very rarely by North Americans. There is a range of weights, and the bold versions are gracefully designed. Photina's proportions are deliberately close to those of Univers, which makes an excellent sanserif companion. This is arguably the first Postmodern text face. Text figures and small caps are basic to the design.

*eabābcefghghijnopōp 123 AOsrym*

*Poetica*

*Poetica* D A chancery italic designed by Robert Slimbach and issued by Adobe in 1992. The basic family consists of four variations on one italic, with varying amounts of swash. There are also five fonts of swash capitals, two of alternate lowercase letters, two fonts of lowercase initials and two of lowercase terminals, two sets of small caps (both ornamented and plain),

*Prowling the Specimen Books*

*

181

a font of fractions and standard ligatures, another of ornamental ligatures, one font of analphabetic ornaments, and one font entirely of ampersands. The basic face is a plain neohumanist italic, suited for extended text. The supplementary fonts permit any desired amount of ostentation. (See also p 115.)

(See also p 115.)

*Bembo*

abcefghijop 1 2 3 AO *abcefghijop*

*Poliphilus & Blado*

abcefghijop 123 AO *abcefghijop*

\* *Poliphilus & Blado* ʜ Poliphilus is the Monotype Corporation's copy, made in 1923, of a roman font cut in Venice in 1499 by Francesco Griffo. It was an early experiment in the resuscitation of Renaissance designs, and the Monotype draftsmen copied the actual letterpress impression, including much of the ink squash, instead of paring back the printed forms to intuit what the punchcutter had carved. The result is a rough, somewhat rumpled yet charming face, like a Renaissance aristocrat, unshaven and in stockinged feet, caught between the bedroom and the bath. A second experiment in the same direction produced a very different result: Monotype Bembo, which is based on another of Griffo's romans.

The italic companion to Poliphilus is based not on one of Griffo's own superb italics but on a font designed by Ludovico degli Arrighi about 1526. (Arrighi died not long after finishing this type – probably his sixth italic – and it was acquired by the typographer Antonio Blado of Rome. No type called Arrighi existed when the 1923 revival was made, but Monotype chose nonetheless to give it Blado's name.)

Text figures and small caps are quintessential to these faces.

*Pontifex*

abcefghijop 123 AO *abcefghijop*

*Pontifex* ꜰ Designed by Friedrich Poppl in Wiesbaden, and issued in 1976 by Berthold in Berlin.

Pontifex is one of several eminent twentieth-century faces built on Mannerist lines. The others include Adrian Frutiger's Méridien, Georg Trump's Trump Mediäval, and Matthew Carter's Galliard. These are four quite different faces, designed by four quite different artists for four different typographic media, but they share several structural presumptions. All have a humanist axis in the roman but an unusually large x-height, a tendency toward sharpness, angularity and tension in the conformation of individual letters, and a considerable slope – generally 14° – in the italic. These are features inherited from French Mannerist typecutters such as Jacques de Sanlecque, Guillaume Le Bé and Robert Granjon. Galliard is in fact a revival of Granjon's letters, while Pontifex, Trump and Méridien are independent creations in a similar spirit. Together they demonstrate the range and depth of what one could call the neomannerist aspect of the Modernist tradition.

The titling figures of Pontifex are particularly well formed, but small caps and text figures are implicit in the design. (See also pp 76, 122.)

abcdefghijop 123 *A* A O *abcdefghijop*

*Romanée* H Designed by Jan van Krimpen and cut at the Enschedé Foundry in Haarlem, Netherlands. The roman owes much to the spirit of Garamond. Van Krimpen designed it in 1928 as a companion for an italic cut in the middle of the seventeenth century by another of Garamond's admirers, Christoffel van Dijck. But Van Krimpen remained dissatisfied with the relationship between the two faces, cut in the same land three hundred years apart. In 1948 he designed an italic of his own to go with Romanée roman. The new italic is distinguished by its prominent descenders, serifed on both sides, and it has much less slope than the italic of Van Dijck. Like the italics of the early sixteenth century, it uses upright capitals.

"United they fall, apart they stand as fine designs," said Van Krimpen's younger colleague, Sem Hartz. And it is true that Romanée italic stands very well on its own. Perhaps these faces are best used in the Renaissance manner – the manner of Garamond and his colleagues – with the italic set in separate passages rather than laced into the midst of roman text. Small caps and text figures are essential to the design.

abcefghijop 123 AO *abcefghijop*

*Sabon* H/M Designed by Jan Tschichold. The foundry type was issued by Stempel in 1964, with machine versions by Monotype and Linotype in 1967. The series consists of a roman, italic and semibold, based on the work of Claude Garamond and his pupil Jacques Sabon. The structure of the letterforms is faithful to French Renaissance models, but Tschichold's face has greater x-height than any but the tiniest sizes cut by Garamond. The type was intended as a general-purpose book face, and it serves this purpose extremely well, though it is bland in comparison with Garamond's originals. Small caps and text figures are essential to the design. (See also p 50.)

(See also p 50.)

*Scala*     abcefghijop 123 AO *abcefghijop*

*Scala* D  A crisp, neohumanist text face with sharp serifs and low contrast, designed by Martin Majoor and issued by Font-Shop International, Berlin, in 1991. This face has many of the merits of Eric Gill's Joanna – not to mention several merits distinctively its own – without Joanna's eccentricities. Small caps and text figures are implicit in the design. Licensed copies are sold under the trade name FF Scala.

*Spectrum*     abcefghijop 123 AO *abcefghijop*

*Spectrum* H/M  Designed in the 1940s by Jan van Krimpen and issued by both Enschedé and Monotype in 1952. This was Van Krimpen's last general text face, and it is the one most widely used and admired. The roman and italic are reserved, elegant and well matched. The axis is humanist, the aperture large, and the serifs simultaneously sharp and flat (a feature neither unwelcome nor contradictory in typography). Small caps and the distinctive Spectrum text figures, with their short extenders, are essential to the design. Spectrum semibold – which Van Krimpen refused to design – was added to the family by Monotype in 1972, long after his death.

*Stone Serif*     abcefghijop 123 AO *abcefghijop*

*Stone Serif* D  Designed by Sumner Stone, issued in digital form by Adobe in 1987, and in 1989 by ITC. Stone is an extended family, consisting of serifed roman and italic, unserifed roman and italic, and a so-called 'informal' roman and italic, all in a wide range of weights. Informal in this case means that the contrast is reduced, the serifs are flattened, thickened and shortened, a few serifs are amputated entirely from the upper case, and cursive forms of *a* and *g* have slipped, like vacationing italics, into the otherwise proper company of the roman.

The structural dissonances between the text face (called Stone Serif) and Stone Informal, make it questionable whether the two can work productively together, but the two remaining permutations – Serif plus Sans, or Informal plus Sans – cause no such interference. Their structural similarities hold them together, and their differences in finish make them easy to distinguish.

The foreshortened terminals on a, f and r, and the abnormally large x-height, give the roman a rather Edwardian tone, not dispelled by its sharp detailing. In Stone Informal, this premodern aura is further amplified by the dulled serifs. Given the large eye and the overall absence of humanist spirit, text figures are unnecessary, but they are included in the master artwork. A matching set of phonetic characters, designed by John Renner and issued by Adobe, makes the Stone family useful for a range of academic work.

*Prowling the Specimen Books*

abcefghijop 123 AO *abcefghijop*

*Swift*

*Swift* D  Designed in Holland by Gerard Unger and issued in 1987 by Dr-Ing Rudolf Hell GMBH in Kiel, Germany. Swift is avowedly a newspaper type and has many uses in general printing. The eye is large and the set is narrow, but the letters are crisp and open, with chisel-tipped wedge serifs. The axis is humanist and the aperture large. The italic is somewhat lighter in color than the roman, but taut and fluent. There is a range of weights. Despite its debt to the Dutch Baroque tradition, Swift functions well with or without text figures. The same designer's sanserif Praxis, and his upright sanserif italic Flora, make useful companion faces for Swift.

abcefghijop 123 AO *abcefghijop*

*Trajanus*

*Trajanus* M  Designed by Warren Chappell, issued in 1939 as a foundry face by Stempel and in machine form by Linotype. The angular, black forms of Trajanus echo the early humanist scripts of the Renaissance and some of the earliest roman printing types, used in Italy and Germany until they were superseded by Nicolas Jenson's Venetian whiteletter, the ancestor of Centaur. But Trajanus has none of the crudity of those earliest fonts, and the roman is matched by an equally crisp yet fluent italic. A digital version has been issued by Mergenthaler. The figures are three-quarter height. There is a companion bold face designed by Chappell and a Cyrillic companion face designed by Hermann Zapf. Chappell's sanserif, Lydian, is another related design, slightly darker than Trajanus but of similar angularity, with an equally good unserifed italic.

*Trinité*

# HadddpppeH *HaddddppppeH*

\* *Trinité* F This is a text family designed by Bram de Does of the Enschedé Foundry in Haarlem, Netherlands, and issued in phototype form in 1982 by Bobst/Autologic in Lausanne. There is a narrow roman, a wide roman, an italic and a bold, and there are swash versions of each of these, as well as chancery variants for the italic. Moreover, each face in the family is available in three different *heights*. The capitals do not vary in height, nor does the eye or torso of the lower case, but the extenders range to different depths and altitudes. In keeping with Aldine tradition, however, the slightly sloped capitals of the italic are shorter than their roman counterparts.

Despite the technical complexities of the series, this is one of the most aristocratic, supple and distinguished type families ever designed. The structure is based on Italian and Dutch Renaissance forms. Small caps and text figures are essential.

*Trump Mediäval*

# abcefghijop 1 2 3 AO *abcefghijop*

*Trump Mediäval* H/M Designed by Georg Trump. This was first issued in 1954 by the Weber Foundry, Stuttgart, and in machine form by Linotype. It is a strong, angular roman and italic with humanist axis but Mannerist torque and proportions. The aperture is moderate, the serifs abrupt and substantial. The titling figures are well designed, but text figures and small caps are available and contribute much to the elegance of the face. There is a series of weights, and there are several excellent script faces by the same designer, potentially useful as companions. (See also pp 50 and 81.)

*Monotype*
*Van Dijck*

# abcefghijop 123 AO (&) *abcefghijop*

\* *Van Dijck* H The family now called Van Dijck – first issued by Monotype in 1935 – is based on an italic cut about 1660 by Christoffel van Dijck and a roman which may or may not also be his. These are graceful Dutch Baroque faces with modest x-height, narrow in the italic but comparatively spacious in the roman. A comparison of Van Dijck with Kis shows some of the range of Dutch Baroque typographic tradition. Text figures and small caps are essential to the design. (See also p 48.)

abcefghijop 123 AO *abcefghijop*     *Veljović*

*Veljović* F Designed by Jovica Veljović and issued in 1984 by ITC. Veljović is a Postmodern face, with inherent movement in spite of its rationalist axis, and a prickly energy, emerging in the sharp, abrupt wedge serifs. There is a wide range of weights. Small caps and text figures are included in the ITC master artwork. (See also p 15.)

*Walbaum* H Justus Erich Walbaum, who was a contemporary of Beethoven, ranks with Giambattista Bodoni and Firmin Didot as one of the great European Romantic or late Neoclassical type designers. He was the latest of the three, but he may well have been the most original. Walbaum cut his fonts at Goslar and Weimar in the first years of the nineteenth century. His matrices were bought by the Berthold Foundry a century later, and Berthold Walbaum, in its metal form, is his type. Other versions have also been digitized. Text figures and small caps are required by the design. (See also p 119.)

abcefghijop 123 AO *abcefghijop*     *Berthold Walbaum*

abcefghijop 123 AO *abcefghijop*     *Zapf Book*

abcefghijop 123 AO *abcefghijop*     *Zapf International*

*Zapf Book* F Designed by Hermann Zapf in 1970–75 and issued by ITC. Zapf Book, and the related, much more potent, display face, Zapf International, are a twentieth-century designer's meditations on Neoclassical and Romantic form, and in particular on the letters of Justus Walbaum. The axis in Zapf Book is insistently vertical, and the serifs are horizontal hairlines. The bowls in both upper and lower case take the form of a superellipse – which is, roughly speaking, an ellipse inflated within a rectangle, or a circle swollen within a square. There is a wide range of weights.

*Zapf Renaissance* D Designed by Hermann Zapf in 1984–85 and issued in 1987 by Scangraphic (Scangraphic Dr Böger GMBH) in Hamburg. This family returns, after forty years, to many of the principles that animated Zapf's Palatino – but Zapf Renaissance is designed for the high-technology, two-dimensional world of digital imaging, instead of the low-technology, multidimensional world of letterpress. The result is a less *printerly* and more *scribal* typeface. The family includes a roman, italic and semibold, each with a standard character set for conventional text composition, but for display work there are many alternate forms, especially in the italic.

*Zapf Renaissance*
*italic*

*a a b c d d e′ e e f f f g g g g h i j k k*

## 10.2 UNSERIFED FACES

Unserifed letters have a history at least as long, and quite as distinguished, as the history of serifed letters. Unserifed capitals appear in the earliest Greek inscriptions. They reappear at Rome in the third and second centuries BC and in Florence in the early Renaissance. Perhaps it is a fluke of history that the unserifed letters of fifteenth-century Florentine architects and sculptors were not translated into metal type in the 1470s.

At Athens and again at Rome, the modulated stroke and bilateral serif were the scribal trademarks and symbols of empire. Unserifed letters, with no modulation or, at most, a subtle taper in the stroke, were emblems of the Republic. This link between unserifed letterforms and populist or democratic movements recurs time and again, in Renaissance Italy and in the eighteenth and nineteenth centuries in northern Europe.

The first unserifed Latin printing type was actually an upright italic cut for Valentin Haüy, Paris, in 1786. But Haüy's type was meant to be invisible. It was embossed, without ink, for the blind to read with their fingers. The first unserifed type for the sighted – cut by William Caslon IV, London, 1816 – was based on signwriters' letters, and it consisted of capitals only. Bicameral (upper- and lowercase) unserifed roman fonts were first cut in Germany in the 1830s.

Most, though not all, of the unserifed types of the nineteenth century were dark, coarse and tightly closed. These characteristics are still obvious in faces like Helvetica and Franklin Gothic, despite the weight-reductions and other refinements

The importance of the Haüy italic was first pointed out by James Mosley. For more information on the history of unserifed letters, see Mosley's essay "The Nymph and the Grot," *Typographica* n.s. 12 (December 1965) and Nicolete Gray, *A History of Lettering.*

worked on them over the years. These faces are cultural souvenirs of the bleakest days of the Industrial Revolution.

During the twentieth century, sanserifs have evolved toward much greater subtlety, and in this evolution there seem to be three major factors. One is the study of archaic Greek inscriptions, with their light, limber stroke and large aperture. Another is the pursuit of pure geometry: typographic meditation on the circle and the line. The third is the study of Renaissance calligraphy and humanistic form – vitally important in the recent history of serifed and unserifed letters alike.

A O *abcdefghijklmnopqrstuvwxyz*     *Flora*

*Flora* D Designed by Gerard Unger, released by Dr-Ing. Rudolf Hell GmbH in 1985 and by ITC in 1989. Flora is a true sanserif italic – and the first unserifed italic that approximates chancery form. It can be used alone but is designed to function also as a companion to Unger's Praxis (unserifed roman) and Demos (serifed roman and italic). Because the slope is only 2½°, Flora works best with Praxis when used for separate blocks of text, rather than to emphasize individual letters or words. (There is a secondary version of the face, produced by Hell, which has no slope at all.)

abcefghijop 123 AO *abcefghijop*     *Formata*

*Formata* D Designed by Bernd Möllenstädt and issued by Berthold in 1984. The proportions of Formata are close to those of Frutiger, but the oblique ends of the strokes, as well as the shapes of the bowls, imply a predominantly humanist axis. The face has other subtleties which are all but lost at normal resolutions in text sizes. At first sight, Formata may appear to be just one more stick-and-ball sanserif, but every stroke in every letter, straight or curved, has a subtle and asymmetrical taper. There is a wide range of weights.

abcefghijop 123 AO *abcefghijop*     *Frutiger*

*Frutiger* F Designed in 1975 by Adrian Frutiger and issued by Mergenthaler. Frutiger was first designed for signage at the Paris-Roissy Airport. It lacks some of the humanist features of other recent sanserifs, but its balance and openness nevertheless commend it for many purposes. It works particularly well with the same designer's Méridien. There are upright and sloped versions in a range of weights. (See also p 102.)

*Futura*

abcefghijop 123 AO *abcefghijop*

\* *Futura* H Designed by Paul Renner in 1924–26 and issued by the Bauer Foundry, Frankfurt, in 1927. Futura is a subtly crafted geometric sanserif. The stroke appears to be unmodulated, but in fact it is carefully shaped to give optical balance. The extra-bold weights and other less graceful additions to the family are not Renner's designs. Spartan and Twentieth Century are other founders' copies of Futura. (See also pp 14, 102, 121.)

*Gill Sans*

abcefghijop 123 AO *abcefghijop*

\* *Gill Sans* M Designed by Eric Gill and issued by Monotype in 1927. Gill Sans is a distinctly British but highly readable sanserif, composed of latently humanist and overtly geometric forms. The aperture is large. The italic – which is a true sanserif italic instead of a sloped roman – was a revolutionary achievement in its time. Books have been set successfully in Gill Sans, though it requires a sure sense of color and measure.

*ITC Goudy Sans*

abcefghijop 123 AO *abcefghijop*

*Goudy Sans* M Designed by Frederic Goudy in 1929–30 and issued by Lanston Monotype. This was one of the first sanserifs to break from the industrial model by opening the aperture and implying an oblique axis in the bowls. But Goudy Sans is not as sans as the name suggests. There are in fact residual serifs in many of the forms. The digital version, issued in 1986 by ITC, is in several respects an improvement on the original.

*ITC Kabel*

A O abcdefghijklmnopqrstuvwxyz

*Kabel* H Designed by Rudolf Koch and issued in various weights by the Klingspor Foundry, Offenbach, in 1927–30. In Koch's original design, the lighter weights of Kabel have a very small eye or x-height, while the eye in the black weight is large. The series was redrawn by ITC in the 1980s with the eye uniformly large throughout. Both versions have now been digi-

190

tized. The original may have greater historical merit, but ITC Kabel has greater vigor, functions much better in smaller sizes and serves more comfortably for extended text.

abcefghijop 123 AO *abcefghijop*

*Laudatio* F Designed by Friedrich Poppl and issued by Berthold in 1982. Laudatio, like Optima, lives on the borderline between serif and sanserif. The ends of the stems are flared, and in the lower case, at the upper ends of the strokes, where a head serif would occur on the left side in a normal roman or italic, the stroke end is canted and flared toward the left. The eye is large and open, and the axis varies, but there is restrained calligraphic power in this face, along with inscriptional dignity. There is a true italic and a range of weights.

abcefghijop 123 AO ABCEFGHJOP

*Meta* D Designed by Erik Spiekermann and issued by Font-. Shop in 1991. The forms are compact and erect, the stroke is subtly modulated, and the ends of the stems are slightly bent and cropped at an angle, giving a faint reminiscence of serifs. Text figures and small caps are included in the design, but there is no italic. Licensed copies are sold as FF Meta.

abcefghijop 123 AO *abcefghijop*

*Optima* H/M Designed by Hermann Zapf in 1952–55 and issued both by Stempel and by Linotype in 1958. The stroke weight is more variable in Optima than in Laudatio, but the degree of taper is less. Of the two, Optima is more purely a sanserif. The taper of the stroke derives from unserifed Greek inscriptions and the unserifed roman inscriptions of Renaissance Florence, but in other respects the architecture of Optima is Neoclassical. In lieu of an italic, there is a sloped roman. There is a range of weights, and there is a matching text Greek, designed by Zapf and issued by Linotype in 1971.

abcefghijop 123 AO *abcefghijop*

*Shannon* D Designed by Kris Holmes and Janice Prescott Fishman, and issued by Compugraphic in 1981. Shannon is a sanserif with humanist axis and large aperture. It is further humanized by a slight flaring and bending of the stroke, and in fact draws its architecture in part from semiserifed letterforms in the Book of Kells. There is an oblique but no true italic.

## abcefghijop 123 AO *abcefghijop*

*Stone Sans* D Designed by Sumner Stone and issued by Adobe in 1987 and by ITC in 1989. A sanserif of variable axis, large aperture, large x-height, and subtle modulation of the stroke. This is part of the comprehensive Stone family, including serifed, unserifed, 'informal' and phonetic faces. Its primary value may lie in the typographical possibilities of this family relationship. The ITC master artwork includes small caps and text figures, but these are omitted by most manufacturers.

## abcefghijop 123 AO *abcefghijop*

For the Bigelow & Holmes version of Syntax , see Dell Hymes's essay, "Victoria Howard's 'Gitskux and His Older Brother,'" in Brian Swann, ed., *Smoothing the Ground: Essays on Native American Oral Literature.* Berkeley, CA, 1983.

*Syntax* H Designed by Hans Eduard Meier and issued by the Stempel foundry in 1969. The roman is a true neohumanist sanserif, in which Renaissance forms are clearly visible. The italic, however, is a hybrid, part italic, part sloped roman. Close analysis will show that Syntax roman is sloped too. The italic slopes at 11° and the roman at about half a degree. Little as it is, half a degree is enough to add a perceptible vitality and motion to the forms. And the stroke is subtly modulated. There are several weights, but with this as with neohumanist faces generally, the weights above semibold are severely distorted.

An extended Syntax character set, intended specifically for setting Native American languages, was designed in 1981 by Charles Bigelow and Kris Holmes.

## abcefghijop 123 AO *abcefghijop*

*Today* D Designed by Volker Küster and issued by Scangraphic in 1988. The name suggests an ephemeral creation, but the letterforms suggest otherwise. This is a neohumanist face, gentler in its design than Syntax, with a true italic of modest Renaissance inclination (8°). Like Goudy Sans, it also retains a few vestigial links with the serif tradition. There are exit strokes – unilateral serifs, by another name – on the *d* and *u* in both roman and italic, and on the *p* in italic only.

All typefaces are, one way or another, edited or paraphrased versions of a written hand, and the evolution of photographic and digital imaging and offset printing has blurred still further the imprecise boundaries between typography and writing. There are thousands of typefaces that stand outside the conservative and tradition-bound world of text type, and that look as if they might have been handwritten rather than drawn, carved or inscribed. Some are formal, some informal, some connected and some made of separate letters. Typographers often lump them together unscientifically as script types.

*Prowling the Specimen Books*

Scripts had an importance in the world of commercial letterpress that they lack in the world of two-dimensional printing. Handwritten originals are expensive to photoengrave for letterpress reproduction. But specially commissioned calligraphy is easy to incorporate into artwork destined for the offset press. The best script to supplement a typographic page is now therefore more likely to be custom made.

In general, scripts are also more closely tied to particular moods, places and times than text types are, and types that pass quickly in and out of fashion are extraneous to the subject of this book. But scripts remain important in typography for the contrast they provide when a single word or line must be set off from a block of formal text.

In recent years, a whole new class of script types has arisen. Faces like Gottfried Pott's Carolina and David Siegel's Tekton are lucid and cool enough for setting extended texts, yet they continue to evoke the scriptorial more than the typographic tradition. Like most real scripts, these typefaces are technically complex. Skillfully used, they are more likely to appear – as good type almost always does – quite simple. They make a virtue out of the incorporeality of contemporary printing: the permeability of the digital type body and the two-dimensionality of letterforms as rendered by the offset press.

## eeeeeeeee eeeeeeeee eeeeeeeee

*Beowolf*

*Beowolf* D Designed in the late 1980s by Jùst van Rossum and Erik van Blokland, and issued by FontShop in 1990. This is not a script type in the conventional sense, but a font that uses the resources of digital imaging to reproduce some of the unpredictabilities of true script. The letterforms have fixed widths, but they are output through a digital randomizer, altering their shapes within predetermined limits in unpredetermined ways. Each incarnation of each character therefore differs from the last. There is also an unserifed companion face, BeoSans.

A O abcdefghijklmnopqrstuvwxyz

*Carolina* D  Designed by Gottfried Pott and issued by Linotype in 1990. Carolina is based on the Carolingian minuscule script, which is the immediate scriptorial grandmother of the roman and italic scripts of the Renaissance, and thus of roman and italic type. (See also p 110.)

*A O abcdefghijklmnopqrstuvwxyz*

*Legende* H  A wide, dark, disconnected script with a small eye but excellent legibility. It was designed by Ernst Schneidler and issued by the Bauer Foundry, Frankfurt, in 1937. This is one of the best modern exemplars of a class of Mannerist scripts that have been cut and cast as type since the High Renaissance. Typographers call them *civilités*.

abcdefghijklmnopqrstuvwxyz

*Ondine* H  A dark but open, lucid, disconnected pen script designed by Adrian Frutiger and originally issued by Deberny & Peignot, Paris, in 1954.

A O abcdefghijklmnopqrstuvwxyz

*Present* F  A light, broad, disconnected brush script designed by Friedrich Sallwey and issued by the Stempel Foundry, Frankfurt, in 1974.

A O abcdefghijklmnopqrstuvwxyz

*Salto* H  A vigorous, simple and dark brush script designed by Karlgeorg Hoefer, issued by Stempel in 1953. The caps are oversize, with the brush marks freely shown. There is a soberer variant, Saltino, in which the same lower case is mated with decorous capitals tamed to normal size.

abcdefghijop 123 A O abcefghijop

*Tekton* D Designed by David Siegel, based on the lettering of Frank Ching. This is a script face derived directly from architectural lettering. It has tiny bead serifs and an unmodulated stroke but is readable enough for extended text. There are upright and oblique versions in two weights. The original script can be seen in Ching's book *Architectural Graphics* (New York, 1985), which is printed entirely from handwritten pages.

*Prowling the Specimen Books*

## 10.4 TITLING & DISPLAY FACES

A handlettered title by a great calligrapher is almost always superior to typesetting, but a titling font designed by a great calligrapher and used by a competent typographer is almost always better than custom lettering by a mediocre scribe.

Often the best titling face is the same face used for the text. Sometimes it is another text face of related design. On other occasions, the best titling face is the most unpredictable and unlikely face to be found. Potential choices exist by the thousand, and new ones are constantly appearing. Old ones are also rapidly being revived in digital form. Metal type, wood type, pen script, brush script, letters cut into stone or lead or linoleum are all possibilities. But a select few alphabets have established themselves as typographical titling faces of stature and probable longevity. Often typographers use them only for versals, one letter at a time, and often these faces are unicameral alphabets, consisting of capitals only.

Typefaces are usually chosen for versals and titles on the basis of one of two contradictory virtues. They either harmonize with the text face – as Hermann Zapf's Michelangelo harmonizes closely with its sister text faces Aldus and Palatino – or they contrast with the text face, as Rudolf Koch's Neuland does with almost anything.

*Albertus* M Inscriptional roman capitals and lower case. Some strokes are flared; others have minimal inscriptional serifs. The face was designed by Berthold Wolpe and originally issued by Monotype in 1934. The italic (which is a condensed, sloped roman, except for *a* and *f*) is a peculiarly narrow later addition, lacking the authority of the original design.

For specimen letters of this and the following faces, see p 199.

*Augustea* ʜ Sharply serifed, formal inscriptional capitals, designed by Aldo Novarese and Alessandro Butti, issued in metal by the Nebiolo Foundry, Torino, in 1955. An impressive lower case was later added to the capitals. There is also an inline version, known as Augustea Filettata or Augustea Inline.

*Avant Garde* ꜰ This is a bicameral stick-and-ball sanserif with very large x-height, designed in New York by Herb Lubalin and Tom Carnase about 1968 and issued by ɪᴛᴄ in 1970. There are many decorative ligatures specific to the face, and there is a range of weights. There is also a slab-serifed variant called Lubalin Graph.

*Cartier* A O abcdefghijklmnopqrstuvwxyz

*Cartier* ꜰ Designed in Toronto by Carl Dair and issued for photosetting in 1967. The roman is based on the earliest proto-Renaissance roman faces, cut in Italy and Germany in the second half of the fifteenth century. There is also a narrow and spidery italic lower case, but it does not match the roman in quality or color. There is a slicker, blander version of the roman, drawn in England in the 1970s, known as Raleigh.

*Castellar* ᴍ Inline capitals, asymmetrically inscribed, so that the hollowed strokes are light on the left, dark on the right. The face was designed by John Peters and issued by Monotype in 1957. (See pp 62, 144.)

*Charlemagne* ᴅ Caroline capitals, based on the Carolingian titling scripts and versals of the ninth and tenth centuries. Designed by Carol Twombly and issued in digital form by Adobe in 1989. (See p 110.)

\* *Codex* ʜ Designed by Georg Trump and issued by Weber in 1955. A sophisticated bicameral face combining serifed and unserifed, roman and italic forms. The splayed, unserifed strokes in the upper case are inherited from late classical scripts; the lower case is derived in part from Carolingian models.

\* *Cristal* ʜ Double-inline formal capitals with sharp, triangular serifs. Designed by Rémy Peignot and issued in metal by Deberny & Peignot, Paris, in 1957.

*Delphin*  ʜ  Designed by Georg Trump and issued by Weber in the early 1950s. The upper case is a conventional roman, but in Trump's distinctive style, similar to the capitals of his Trump Mediäval. The lower case is a pen-formed italic with several unusual permutations. There are two weights, with subtle differences in the serifs and other details.

abcefghijop 123 AO *abcefghijop*    *Ellington*

*Ellington*  ᴅ  Designed by British calligrapher and stonecutter Michael Harvey and issued in digital form by Monotype in 1990. A narrow but vigorous bicameral roman and italic, with large x-height and lining figures, in a range of weights. There is a rationalist axis in the roman, a humanist axis in the italic.

*Lithos*  ᴅ  Unserifed capitals with light stroke and large aperture, based on early Greek inscriptional letters. Designed by Carol Twombly and issued by Adobe. There are several weights. There are many subtle modulations in the stroke. (See p 108.)

*Michelangelo*  ʜ  Serifed roman capitals designed by Hermann Zapf as a titling face for use in combination with Palatino and Aldus. Issued in metal by Stempel in 1950. There is a matching set of Greek capitals, known as Phidias.

*Monument*  ʜ  Open inline capitals, designed by Oldřich Menhart and cast in 1950 by the Grafotechna Foundry, Prague. The imperial stillness typical of inscriptional roman letters is transformed to a kind of stately folk dance under Menhart's hand.    *

*Neuland*  ʜ  Dark, rugged, unserifed roman capitals, designed and cut by Rudolf Koch and issued in metal by the Klingspor Foundry, Offenbach, in 1923. Koch cut the original punches freehand, without pattern drawings. Each size in the foundry version therefore has many idiosyncracies of its own. These subtleties are lost in the existing digital versions.

*Pericles*  ʜ  Unserifed capitals, based on Greek inscriptional letters, designed in Brooklyn by the sculptor Robert Foster and issued in metal by ᴀᴛꜰ in 1934. Foster's Pericles, like Twombly's Lithos, captures some of the playfulness, the openness and the spare, athletic dignity of early Greek inscriptional letterforms.    *

# abcefghijop AO abcefghijop

\*   *Preissig* H  A rugged expressionist face – roman in form and yet more angular than many blackletters – designed in New York in 1924–25 by the Czech artist Vojtěch Preissig and cast by the Státni tiskárna (the Czechoslovak state foundry), Prague.

\*   *Romulus Open Capitals* H  Light, sharply serifed, inline roman capitals, designed by Jan van Krimpen and issued by Enschedé in 1936.

*Sistina* H  Dark, serifed roman capitals designed by Hermann Zapf as part of the family that includes Palatino, Aldus and Michelangelo. The original was issued by Stempel in 1951. Sistina and Michelangelo together represent a typographic inquest into the dark and light, the yin and yang, the ecclesiastical and the humanist aspects of the Italian Renaissance.

*Trajan* D  Serifed capitals, based on the inscription at the base of Trajan's Column, Rome, carved at the beginning of the second century AD. Drawn by Carol Twombly and issued in digital form by Adobe. (See p 110.)

*Vendôme* H  Designed by François Ganeau in collaboration with Roger Excoffon and cut by the Fonderie Olive, Marseille, in 1951. Vendôme is an exaggeratedly Gallic and playful variation on the roman of Jean Jannon. There is a sloped roman in lieu of an italic, and there are several weights. (See p 97.)

For a specimen of Zapf International, see p 187.

*Zapf International* F  Designed by Hermann Zapf and issued in 1976 by ITC. The axis and serifs appear at first sight properly Neoclassical, but the forms are full of energy. The eye is super-elliptical and slightly asymmetrical, as if it were under pressure. The axis varies slightly both to left and right; and the vertical strokes, especially in the upper case, are prominently tapered. The result is a kind of Blues on Baskerville, or Didot reconstructed by Duke Ellington. It makes an excellent titling and display face with Baskerville, Walbaum, Zapf Book or other text faces of Neoclassical or Romantic persuasion. Text figures are included in the master artwork, and there is an extensive range of weights. (See pp 100, 123.)

From left to right:

*Albertus,*
*Augustea,*
*Avant Garde*

*Cartier,*
*Castellar,*
*Charlemagne*

*Codex,*
*Cristal,*
*Delphin*

*Michelangelo,*
*Monument,*
*Neuland*

*Pericles,*
*Romulus Open,*
*Sistina*

The earliest types cut in Europe, those used by Gutenberg, were blackletters. Scripts and typefaces of this class were once used throughout Europe – in England, France, the Netherlands and Spain, as well as Germany – and some species thrived even in Italy. They are the typographic counterpart of the Gothic style in architecture, and like Gothic architecture, they are a prominent part of the European heritage, though they flourished longer and more vigorously in Germany than anywhere else.

Blackletter scripts, like roman scripts, exist in endless variety. Blackletter types are somewhat simpler, and not all of them need concern us here. But it is worth noting the presence of four major families: *textura, fraktur, bastarda* and *rotunda*. (Another genus of blackletter often listed in type catalogues is Schwabacher. This is bastarda by its domestic German name.) None of these families is confined to a particular historical period. All four of them have survived, like roman and italic, through many historical variations. Their differences are many and complex, but they can usually be distinguished by reference to the lowercase *o* alone. Though it is written with only two penstrokes, the *o* in a textura looks essentially hexagonal. In a fraktur, it is normally flat on the left side, curved on the right. In a bastarda, it is normally pointed at top and bottom and belled on both sides. In a rotunda, it is essentially oval or round.

Typical lowercase forms in textura, fraktur, bastarda, and rotunda

The heavily ornamented and tightly set blackletters of the High Gothic period are difficult to read without long practice, and the elaborate, often delicate frakturs of the eighteenth century are nearly as challenging. But some of these faces – notably those of Johann Unger and Johann Breitkopf – are as important to the history of German typography as Baskerville's letters to the typographical history of England, France and the USA.

Blackletter can be used in many contexts for emphasis or contrast, and need not be confined to the mastheads of newspapers and the titles of religious tracts. Type designers have also not abandoned it. Some excellent blackletters have been drawn in the twentieth century – by German artists such as Rudolf Koch and by the American Frederic Goudy.

A O abcdefghijklmnopqrstuvwxyz

*Clairvaux* D Designed by Herbert Maring and issued in digital form by Linotype in 1990. Clairvaux is a bastarda, but closer than most to the Caroline minuscule, which makes it more legible to modern eyes.

A O abcdefghijklmnopqrstuvwxyz

*Claudius* H A light, legible and unornamented fraktur of generous character width, with decorative capitals, designed by Rudolf Koch in 1934 and issued by Klingspor in 1937.

A O abcdefghijklmnopqrstuvwxyz

*Duc de Berry* D A light French bastarda, designed by Gottfried Pott, issued in digital form by Linotype in 1991.

A O abcdefghijklmnopqrstuvwxyz

*Fette Fraktur* H This heavy, Romantic fraktur was designed by Johann Christian Bauer and issued by his foundry at Frankfurt about 1850. It provides strong evidence that the Victorian 'fat face' is inherently more congenial to blackletter than to roman.

A O abcdefghijklmnopqrstuvwxyz A O

*Goudy Text* M Designed by Frederic Goudy and issued by Monotype in 1928. A narrow, smooth, slightly ornamented textura, legible in the upper as well as the lower case. There is a second set of capitals, known as Lombardic caps.

A O abcdefghijklmnopqrstuvwxyz

*Goudy Thirty* M This was one of Frederic Goudy's last typefaces, deliberately conceived as his memorial to himself. It is a light and simple rotunda, designed in 1942 and issued by Lanston Monotype in 1948.

ℝ O abcdefghijklmnopqrs|tuvwxyz

*Rhapsodie* ʜ This is an energetic, legible Schwabacher (German bastarda) designed by Ilse Schüle and issued by Ludwig & Mayer, Frankfurt, in 1951. There is an alternate set of ornamental but legible capitals.

A ☉ abcdefghijklmnopqrstuvwxyz

*San Marco* ᴅ Designed by Karlgeorg Hoefer and issued by Linotype in 1991. The lower case is a rotunda – the genus of blackletter most closely connected to Italy and structurally closest to roman forms. The capitals are more ornate, doublestroke gothics.

A abcdefghijklmnopqrſstuvwxyz

*Trump-Deutsch* ʜ Designed by Georg Trump and issued in metal by the Berthold Foundry in 1936. This is a dark, wide, concave, unornamented and energetic textura. Both upper and lower case are open and easily legible forms.

10.6 UNCIALS

Uncial letters were widely used by European scribes from the fourth through the ninth century ᴀᴅ, both for Latin and for Greek, but they had vanished from common use in the time of Gutenberg. Uncials were not cut into type until the nineteenth century, and then only for scholarly or antiquarian purposes. In the twentieth century, many designers – Sjoerd de Roos, W.A. Dwiggins, Frederic Goudy, Oldřich Menhart and Günter Gerhard Lange, among others – have taken an interest in uncial forms. One twentieth-century artist and printer, Victor Hammer, devoted his life to them.

Historically, uncials are unicameral – they have only one case, as all European alphabets did until the late Middle Ages. Many recent uncial designs preserve this feature; others have mated roman capitals to an uncial lower case. Early uncials, like recent ones, are sometimes serifed, sometimes not, but most have a highly modulated stroke. They are often used for display, but some are quiet enough for setting extended texts.

A O abcðefghíjklmnopqrstuvwxyz

*American Uncial* ʜ Round uncials with vertical axis. Unserified roman capitals are supplied as an upper case. The original version was designed and cut by Victor Hammer in the early 1940s. The face was cast privately in Chicago in 1945 and commercially by the Stempel Foundry in 1953.

ABCðEFGhIJKLMNOPQRSTUVWXYZ

*Omnia* ᴅ Lightly serifed, round, cursive uncials with a large aperture and humanist axis, designed by Karlgeorg Hoefer and issued by Linotype in 1991.

ABCðEFGhiJkLMNOPQRSTUVWXYZ

*Solemnis* ʜ Serifed, square uncials with a humanist axis, designed by Günter Gerhard Lange and issued in metal by Berthold in 1953.

10.7 GREEKS

Greek type has a long and complex history peculiarly its own, yet closely entwined with the history of roman. The first Greek types were cut in Venice by Nicolas Jenson, Francesco Griffo and others who were simultaneously cutting the first roman and italic faces. Claude Garamond spent years of his life cutting Greek letters on commission from the King of France. Robert Granjon, Miklós Kis and William Caslon cut excellent Greeks as well. Yet the first Greek books printed in Greece itself were printed by a visitor from Paris in 1821. Even now, typography and type design in Greece lean oddly in a nineteenth-century French direction. But in the multinational world of classical studies, Greek types that will harmonize with humanist romans are perennially needed and in perennial short supply.

Greek adaptations of popular roman faces – Baskerville, Caledonia, Times New Roman, Souvenir, Helvetica and Univers, among others – have been issued by both Linotype and Monotype, and are widely used in Greece. But there, as in much of Eastern Europe, the more lyrical forms of modernism have been slower to arrive.

Greek, like Latin, evolved into bicameral form in the late Middle Ages. The upper case in the two alphabets shares the same ancient heritage, and more than half the uppercase forms remain identical. But the Greek lower case has evolved along a different path. There is a quiet and formal Greek hand, not dissimilar in spirit to the roman lower case, and there are typefaces (New Hellenic, for example) derived from it. But the normal Greek lower case is cursive. Thus, most Greek faces are like Renaissance italics: upright, formal capitals with a flowing, often sloping, lower case. No supplementary face has developed in the Greek typographic tradition: no face that augments and contrasts with this primary alphabet as italic does with roman.

Twentieth-century designers have sometimes added bold and inclined variants to their Greeks, in imitation of Latin models. But most of the faces listed below are solitary: designed to be used alone or as supplementary faces themselves, for setting Greek intermixed with roman.

*Antigone*

αβγδεζηϑικλμνξοπρσςτυφχψω

\* *Antigone* H Designed by Jan van Krimpen and issued by Enschedé in 1927. This is a delicately drawn and sculpted face, intended for the setting of lyric poetry. It composes well with the same designer's eminent Latin faces: Lutetia, Romanée and Spectrum. (See also p 103.)

*Attika*

αβγδεζηθικλμνξοπρσςτυφχψω

\* *Attika* H/M Designed by Hermann Zapf for the Stempel Foundry in 1953 as a Greek companion to Neuzeit, C.W. Pischner's unserifed roman. Issued in machine form by Linotype. It is a rigorously modernist, geometric face, more purely sanserif and larger in the eye than Gill Sans Greek.

*Gill Sans Greek*

αβγδεζηθικλμνξοπρστυφχψω

\* *Gill Sans* M Light, medium and bold, upright and inclined. This face was designed in the 1950s, not by Eric Gill but by Monotype draftsmen as a companion for and extension to Gill Sans roman. Since the roman was itself much modified from Gill's drawings, Gill Sans Greek is twice removed from the artist for whom it is named. The capitals are very clean. The lower case, like its roman counterpart, includes a few residual serifs. It combines transparently with Gill Sans roman. It can also be used effectively with serifed humanist faces, playing off the distinction between archaic, inscriptional Greek and the Renaissance scribal tradition whose alphabet is Latin.

αβγδεζηθικλμνξοπρσςτυφχψω                    *Heraklit*

*Heraklit* H/M  Designed by Hermann Zapf and issued both by        *
Stempel and by Linotype in 1954. This is a humanist Greek, designed to harmonize with the same designer's Palatino and Aldus. (See also p 103.)

ἐκλίνθη ἰάχων, πατρὸς φίλου ὄψιν          *New Hellenic*

*New Hellenic* M  Designed by Victor Scholderer and issued by        *
Monotype in 1927. This is a modern variation on a Greek font cut by Arnaldo Guillén de Brocar at Alcalá de Henares, near Madrid, in 1510. The original font – called the Complutensian Greek – was intended for use in a polyglot Bible but was diverted at once into printing the pagan classics. Scholderer's version is open, erect, gracious and stable, with minimal modulation of the stroke and minimal serifs.

αβγδεζηθικλμνξοπρσςτυφχψω                *Monotype Porson*

*Porson* H  Designed by Richard Porson and first cut in metal        *
by Richard Austin in 1826. The face was soon copied by several founders, and in 1912 an edited and polished version was issued by Monotype. This has been the standard Greek face for the Oxford Classical Texts for close to a century. It is a calm and restful yet energetic face that composes well with many romans, especially those of Baroque or Neoclassical design. In spirit it is close to Baskerville, but it is far less spindly and timid than the Greek that John Baskerville actually designed.

10.8  CYRILLICS

The Cyrillic alphabet was adapted from Greek in the ninth century, and the first Cyrillic type was cut in Kraków by Ludolf Borchtorp in 1490. The subsequent history of Cyrillic is largely parallel to that of Latin type, with the important exception that there is no humanist or Renaissance phase. Slavic type, like Slavic literature, passed more or less directly from the medieval to the Baroque. For this and for other, more overtly political reasons, the neohumanist movement in type design also came late to Cyrillic letters.

*Cyrillics*

With minor variations, Cyrillic is used by perhaps a third of a billion people, writing in Russian, Ukrainian, Belorussian, Bulgarian, Macedonian and other Slavic languages. In Serbia and Montenegro it is used for Serbo-Croatian, and in Moldova for Rumanian. It is also now the common alphabet for a host of unrelated languages, from Azerbaijani to Udmert, spoken and written across what once was the Soviet Union.

Several excellent type designers have worked in Russia and the neighboring republics in this century. The list includes Vadim Lazurski from Odessa, Galina Bannikova from Sarapul, Anatoli Shchukin from Moscow, Pavel Kuzanyan and Solomon Telingater from Tbilisi. Few of their designs have been available in the West; many, in fact, have yet to be produced in type at all.

Monotype, Linotype and other digital foundries have issued Cyrillic adaptations and derivatives of many well-known roman faces, including Univers, Helvetica, Baskerville, Bodoni, Caslon, Plantin and Times. These have their uses, especially for multilingual work, when matching Latin and Cyrillic fonts may be required. But not all of these derivative Cyrillics can claim to be distinguished designs, and few are suited to running text.

In its normal upright form (called *pryamoĭ* in Russian), Cyrillic is primarily an alphabet of small caps. There are fewer than half a dozen recognizably minuscule forms in the *pryamoĭ* lower case. The customary companion face, however, is an inclined cursive (*kursiv* in Russian), with an abundance of minuscule forms, structurally close to Latin italic. Unserifed Cyrillics, following the model of unserifed Latins, often include a sloped *pryamoĭ* in place of a *kursiv*.

Text figures are essential for most Cyrillic faces, including all of those listed below.

*Monotype*
*Baskerville Cyrillic*

абвгдежоф 1 2 3 АО *абвгдежоф*

*Baskerville* м Baskerville himself designed no Cyrillic, but Cyrillic adaptations of his roman and italic have been issued by Monotype, both in metal matrices and in digital form. For many Russian texts of the eighteenth century and later, a face of obviously Western origin and French Enlightenment spirit seems appropriate. Baskerville Cyrillic is one obvious choice for this purpose, especially if the text is bilingual and Baskerville roman and italic will suit the translation.

абвгдежоф АО *абвгдежоф*

*Lazurski* м This is a neohumanist Cyrillic with its own companion roman and italic, designed by Vadim Lazurski and issued in 1991 in digital form by ParaGraph International, Moscow. The immediate ancestor of this face is the Pushkin Cyrillic, designed by Lazurski and revised by Giovanni Mardersteig for his own press, the Officina Bodoni in Verona. Pushkin was cut in metal by Ruggiero Olivieri in 1967.

*

а б в г д е ж ф А О Ф *а б в г д е ж з ф*

*Manuscript* н A vigorous, expressionist Cyrillic designed in 1952 by Oldřich Menhart as a companion to his Manuscript roman. It was issued by Grafotechna, Prague in 1953.

*

абвгдежоф АО *абвгдежоф*

*Minion* D A neohumanist Cyrillic designed by Robert Slimbach as a companion to his Minion roman and italic. It was issued by Adobe in 1992.

абвгдежзийклмнопрстуфхцчшщъыьэюя

*Trajanus* м Upright and cursive Cyrillic companions to Warren Chappell's Trajanus were designed in 1957 by Hermann Zapf and issued by the Stempel Foundry. No other Cyrillic of Western origin comes so close to the pre-Renaissance spirit of much Slavic art and literature.

*

10.9 CROSS LISTING OF TYPE DESIGNERS

A biographical index of designers important to typographical history, and of all those doing important work at the present day, would be hundreds of pages long. The following list is merely a brief cross-reference to important designers whose work is mentioned elsewhere in this book.

LUDOVICO DEGLI ARRIGHI (*c.* 1480–1527) Italian calligrapher and designer of at least six chancery italics. Frederic Warde's Arrighi is based on one of his faces. Monotype Blado (the italic companion to Poliphilus) is a rough reproduction of another.

RICHARD AUSTIN (*c.* 1765–1830) English punchcutter producing Neoclassical and Romantic faces. He cut the original Bell type, the first Scotch Roman, and the original version of Porson Greek. W. A. Dwiggins's Caledonia is based primarily on Austin's work.

JOHN BASKERVILLE (1706–1775) English calligrapher, printer and businessman. Designer of a series of Neoclassical romans, italics and a Greek. Most of the faces sold in his name are based on his work. His punches are now at the University Library, Cambridge, and the St Bride Printing Library, London. A set of original matrices, formerly in Paris, is now in Münchenstein, Switzerland.

GIAMBATTISTA BODONI (1740–1813) Italian punchcutter, printer and prolific designer of type, working at Rome and Parma. Bodoni is best known for his dark and razor-sharp Romantic romans, italics and Greeks, but he also designed and cut a large number of Neoclassical fonts. Bauer Bodoni, Berthold Bodoni, and other faces now sold in his name are based on his work. His punches are in the Bodoni Museum, Parma.

MATTHEW CARTER (1937– ) English type designer and scholar, working primarily in Europe and the USA. His text faces include Auriga, Charter and Galliard.

WILLIAM CASLON (1692–1766) English gunsmith, punchcutter and typefounder; author of many Baroque romans, italics, Greeks and other non-Latin faces. ATF Caslon, Monotype Caslon, and Carol Twombly's Adobe Caslon are closely based on his work. Caslon's surviving punches are in the St Bride Printing Library, London.

WARREN CHAPPELL (1904–1991) American designer and scholar, trained in Germany, where he studied with Rudolf Koch. His typefaces include Trajanus, Lydian, and a script known as Lydian Cursive.

BRAM DE DOES (1934– ) Dutch typographer. Designer of the Trinité family.

FIRMIN DIDOT (1764–1836) French printer and punchcutter; student of Pierre-Louis Vafflard. He cut many French Romantic fonts. Deberny & Peignot's Didot is cast from his punches. Monotype Didot and Linotype's digital Didot (drawn by Adrian Frutiger) are based on his work. André Gürtler's Basilia is also, in a large measure, derived from it.

WILLIAM ADDISON DWIGGINS (1880–1956) American designer and typographer. Dwiggins designed typefaces exclusively for the Linotype machine. In the 1930s and 1940s, he also created the typographic house style at Alfred Knopf, New York. His serifed faces include Caledonia, Eldorado, Electra and Falcon. His only completed sanserif is Metro. His uncial is Winchester. Many of his type drawings are now in the Boston Public Library.

ALFRED FAIRBANK (1895–1982) English calligrapher. Designer of the Fairbank italic.

KARL-ERIK FORSBERG (1914–  ) Swedish calligrapher. His text face is Berling. His titling faces include Carolus, Ericus and Lunda.

PIERRE SIMON FOURNIER (1712–1768) French printer and punchcutter. Author of many French Neoclassical fonts and typographical ornaments. Nearly all of his original material has been damaged or lost. Monotype Fournier and Barbou are based on his work, and W.A. Dwiggins's Electra owes much to the study of it.

ADRIAN FRUTIGER (1928–  ) Swiss, working in France. His serifed faces include Apollo, Breughel, Glypha, Iridium and Méridien. His sanserifs include Avenir, Frutiger and Univers. His script types include Ondine.

CLAUDE GARAMOND (c. 1490–1561) French punchcutter, working chiefly at Paris. Author of many fonts of Renaissance roman, at least two italics, and a full set of cursive Greeks. Many of his punches and matrices survive at the Plantin-Moretus Museum in Antwerp and at the Imprimerie National, Paris. Stempel Garamond, Linotype Granjon roman, Jan Tschichold's Sabon roman, G.G. Lange's Berthold Garamond roman and Robert Slimbach's Adobe Garamond roman are all based on his designs.

ERIC GILL (1882–1940) English stonecutter, working in Wales. His serifed faces include Joanna, Perpetua and Pilgrim. His one unserifed face is Gill Sans. Perpetua Greek is also his, but Gill Sans Greek is by other hands. Gill's type drawings are now in the St Bride Library, London. Some of his matrices and punches are at the University Library,

Cambridge; others are in the Clark Library, Los Angeles – but none of these punches were cut by Gill himself.

FREDERIC GOUDY (1865–1947) American. His serifed faces include University of California Old Style (also known as Californian), Deepdene, Italian Old Style, Kaatskill, Kennerley, Village № 1 and Village № 2. His blackletters include Franciscan, Goudy Text and Goudy Thirty. His titling faces include Forum, Goudy Old Style and Hadriano. Goudy Sans is his only unserifed face. His only uncial is Friar. ITC Berkeley is based on his Californian. Most of Goudy's original material was destroyed by fire in 1939. What survives is at the Rochester Institute of Technology.

ROBERT GRANJON (c. 1513–1590) French, working at Paris, Lyon, Antwerp, Frankfurt, Rome. Author of many Renaissance and Mannerist romans, italics, scripts, several Greeks, a Cyrillic, some Hebrews, and the first successful fonts of Arabic type. Some of his punches and matrices survive at the Plantin-Moretus Museum, Antwerp and the Nordiska Museet, Stockholm. Matthew Carter's Galliard is based primarily on his Ascendonica roman and italic.

FRANCESCO GRIFFO (c. 1450–1518) Italian, from Bologna, working primarily in Venice. Author of at least seven romans, three italics, four Greeks and a Hebrew. None of Griffo's actual punches or matrices are known to survive, and the house of Aldus Manutius in Venice, where he did most of his work, has vanished. (The site is now occupied by a bank.) Griffo's letterforms have nonetheless been patiently reconstructed from the printed books in which his type appears. Giovanni Mardersteig's Griffo type is an exacting replica of one of Griffo's fonts. Monotype Bembo roman is based more loosely on the same font. Monotype Poliphilus is a rough reproduction of another. Mardersteig's Dante is also based on a close study of Griffo's work.

VICTOR HAMMER (1882–1967) Austrian immigrant to the USA. All of Hammer's types are uncials. These include American Uncial, Andromache, Hammer Uncial, Pindar and Samson. His designs and punches are now at the University of Kentucky, Lexington.

JEAN JANNON (1580–1658) French punchcutter and printer. Author of a series of Baroque romans and italics. Much of his material survives at the Imprimerie Nationale, Paris, where his type is known as the *caractères de l'université*.

Monotype 'Garamond,' Linotype 'Garamond' 3, ATF 'Garamond,' Lanston 'Garamont,' and Simoncini 'Garamond' are all based on his work. (See p 177.)

NICOLAS JENSON (*c.* 1420–1480) French punchcutter and printer, working in Venice. Author of at least one roman, one rotunda, one Greek. Jenson's punches have vanished, but his type has often been copied from his printed books. Bruce Rogers's Centaur is based on Jenson's roman.

MIKLÓS TÓTFALUSI KIS (1650–1702) Hungarian scholar, printer and typecutter. Kis was trained in Amsterdam and worked there and in Kolozsvár (now Cluj, Romania). Stempel Janson is cast from his surviving punches. Linotype Janson and Monotype Erhardt are based on his work.

RUDOLF KOCH (1876–1934) German calligrapher and artist. His titling faces include Koch Antiqua and Neuland. His blackletters include Claudius, Jessen, Wallau and Wilhelm-Klingspor Schrift. Kabel is his only sanserif. Much of his material, formerly in the Klingspor Archive, Offenbach, is now in the Stempel Collection, Darmstadt.

GÜNTER GERHARD LANGE (1921– ) German. Art director at the Berthold Foundry, Berlin. His titling faces and scripts include Derby and El Greco. Solemnis is his uncial face.

VADIM VLADIMIROVICH LAZURSKI (1909– ) Russian. His many Cyrillics include Pushkin (in collaboration with Giovanni Mardersteig). His Lazurski family includes both Cyrillic and Latin alphabets.

GIOVANNI MARDERSTEIG (1892–1977) German immigrant to Italy. His serifed faces include Dante, Fontana, Griffo and Zeno. His material is at the Officina Bodoni, Verona.

HANS EDUARD MEIER (1922– ) Swiss. Designer of Barbedor, Syndor and the Syntax sanserif.

JOSÉ MENDOZA Y ALMEIDA (1926– ) French. His faces include Mendoza, Photina, Pascal, Fidelio (a chancery script), Sully Jonquières (an upright italic) and Convention.

OLDŘICH MENHART (1897–1962) Czech. His serifed Latin faces include Figural, Menhart and Parliament. His Manuscript family includes both Latin and Cyrillic faces. His titling faces include Czech Uncial and Monument.

FRIEDRICH POPPL (1923–1982) German. His serifed faces include Pontifex and Poppl Antiqua. His sanserif is Laudatio. His titling faces include Nero and Saladin. His script types include Poppl Exquisit and Residenz.

*Prowling the Specimen Books*

RICHARD PORSON (1759–1808) English classical scholar. Designer of the original Porson Greek. Monotype Porson is based on his work.

VOJTĚCH PREISSIG (1873–1944) Czech artist, typographer and teacher, working in Czechoslovakia and in New York City. Preissig designed several text and titling faces, including the one that bears his name. His surviving drawings are in the Strahov Abbey, Prague.

*Type Designers*

PAUL RENNER (1878–1956) German. Designer of the Futura sanserif. His drawings for this face are now in the Fundición Tipográfica Neufville, Barcelona.

BRUCE ROGERS (1870–1957) American typographer, working chiefly in Boston, London and Oxford. Designer of Montaigne and Centaur. The original drawings for Centaur are now in the Newberry Library, Chicago.

RUDOLF RŮŽIČKA (1883–1978) Czech immigrant to the USA. Designer of Linotype Fairfield and Primer.

VICTOR SCHOLDERER (1880–1971) English classical scholar and librarian. Designer of the New Hellenic Greek.

ROBERT SLIMBACH (1956– ) American. His serifed faces include Giovanni, Minion, Poetica, Slimbach, Utopia and Adobe Garamond. The sanserif Myriad is a joint design by Slimbach and Carol Twombly.

SUMNER STONE (1945– ) American. Author of the Stone typeface family, which includes both serifed and unserifed forms.

GIOVANANTONIO TAGLIENTE (*fl.* 1500–1525) Italian scribe and designer of at least one chancery italic type. Monotype Bembo italic is based on this font.

GEORG TRUMP (1896–1985). German artist. Trump studied lettering with Ernst Schneidler. His serifed text faces include Mauritius, Schadow and Trump Mediäval. His blackletters include Trump-Deutsch. His titling faces and scripts include Codex, Delphin, Jaguar and Time.

JAN TSCHICHOLD (1902–1974) German immigrant to Switzerland. A number of Tschichold's phototype designs were destroyed in the Second World War. His only publicly issued face is Sabon.

CAROL TWOMBLY (1959– ) American. Her titling faces include Charlemagne, Lithos and Trajan. Adobe Caslon is her work, based on William Caslon's originals. With Robert Slimbach, she is co-designer of the Myriad sanserif.

GERARD UNGER (1942– ) Dutch. His serifed faces include Amerigo, Demos, Hollander and Swift, and his unserifed, Flora and Praxis.

CHRISTOFFEL VAN DIJCK (1606–1669) Dutch punchcutter. Author of several Baroque romans and italics. Monotype Van Dijck is based on his work. Jan van Krimpen's Romanée and Gerard Unger's Hollander echo it in various ways. Most of Van Dijck's material has been destroyed. The surviving punches and matrices are at Johann Enschedé en Zonen, Haarlem, Netherlands.

JAN VAN KRIMPEN (1892–1958) Dutch typographer. His serifed faces include Lutetia, Romanée, Romulus, Spectrum, and the chancery italic called Cancelleresca Bastarda. His only sanserif is Romulus Sans. His Greek is Antigone. His titling faces include Double Augustin Open Capitals, Lutetia Open Capitals and Romulus Open Capitals. His original material is at Johann Enschedé en Zonen, Haarlem.

JOVICA VELJOVIĆ (1954– ) Serbian. His Latin faces include Esprit, Gamma and Veljović.

JUSTUS ERICH WALBAUM (1768–1837) German typefounder and printer, author of several Neoclassical and Romantic faces. Berthold Walbaum is based on his surviving punches and matrices.

FREDERIC WARDE (1894–1939) American, working chiefly in France, Italy and England. Designer of the Arrighi italic. Some of Warde's drawings are in the Newberry Library, Chicago. Punches and matrices for the early (handcut) Arrighi are now at the Rochester Institute of Technology.

BERTHOLD WOLPE (1905–1989) German immigrant to England. Pegasus is his text face. His titling faces include Albertus and Hyperion.

HERMANN ZAPF (1918– ) German. His serifed faces include Aldus, Comenius, Marconi, Melior, Orion, Palatino, Zapf Book and Zapf Renaissance. His sanserifs include Optima, and his blackletters include Gilgengart, Hallmark Winchester and Stratford. His titling faces and scripts include Kompakt, Michelangelo, Sistina, Venture, Zapf Chancery, Zapf Civilité and Zapf International. His Greeks include Attika, Heraklit, Optima and Phidias.

GUDRUN ZAPF-VON HESSE (1918– ) German calligrapher. Her text and titling faces include Carmina, Diotima, Nofret, Christiana, Ariadne and Smaragd.

| Single Stroke | Double Stroke | Letterforms and Modified Letters |
|---|---|---|
| ˙ overdot | ¨ umlaut / diaeresis | æ aesc |
| · midpoint | : colon | Æ aesc |
| . period | ; semicolon | @ at |
| . underdot | " " quotation | © copyright |
| • bullet | „ " quotation | ¢ cent |
| ' apostrophe | ¡ ! exclamation | ð eth |
| ' inverted comma | ¿ ? question | đ dyet |
| , comma | ¦ pipe | Đ eth / dyet |
| \| bar | ‖ double bar | & ampersand |
| ´ acute | " double prime | ⅋ ampersand |
| ` grave | ˝ double acute | ƒ florin |
| ' prime | = equal | ħ barred H |
| ¯ macron | + addition | Ħ barred H |
| - hyphen | × multiplication | ı dotless I |
| – subtraction | « » guillemets | ł barred L |
| – en dash | ♮ natural | Ł barred L |
| — ¾ em dash | ♭ flat | £ sterling |
| —— em dash | | µ mu |
| _ lowline | | ŋ eng |
| / solidus | **Multiple Stroke** | Ŋ eng |
| / virgule | | ø barred O |
| \ backslash | | Ø barred O |
| ( ) parenthesis | … ellipsis | œ ethel |
| { } brace | ÷ division | Œ ethel |
| ˛ ogonek | ± plus-or-minus | ¶ pilcrow |
| ¸ cedilla | # octothorp | ® registration |
| ˘ breve | ♯ sharp | § section |
| ˜ tilde | | $ dollar |
| ~ swung dash | | ß eszett |
| ¬ negation | **Pictograms** | þ thorn |
| [ ] bracket | | Þ thorn |
| > greater than | | ŧ barred T |
| < less than | * asterisk | Ŧ barred T |
| ⟨ ⟩ bracket | † dagger | ™ trademark |
| ‹ › guillemet | ‡ double dagger | ¥ yen |
| ˇ caron / háček | ¤ currency | ȝ yogh |
| ˆ circumflex | ☞ fist | % per cent |
| ∧ caret | | ‰ per mil |
| ˚ ring / kroužek | | |
| ° degree | | |

There is, of course, no limit to the number of typographic characters. This appendix lists only those included on standard ISO Latin alphabet text fonts, and a tiny handful of additional characters of traditional typographic importance. (To date, ISO has defined nine separate official Latin character sets, but these differ little among themselves, and there is no impediment to putting all characters on a single font. Characters from all nine are therefore listed here together.) The hundreds of additional common characters required for mathematical and scientific work must generally be sought on specialized technical or pi fonts.

**acute** An accent used on vowels – á é í ó ú – in French, Spanish, Italian, Icelandic, Hungarian, Navajo, Gaelic, Czech, and many other languages, and on consonants – ć ŕ ś ń – in Basque, Croatian, Polish and romanized Sanskrit. In romanized Chinese, it is used with vowels to mark the rising tone. The accented vowels are on normal fonts as composite characters.

´

**aesc** This ligature is a letter of the alphabet in Danish, Norwegian and Anglo-Saxon, corresponding to the Swedish ä. In English, words of Greek origin were formerly spelled with æ corresponding to Greek αι (alpha iota). Thus *aesthetics* in older texts is *æsthetics*. Deliberate archaism and pedantically correct quotation still, therefore, require the ligature even in English. *Aesc* (*æsc* in the older spelling) is pronounced *ash*.

æ

Æ

**ampersand** A scribal abbreviation for *and*. It takes many forms – ℰ & & & &c – all derived from the Latin word *et*.

&

**apostrophe** Also called *raised comma* or *single close-quote*. A mark of elision in many languages. It grew from that use in English to become also a sign of the possessive. [*It's* = *it is*, but *John's* = *Johnes* = *John his* = belonging to John.] In many Native American and Slavic languages written in Latin script, it is used with consonants – d' k' t' x' – to indicate modified pronunciation. Used alone, it serves in many languages as a sign for the glottal stop. See also *glottal stop* and *quotation*.

’

**± =**
**< + >**
**× ÷**

**arithmetical signs** Only eight basic signs, $+ - \pm \times \div < = >$, are in the standard ISO character set, and the subtraction sign and en dash are often identical. When other symbols, such as $\neq \approx \cong \equiv \surd \leq \geq$ , are required, it is generally best to take all signs, including the basic ones, from the same technical font so that all forms match in color and size.

**✶**

**asterisk** A superscript, used primarily to mark referents and keywords. In European typography, it is widely used to mark a person's year of birth (as the dagger, substituting for a cross, is used to mark the year of death). In philology and other sciences, it is used to mark hypothetically reconstructed or fetal forms. The asterisk takes many forms: * * * , for example. It appears in the earliest Sumerian pictographic writing and has been in continuous typographic use for at least 5000 years.

**@**

**at** A commercial symbol meaning *at* or *at the rate of*. It is often used in electronic mail addressing and computer coding, precisely because it has no typographic function in normal text.

**\\**

**backslash** This is an unsolicited gift of the computer keyboard. Basic though it may be to elementary computer operations, it has no accepted function in typography.

**|**

**bar** The bar is used in mathematics as a sign of absolute value, in prosodical studies to mark a caesura, and in propositional calculus (where it is called *Sheffer's stroke*) as a sign of nonconjunction. In bibliographical work, both single and double bars are used. Also called *caesura*.

**ħ Ħ**

**barred H** This is one of the ISO characters, but it is omitted from most fonts. It is a basic letter of the alphabet in Maltese, corresponding to the Arabic *ḥ*.

**ł Ł**

**barred L** A basic letter of the alphabet in Polish, Navajo, Chipewyan and many other languages. The barred L (or *l-slash*, as it is known in PostScript) is now routinely included in standard text fonts.

**ø Ø**

**barred O** This is a basic letter of the alphabet in Norwegian and Danish, corresponding to the Swedish *ö*. In PostScript jargon, it is known as *o-slash*.

**barred т** This is a basic letter of the alphabet in Lapp, and it is therefore one of the standard ɪsᴏ characters, but it is absent from most fonts.

ŧ Ŧ

**braces** Braces are rarely required in text work, but they can function as an extra and outer set of parentheses: { ( [ – ] ) }. Their primary use is marking mathematical phrases and sets.

{ }

**brackets** Square brackets are essentials of text typography, used for interpolations into quoted matter and as a secondary and inner set of parentheses. Angle brackets, which are useful for many editorial purposes, and for mathematics, are missing from the standard ɪsᴏ character set.

[ ]

⟨ ⟩

**breve** An accent used on consonants and vowels – ă ĕ ğ – in Rumanian, Malay and Turkish. In English, it is used in informal phonetic transcriptions to mark lax vowels. In writings on metrics and prosody, it is the sign of a quantitatively short vowel or syllable. The breve is always rounded, and should not be confused with the angular caron. (*Breve* is two syllables, with the stress on the first, as in *brave, eh?*) Also called *short*.

˘

**bullet** A large version of the midpoint, used chiefly as a typographic flag. Bullets are commonly hung, like numbers, in the left margin to mark items in a list, or centered on the measure to separate blocks of text. See also *midpoint*.

●

**caret** This is a stray, like the backslash, inherited from the ᴀsᴄɪɪ computer keyboard. Along with the *dele* or delete sign, it is one of the most basic editorial symbols, but its only stock role in typography is as the sign of partial conjunction in symbolic logic. It is useless in that regard without the other standard logical operators, and with two exceptions (I and ¬) they are missing from the standard ɪsᴏ character set.

∧

**caron** An inverted circumflex. It is used on consonants and vowels – č ě ň ř š ž – in Slovak, Croatian, Czech, Lapp, Lithuanian and other scripts. In romanized Chinese, it is used on vowels to mark the retroflexive third tone (falling/rising tone) of the Mandarin dialect, and it is increasingly used in new scripts for Native American languages. For no apparent reason, ɪsᴏ character sets include a prefabricated upper- and lowercase

∨

š and ž, while other combinations, no less frequent in normal text, must be built with the floating accent. Typographers know the caron also by its Czech name, *háček*, pronounced *haa-check*.

**cedilla**  An accent used with consonants – such as the ç in French, Portuguese, Catalan and Nahuatl, the ç and ş in Turkish, the ş and ţ in Rumanian, and the ŋ in Latvian. Not to be confused with the *ogonek* or nasal hook, which curves the other way and is used with vowels. The name means *little z*. Only Ç and ç appear on most fonts in prefabricated form.

**circumflex**  An accent used on vowels – â ê î ô û ŵ ŷ – in French, Portuguese, Rumanian, Turkish, Welsh and other languages. In transliterated texts (e.g., from Arabic, Hebrew, Sanskrit and Greek), it is sometimes used as a substitute for the macron, to mark long vowels. Normal fonts include all the circumflected vowels except the Welsh ŵ and ŷ in prebuilt form.

**colon**  A grammatical marker inherited from the medieval European scribes. It is also used in mathematics to indicate ratios and in linguistics as a mark of prolongation. The name is from Greek. In classical rhetoric and prosody, a *colon* (plural, *cola*) is a long clause, and a *comma* is a short one.

**comma**  A grammatical marker, descended from early scribal practice. In German, and often in Eastern European languages, the comma is used as an open quote. Throughout Europe, it is also used as a decimal point, where most North Americans expect a period. And in North American usage, the comma separates thousands, while a space is preferred in Europe. Thus 10,000,000 = 10 000 000, but a number such as 10,001 is typographically ambiguous. In Europe it means ten and one one-thousandth; in North America, ten thousand and one.

**copyright**  On poorly designed fonts, the copyright symbol sometimes appears as a superscript, but its rightful place in typography is on the baseline.

**currency symbols**  Standard ISO character sets include five real currency signs – $ £ ƒ ¥ ¢ – and one imaginary sign, ¤ . The latter symbol, the so-called general currency sign, has no function except to hold a place on the font to which a real symbol for local currency (rupee, cruzeiro, peseta, etc) can be assigned. The cent sign (¢), now an American typographical heirloom, is equally irrelevant for most work. It remains in the character set chiefly out of nostalgia. The dollar sign, a slashed s, is descended from an old symbol for the shilling. The same sign has come to be used for currencies with many other names: sol, peso, escudo, yuan, etc. The sign of the pound sterling is a stylized L, standing for the Latin *libra* (also the source of the abbreviation *lb*, used for the pound avoirdupois). This sign is now used not only for British currency but for the pound, lira or livre of many African and Middle Eastern states. The sign for Dutch guilders is *f*, for *florin*, which is the old name for the currency. It is often designed to a greater width than the italic lowercase *f*.

$ £

*f* ¥

¢

**dagger** A reference mark, used chiefly with footnotes. In European typography, it is also a sign of mortality, used to mark the year of death or the names of deceased persons, and in lexicography to mark obsolete forms. Also called *obelisk* or *long cross*.

†

**dashes** Standard fonts include, at minimum, an em dash, en dash and hyphen. A figure dash and three-quarter em dash are often included as well, and a one-third em dash more rarely.

**degree** Used in mathematics and in normal text to give temperatures, inclinations, latitudes, longitudes and compass bearings. Not to be confused with the *superior o* used in abbreviations such as Nº, nor with the *ring*, which is a diacritic.

o

**diaeresis / umlaut** An accent used with vowels – ë ï ö ü ẅ ÿ – in many languages, including Albanian, Breton, Estonian, Finnish, German, Swedish, Turkish and Welsh, and less frequently also in English, Spanish, Portuguese and French. Linguists distinguish between the *umlaut*, which marks a *change* in pronunciation of a single vowel (as in the German *Schön*) and the *diaeresis*, which marks the *separation* of adjacent vowels (as in naïve and Noël). The typographical symbol is the same, but in reference to English and the Romance languages, the correct term is diaeresis, while umlaut is correct in reference to most other languages in which the symbol is used. The umlauted or diaeretic vowels appear on normal fonts in composite form.

··

**dimension sign**  Same as the multiplication sign. See *arithmetical symbols.*

**1**

**dotless i**  A letter of the alphabet in Turkish. It is also used with floating accents to set í ì î ï ǐ. Only the first four of these characters are included in the ISO character sets in composite form.

**″**

**double acute**  An accent used on the vowels ő and ű in Hungarian. It is sometimes called the Hungarian umlaut – an unhelpful name, since the umlauted vowels ö and ü also appear in Hungarian. Not to be confused with the double prime nor with the close quote.

**‖**

**double bar**  This is a standard symbol in bibliographical work and an old standard reference mark in European typography. It is nevertheless missing from the ISO character list. It is easily made by kerning two bars together.

**‡**

**double dagger**  A reference mark for footnoting. Also called *double obelisk.*

**″**

**double prime**  An abbreviation for inches (1″ = 2.54 cm) and for seconds of arc (360″ = 1°). Not to be confused with quotation marks nor with the double acute. See also *prime.*

**đ Ð**

**dyet**  A basic letter of the alphabet in Croatian. It is also required for romanized Macedonian and Serbian. The uppercase form of the letter is the same as the uppercase *eth.*

**• • •**

**ellipsis**  The sign of elision and of rhetorical pause.

**ŋ Ŋ**

**eng**  A basic letter of the alphabet in Lapp, and in its lowercase form, widely used in linguistics and lexicography. It represents the *ng* sound in the word *wing.* (Note the different sounds represented by the same letters in the words *wing, Wingate, singlet* and *singe.*) Though it is an ISO character, the eng is missing from most text fonts.

**ß**

**eszett**  The ss ligature, once essential for setting English and still essential for setting German. Not to be confused with the Greek beta, β. Also known as *sharp s.*

**eth**  A basic letter in the alphabet in Icelandic, Old English and Faroese. The uppercase eth is the same as the uppercase *dyet*, but the lowercase forms are not interchangeable, and the letters represent quite different sounds. (The name *eth*, also spelled *edh*, is pronounced like the *eth* in *whether*.)

ð Ð

**ethel**  A ligature formerly used in English and still essential for setting French. English words and names derived from Greek were formerly spelled with the ethel (or œthel) corresponding to the Greek οι (omicron iota). Thus the old form of *ecumenical* is *œcumenical*, and the Greek name Οἰδίπους, Oidípous, still disguised in English as Oedipus, was formerly written Œdipus. The ligature is required, therefore, for deliberate archaism and for academically correct quotation from older sources, as well as for the correct spelling of French words like *hors d'œuvre*.

œ Œ

**exclamation**  In Spanish, the inverted exclamation mark is used at the beginning of the phrase and the upright mark at the end. In mathematics, the upright exclamation mark is the symbol for factorials ($4! = 4 \times 3 \times 2 \times 1$). It is also often used to represent the palatal clicks of the Khoisan languages of Africa. Thus, for example, the name !Kung.

¡ !

**figures**  A basic text font normally includes only one set of figures, which should normally be text figures. The supporting fonts normally include three further sets: titling figures, superior figures and inferior figures. The superiors are used for exponents, superscripts and the numerators of piece fractions. The inferiors are used for the denominators of fractions. For chemical formulae ($H_2O$ etc) and mathematical subscripts, the inferior figures must usually be lowered.

1 2 3
4 5

**fist**  The typographer's fist is not a blunt instrument but a silent, pointing hand. All too often, however, it is overdressed, with ruffles at the cuff. A Baroque invention, the fist is missing from the ISO character set and must be found on a supplementary font.

**fractions**  Only three fractions – ¼ ½ ¾ – appear on standard ISO text fonts. For fractions beyond these three, whether prefabricated or custom-built from superior and inferior figures, a supplementary font is commonly required.

½

**glottal stop**  The glottal stop is a sound, not a letter, but it is a typographic problem because it is a common and meaningful sound in human speech for which the Latin alphabet lacks a specific symbol. Linguists use the symbol ʔ – a gelded question mark – to represent this sound, but the best symbol to use in roman and italic text is usually the apostrophe. In romanized Arabic or Hebrew, the inverted comma or open quote (ʻ) is used to represent the letter *ain*, whose phonetic symbol is ʕ, and the apostrophe (ʼ) is used to represent the *hamza* or glottal stop. Thus, the Koran in Arabic is *al-Qurʼān*, but Arab is *ʻarab*, and the family is *al-ʻāʼila*. See also *apostrophe, inverted comma* and *quotation mark*.

**grave**  An accent used with vowels – à è ì ò ù – in French, Italian, Portuguese, Catalan and many other languages. In romanized Chinese it signifies a falling tone. The grave vowels are included in the ISO character set in prefabricated form.

**guillemets**  Single and double quotation marks widely used with the Latin, Cyrillic and Greek alphabets in Europe, Asia and Africa. Attempts to introduce them into North America have, unfortunately, met with slight success. In French and Italian, the guillemets almost always point out, « thus » and ‹ thus ›, but in German they more frequently point in. Single guillemets should not be confused with angle brackets nor with the arithmetical operators meaning greater-than and less-than. Guillemet means Little Willy, in honor of the sixteenth-century French typecutter Guillaume [William] Le Bé, who may have invented them. Also called *chevrons, duck feet* and *angle quotes*.

**hyphen**  See *dashes*.

**inverted comma**  Also called a single open-quote, and used for that purpose in English, Spanish and many other languages. In transliterated Arabic and Hebrew, it is also used to represent the letter *ain* or *ayin*, a pharyngeal continuant, while its opposite, the apostrophe, represents the glottal stop. Thus: King Ibn Saʻūd; the Beqaʻa Valley. By convention, the inverted comma and apostrophe used in transliterating Semitic languages must curve (ʻ ʼ). The rigid or German inverted comma and apostrophe (ʹ ʹ), also known as sloped primes, are unsuitable for this purpose. See also *glottal stop* and *quotation mark*.

**krouzek** See *ring*.

**letters** Three varieties of letters appear on an ordinary font of type. There is normally a full alphabet in upper and lower case (or in full and small caps) and a partial alphabet of superior letters. The latter are used in numerical abbreviations such as 1$^{st}$, 2$^{nd}$ 3$^{rd}$, the French 1$^{er}$ and 1$^{ere}$ (*premier, première*) and the Spanish 2$^a$, 2$^o$ (*segunda, segundo*). They are also used in a few verbal abbreviations, such as 4$^o$ = quarto; 8$^o$ = octavo; M$^r$ = mister; N$^o$ = number, but in English most such forms are now archaic. The basic ISO character set includes only two superior letters, the *ordinal a* and *ordinal o*, which are essential for setting text in Romance languages. (They are called ordinals because they are used for ordinal numbers: first, second, third....) The remaining set – conventionally limited to a b d e i l m n o r s t – is usually to be found on a supplementary font. In some faces, the ordinal *a* and *o* are underlined while the superior letters are not. Strange to say, the superior *c*, useful for setting names such as M$^c$Intyre, is not included in the ISO character set.

a b

x$^a$ z

Qu

**ligatures** Basic ISO fonts are limited to two rudimentary ligatures, fi and fl. Rigid definitions of the character set, leaving no provision for additional ligatures such as ff, ffi, ffl, are a hazard to typography. Ligatures required by the design of the individual typeface should always be present on the basic font.

fi ffi

**lowline** This is a basic ISO character. On fonts intended for commercial work, it is sometimes positioned as a baseline rule. On text fonts, it is generally identical with the underscore.

_

**macron** A diacritic used to mark long vowels – ā ē ī ō ū – in many languages: Latvian, Lithuanian, Hausa and Fijian, among others. It is also necessary for romanized Arabic, Greek, Hebrew, Japanese and Sanskrit.

_

**midpoint** An ancient European mark of punctuation, widely used in typography to flag items in a vertical list and to separate items in a horizontal line. A closely spaced midpoint is also sometimes used to separate syllables or letters – e.g., in Catalan when one L is set next to another. (In Catalan as in Spanish, *ll* is normally regarded as a single letter. When the two are adjacent but separate, they are written *l·l*.) The same sign is used in

•

mathematics for scalar multiplication and in propositional calculus for logical conjunction. Also called *small bullet*.

**μ**

**mu**  The Greek lowercase *m*. Alone, it is the symbol for micron (1000 μ = 1 mm). In combination, it represents the prefix *micro-*. Thus milligrams is abbreviated mg and micrograms μg. It is the only lowercase Greek letter included in the ISO Latin character sets.

**♭♯♮**

**musical signs**  Three elementary musical symbols – ♭ ♯ ♮ , the flat, sharp and natural – are needed for setting normal texts that make reference to musical key signatures (Beethoven's Sonata Op. 110 in A♭, Ennemond Gaultier's Suite for Lute in F♯m, etc). These characters are, however, missing from the standard ISO list. The octothorp is not an adequate substitute for the sharp.

**nasal hook**  See *ogonek*.

**¬**

**negation**  The negation sign used in the propositional calculus (symbolic logic) was formerly the swung dash (~). The usual form now is the angled dash (¬). It is part of the standard ISO Latin character set and included on most digital text fonts, even though it is useless without the other logical operators, such as ∪ ∩ ∧ ∨ ≡ , which are usually missing from ISO fonts. Also called *logical not*.

**numeral sign**  See *octothorp*.

**obelisk**  See *dagger*.

**#**

**octothorp**  Otherwise known as the numeral sign. It has also been used as a symbol for the pound avoirdupois, but this usage is now archaic. In cartography, it is also a symbol for village: eight fields around a central square, and this is the source of its name. Octothorp means eight fields.

**ȼ**

**ogonek**  An accent used with vowels – ą ę į ǫ ų – in Navajo, Polish, Lithuanian, and many other languages. Also called a *nasal hook*. Not to be confused with the cedilla, which is used with consonants and curves the other way.

**ordinal ᴀ, ordinal o**  See *letters*.

**overdot** An accent used with consonants – ċ ġ ż – in Polish and Maltese, and with vowels – ė, İ – in Lithuanian and Turkish. It is also required for several Native American languages, and for Sanskrit in romanized form.

•

**paragraph** See *pilcrow.*

**parentheses** Used as phrase markers in grammar and in mathematics, and sometimes to isolate figures or letters in a numerical or alphabetical list. Renaissance parentheses are drawn (thus) as curved rules, generally of the same weight as the em dash. Neoclassical parentheses are drawn (thus) as symmetrical swelled rules, thick in the center and thin at the ends. Neohumanist parentheses are sometimes drawn as asymmetrical pen strokes.

( )

**per cent** Parts per hundred. Not to be confused with the symbol ℅, 'in care of,' which is not part of the ISO character set.

%

**per mil** Parts per thousand (61‰ = 6.1%). Though it is rarely required in text typography, this sign has been given a place in the ISO character set.

‰

**period** The normal sign for the end of a sentence in all the languages of Europe. But it is also a letter of the alphabet in Tlingit, pronounced as a glottal stop. In Catalan, it is sometimes used in the sequence *l.l,* as an alternative to the midpoint. Also called full point or full stop.

•

**pilcrow** An old scribal mark used at the beginning of a paragraph or main text section. It is still used by typographers for that very purpose, and occasionally as a reference mark. Well-designed faces offer pilcrows with some character – ¶ ¶ ❡ ¶ – in preference to the over-used Neoclassical standard, ¶. The symbol is derived from the Greek Π (capital pi), for *parágraphos.*

¶

**pipe** Despite its importance to programmers and its presence on the standard ASCII keyboard, the pipe has no set function in typography. For drawing broken rules and boxes, a separate character from a specialized ruling font is commonly used. Also called a *broken bar* or *parted rule.*

|
|

**prime**  An abbreviation for feet (1' = 12") and for minutes of arc (60' = 1°). Single and double primes may be sloped or vertical, but should not be confused with quotation marks, which in some faces (frakturs especially) also take the shape of sloped primes. See also *double prime.*

**question**  In Spanish, the inverted question mark is used at the beginning of the phrase, in addition to the upright question mark at the end.

**quotation marks**  A standard ISO font includes four forms of guillemet and six forms of Anglo-Germanic quotation mark – ' ' , „ " " – but one of these is identical with the comma and one with the apostrophe. In English and Spanish, common usage is 'thus' and "thus"; in German, it is ‚thus' and „thus".

**raised comma**  See *apostrophe, glottal stop* and *quotation mark.*

**registered trademark**  This is properly a superscript, though the otherwise similar copyright symbol is not.

**ring**  Also called *kroužek.* A diacritic used with å in Scandinavia and with ů in Eastern Europe. Å and å (the *round A*) are a basic letter of the alphabet in Swedish, Norwegian and Danish, and they are included in the ISO character set, but Ů and ů (*u* with kroužek), which are just as common in Czech, must be built from the component parts. The uppercase or small cap round A is also used as the symbol for ångström units ($10^4$Å = $1\,\mu$).

**section**  A scribal form of double s, now used chiefly with reference to legal codes and statutes, when citing particular sections for reference. (The plural abbreviation, meaning sections, is written by doubling the symbol: §§, just as the abbreviation for pages is written *pp.*)

**semicolon**  A grammatical marker, hybrid between colon and comma, derived from European scribal practice. But in classical Greek texts, the same symbol is used as a question mark.

**solidus**  The fraction bar. Used with superior and inferior numbers to construct ad hoc fractions. (The solidus was a Roman imperial coin introduced by Constantine in AD 309.

There were 72 solidi to the libra, the Roman pound, and 25 denarii to the solidus. The British based their imperial coinage and its symbols – £/s/d, for pounds, shillings and pence – on the Roman model, and *solidus* became in due course not only a byword for shilling but also the name of the slash mark with which shillings and pence were written. (Given the design and fitting of the characters on most modern type fonts, the solidus is now best used for fractions alone. An italic virgule is usually the best character for setting references to British imperial money.) See also *virgule*, which is a separate character.

/

**swung dash**  A stock keyboard character, used in mathematics as the sign of similarity ($a \sim b$) and in lexicography as a sign of repetition. The same sign has been used in symbolic logic to indicate negation, but to avoid confusion, the angular negation symbol ($\neg$) is preferred. Not to be confused with the *tilde*.

~

**thorn**  A basic letter of the alphabet in both Icelandic and Anglo-Saxon: *Þótt þu langförull legðir....*

Þ þ

**tilde**  Used on vowels – ã ĩ õ – in Portuguese and Greenlandic, and on consonants – g̃, ñ – in Pilipino, Quechua, romanized Sanskrit, Spanish and a number of other languages. The ã, ñ and õ appear on standard text fonts in prefabricated form. The remaining forms must usually be constructed.

~

**trademark**  A superscript, used in commercial work only.

TM

**umlaut**  See *diaeresis*.

**underdot**  An accent used especially with consonants – ḥ ṃ ṇ ṣ ṭ – in romanized Arabic, Hebrew, Sanskrit and other Asian languages, and often used in African and Native American scripts. In romanized Arabic and Hebrew, the underscore can be substituted, but the underdot is preferable. It is missing from the ISO character set.

•

**underscore**  A diacritic required for many African and Native American languages, and useful for some purposes in English. It is also used as an alternative to the underdot in setting romanized Arabic and Hebrew. To clear descenders, a repositioned version of the character is required. See also *lowline*.

—

**≠**

**unequal**  A useful symbol missing from the ISO character sets. Apart from its importance in mathematics and general text, it has several more specialized uses. In writing the Khoisan (Bushman) languages of Africa, for example, it has often been used as a symbol for alveolar clicks.

**vertical rule**  See *bar.*

**/**

**virgule**  An oblique stroke, used by medieval scribes and many later writers as a form of comma. It is also used to represent a linebreak when verse is transcribed into prose, and in dates, addresses and elsewhere as a sign of separation. In writing the Khoisan languages of western Africa, it is sometimes used to represent dental or lateral clicks. (In the Auen language, spoken in the Kalahari, for example, the word for *sun* is written */m,* one of the words for *feathers* is written *≠xwí,* and the name of the language itself is written *//āū//'ē.*) Not to be confused with the *solidus* or fraction bar, which is usually less steep, nor with the *bar,* which is strictly vertical.

**yen**  See *currency signs.*

**3**

**yogh**  A letter of the early English alphabet, still occasionally used in scholarly editions of Anglo-Saxon and Middle English texts. It is (quite rightly) omitted from the ISO character sets, but it is part of the IPA (International Phonetic Association) alphabet. The lowercase form can therefore be found on any standard font of phonetic characters. (The numeral 3 is not a suitable substitute.)

Names of individual characters and accent marks (circumflex, midpoint, virgule, etc) are not in this glossary. They appear in Appendix A instead. For summary definitions of historical categories (Renaissance, Baroque, etc), see Chapter 7.

10/12 × 18   Ten on twelve by eighteen, which is to say, ten-point (10 pt) type set with 12 pt leading (2 pt extra lead, in addition to the body size of 10 pt, for a total of 12 pt from baseline to baseline) on a measure of 18 picas.

*Adnate*   Flowing into, or smoothly joining. Serifs are either *abrupt* – meaning they break from the stem suddenly at an angle – or they are *adnate*, flowing smoothly to or from the stem. In the older typographical literature, adnate serifs are generally described as bracketed serifs.

*Aldine*   Relating to the publishing house operated in Venice by Aldus Manutius between 1494 and 1515. Most of Aldus's type was cut by Francesco Griffo. Type that resembles Griffo's, and typography that resembles Aldus's, is called Aldine.

*Analphabetic*   A typographical character used with the alphabet but lacking a place in the alphabetical order. Diacritics such as the acute accent, umlaut, circumflex and caron are analphabetics. So are the asterisk, the dagger, the pilcrow.

*Aperture*   The openings of letters such as C, c, S, s, a and e. Humanist faces such as Bembo and Centaur have large apertures, while Romantic faces such as Bodoni and Realist faces such as Helvetica have small apertures. Very large apertures occur in archaic Greek inscriptions and in typefaces such as Lithos, which are derived from them.

ATF   American Type Founders, Elizabeth, New Jersey. This was the largest metal typefoundry in North America, formed in 1892 by amalgamating a number of smaller firms.

*Axis*   In typography, the axis of a letter generally means the axis of the stroke, which in turn reveals the axis of the pen or other tool used to make the letter. If a letter has thick strokes and thin ones, find the thick strokes and extend them into lines. These lines are the axis (or *axes;* there may be several) of the letter. Not to be confused with *slope.*

**f**

*Ball Terminal* A circular form at the end of the arm in letters such as a, c, f, j, r and y. Ball terminals are found in many romans and italics of the Romantic period, and in recent faces built on Romantic lines. Examples: Bodoni, Scotch Roman, Clarendon, Basilia. See also *beak terminal* and *teardrop terminal.*

*Baseline* Whether written by hand or set into type, the Latin lowercase alphabet implies an invisible staff consisting of at least four lines: topline, midline, baseline and beardline.

The topline is the line reached by ascenders in letters like b, d, h, k, l. The midline marks the top of letters like a, c, e, m, x, and the top of the torso of letters like b, d, h. The baseline is the line on which all these letters rest. The beardline is the line reached by descenders in letters like p and q. The *cap line,* marking the top of uppercase letters like H, does not necessarily coincide with the topline of the lower case.

Round letters like e and o normally dent the baseline. Pointed letters like v and w normally pierce it, while the foot serifs of letters like h and m rest precisely upon it.

*Bastarda* A class of blackletter types. See p 200.

*Beak Terminal* A sharp spur, found particularly on the f, and also often on a, c, j, r and y in many twentieth-century romans and, to a lesser degree, italics. Examples: Perpetua, Berling, Méridien, Pontifex, Veljović, Calisto, Ignatius.

**f**

*Bicameral* A bicameral alphabet is two alphabets joined. The Latin alphabet, which you are reading, is an example. It has an upper and a lower case, as closely linked and yet as easy to distinguish as the Senate and the House of Representatives. Unicameral alphabets (the Arabic, Hebrew and Devanagari alphabets, for example) have only one case. Tricameral alphabets have three – and a normal font of roman type can be described as tricameral, if you distinguish upper case, lower case and small caps.

*Bitmap* A digital image in unintelligent form. A letterform can be described morphologically, as a series of reference points and trajectories that mimic its perimeter, or embryologically, as the series of penstrokes that produce the form. Such descriptions are partially independent of size and position. The same image can also be described quite accurately but superficially as the addresses of all the dots (or *bits*) in its digital representation. This sort of description, a *bitmap,* ties the image to one orientation and size.

*Blackletter*   Blackletter is to typography what Gothic is to archi-tecture: a general name for a wide variety of forms that stem predominantly from the north of Europe. Like Gothic buildings, blackletters are generally tall, narrow and poin-ted. They are often massive, but sometimes light. Compare *whiteletter.* The categories of blackletter include *bastarda, fraktur, quadrata, rotunda* and *textura.*

*Bleed*   As a verb, to bleed means to reach to the edge of the page. As a noun, it means printed matter with no margin. If an image is printed so that it reaches beyond the trim line, it will bleed when the page is trimmed. Photographs, rules, solids and background screens or patterns are often allowed to bleed. Type can rarely do so.

*Blind*   In letterpress work, printing blind means printing without ink, producing a colorless impression.

*Blind Folio*   A page which is counted in the numbering sequence but carries no visible number.

*Block Quotation*   A quotation set off from the main text, form-ing a paragraph of its own, often indented or set in a differ-ent face or smaller size than the main text. A *run-in quota-tion,* on the other hand, is run in with the main text and usually enclosed in quotation marks.

*Body*   (1) In reference to foundry type: the actual block of type-metal from which the sculpted mirror-image of the printed letter protrudes. (2) In reference to phototype or digital type: the rectangular face of the metal block that the letter would be mounted on *if it were* three-dimensional metal instead of a two-dimensional image or bitmap. Retained as a fiction for use in sizing and spacing the type.

*Body Size*   The *height* of the *face* of the type, which in let-terpress terms is the *depth* of the *body* of the type. Origi-nally, this was the height of the face of the metal block on which each individual letter was cast. In digital type, it is the height of its imaginary equivalent, the rectangle defining the space owned by a given letter, and not the dimension of the letter itself. Type sizes are usually given in points – but European type sizes are sometimes given in *Didot points,* which are 7% larger than the points used in Britain and North America.

*Bowl*   The generally round or elliptical forms which are the basic bodyshape of letters such as C, G, O in the upper case, and b, c, e, o, p in the lower case. Also called *eye.*

*Cap Height* The distance from baseline to cap line of an alphabet, which is the approximate height of the uppercase letters. It is often less, but sometimes greater, than the height of the ascending lowercase letters. See also *baseline* and *x-height.*

*Chancery* A class of italic letterforms, generally distinguished by lengthened and curved extenders. Many, but not all, chancery letterforms are also *swash* forms.

*Cicero* A unit of measure equal to 12 Didot points. This is the continental European counterpart to the British and American *pica,* but the cicero is slightly larger than the pica. It is equivalent to 4.52 mm or 0.178 inch.

*Color* The darkness of the type as set in mass, which is not the same as the *weight* of the face itself. The spacing of words and letters, the leading of lines, and the incidence of capitals, not to mention the color (i.e., darkness) of the ink and of the paper it is printed on, all affect the color of the type.

*Contrast* In the analysis of letterforms, this usually refers to the degree of contrast between the thick strokes and thin strokes of a given letter. In faces such as Gill Sans and Helvetica, there is no contrast. In Neoclassical and Romantic faces such as Bell and Bodoni, the contrast is high.

*Counter* The white space enclosed by a letterform, whether wholly enclosed, as in *d* or *o,* or partially, as in *c* or *m.*

*Crosshead* A title or subhead centered over the text. Compare *sidehead.*

*Cursive* Flowing. Often used as a synonym for *italic.*

*Dingbat* A typographical character subject to scorn because it has no apparent relation to the alphabet. Many dingbats are pictograms – tiny pictures of telephones, skiers, airplanes, churches, and the like, used in the tourist industry. Others are more abstract symbols – check marks, crosses, cartographic symbols, the emblems of the suits of playing cards, and so on.

*Dot Leader* A row of evenly spaced periods or midpoints, often used by typographers to link flush-left text with flush-right numerals in a table of contents or similar context. (There are none in this book.)

DPI Dots per inch. The usual measure of output *resolution* in digital typography and in laser printing.

*Drop Cap* A large initial capital or *versal* mortised into the text. (See p 62 for examples.) Compare *elevated cap.*

*Drop Folio*  A folio (page number) dropped to the foot of the page when the folios on other pages are carried at the top. Drop folios are often used on chapter openings.

*Dropline Paragraph*  A paragraph marked by dropping directly down one line space from the end of the previous paragraph, without going back to the left margin.

*Elevated Cap*  A large initial capital or versal set on the same baseline as the first line of the text.

*Em*  In linear measure, a distance equal to the type size, and in square measure, the square of the type size. Thus an em is 12 pt (or a 12 pt square) in 12 pt type, and 11 pt (or an 11 pt square) in 11 pt type. Also called *mutton*.

*En*  Half an em. To avoid misunderstanding when instructions are given orally, typographers often speak of ems as *muttons* and ens as *nuts*.

*Extenders*  Descenders and ascenders; i.e., the parts of the letterform that extend below the baseline, as in *p* and *q*, or above the midline, as in *b* and *d*.

*Eye*  Synonym for *bowl*. But large eye means large *x-height*. Open eye means large *aperture*.

FL  Flush left, which means set with an even left margin. By implication, the right margin is ragged. To be more precise, one could write FL/RR, meaning flush left, ragged right.

FL&R  Flush left and right, which is to say *justified*.

*Fleuron*  An aristocratic dingbat. A typographical ornament, generally in the shape of a flower or leaf. Some fleurons are designed to be set in bulk and in combinations, to produce what amounts to typographical wallpaper.

*Flush and Hung*  Set with the first line FL and subsequent lines indented, like the entries in this glossary.

*Folio*  In bibliography, a page or leaf; but in typography, a folio is normally a typeset page *number*, not the page itself.

*Font*  A set of characters. In the world of metal type, this means a given alphabet, with all its accessory characters, *in a given size*. In relation to phototype, it usually means the assortment of standard patterns forming the character set, without regard to size, or the actual filmstrip or wheel on which these patterns are stored. In the world of digital type, the font is the character set itself or the digital information encoding it. (The older British spelling, *fount*, has not only the same meaning but also the same pronunciation.)

*Font Driver* A computer file that mediates between the font and the keyboard, defining which character will be called by a given code.

*Fore-edge* The outside edge or margin of a book page; i.e., the edge or margin opposite the spine.

FR Flush right. With an even right margin. By implication, the left margin is ragged.

*Fraktur* A class of blackletter types. See p 200.

*Gutter* The blank column between two columns of type. Also used for the fold and spine margins between the typeblocks on facing pages of a book.

*Hanging Figures* Text figures.

*Hard Space* A word space that will not translate into a linebreak. Also called *no-break space*.

*Hint* The letterforms that make up a digital font are usually defined mathematically in terms of outlines or templates, which can be freely scaled, rotated and moved about. When pages are composed, these outlines are given specific locations and sizes. They must then be *rasterized*, i.e., converted into solid forms made up of dots at the resolution of the output device. If the size is very small or the resolution low, the raster or grid will be coarse, and the dots will fill the mathematical template very imperfectly. *Hints* are the rules of compromise applied in this process of rasterization. At large sizes and high resolutions, they are irrelevant. At smaller sizes and lower resolutions, where distortion is inevitable, they are crucial. Most, but not all, digital fonts are *hinted*. That is, they include hints as integral parts of the font definition. See *bitmap*.

*Humanist* Humanist letterforms are letterforms originating among the humanists of the Italian Renaissance. They are of two kinds: roman forms based on Carolingian script, and italic forms, which occur for the first time in Italy in the fifteenth century. Humanist letterforms show the clear trace of a broad-nib pen held by a right-handed scribe. They have a *modulated* stroke and a *humanist axis*.

*Humanist Axis* An oblique stroke axis reflecting the natural inclination of the writing hand. See pp 12–13.

*Inline* A letter in which the inner portions of the main strokes have been carved away, leaving the edges more or less intact. Inline faces lighten the color while preserving the shapes and proportions of the original face. *Outline* letters, on the other hand, are produced by drawing a line around the outsides of the letters and removing the entire original form. Outline letters, in consequence, are fatter than the originals and have less definition. Castellar and Romulus Open are examples of inline faces.

ISO  International Organization for Standardization, head-quartered in Geneva. An agency for international cooperation on industrial and scientific standards. Its membership consists of the national standards organizations of roughly one hundred countries.

*Italic*  A class of letterforms more cursive than roman but less cursive than script, first developed in Italy during the fifteenth century.

ITC  International Typeface Corporation, New York. A typeface licensing and distribution agency, founded in 1970.

*Justify*  To adjust the length of the line so that it is flush left and right on the measure. Type is commonly set either justified or FL/RR (flush left, ragged right).

*Kern*  Part of a letter that extends into the space of another. In many alphabets, the roman f has a kern to the right, the roman j a kern to the left, and the italic *f* one of each. As a verb, to kern means to alter the fit of certain letter combinations – *To* or *VA*, for example – so that the limb of one projects over or under the body or limb of the other.

*Lachrymal Terminal*  See *teardrop terminal.*

*Lead*  [Rhyming with red] Originally a horizontal strip of soft metal used for vertical spacing between lines of type. Now meaning the vertical distance from the baseline of one line to the baseline of the next. Also called *leading.*

*Ligature*  Two or more letters tied into a single character. The sequence ffi, for example, forms a ligature in most serifed faces.

*Lining Figures*  Figures of even height. Usually synonymous with *titling figures,* but some lining figures are smaller and lighter than the uppercase letters.

*Logogram*  A specific typographic form tied to a certain word. Example: the nonstandard capitalizations in the names *e.e. cummings* and *WordPerfect.*

*Lowercase Figures*  Text figures.

M/3  One-third of an em: i.e., 4 pt in 12 pt type; 8 pt in 24 pt type.

*Measure* The standard length of the line; i.e., column width or width of the overall typeblock, usually measured in picas.

*Mid Space* A space measuring M/4, a fourth of an em.

*Modulation* In relation to typography, modulation means the usually cyclical and predictable variation in width of the stroke. In *unmodulated* letterforms, such as Helvetica, the stroke is always fundamentally the same width. In a Renaissance face such as Bembo or Garamond, the stroke is based on the trace of a broad-nib pen, which makes thin cross strokes and thicker pull strokes. When letters are written with such an instrument, modulation automatically occurs.

*Mutton* An *em*. Also called mutton quad.

*Negative Leading* Leading of less than the body size. Type set 16/14, for example, is set with negative leading.

*Neohumanist* Letterforms reflecting the twentieth-century revivial of *humanist* principles are called neohumanist.

*Nut* An *en*.

*Old-syle Figures* A poor but common synonym for text figures.

*Pi Font* A font of assorted mathematical or other symbols, designed to be used as an adjunct to the text fonts.

*Pica* A unit of measure equal to 12 points. Two different picas are in common use. (1) In traditional printers' measure, the pica is 4.22 mm or 0.166 inch: close to, but not exactly, one sixth of an inch. This is the customary British and American unit for measuring the length of the line and the depth of the typeblock. (2) The PostScript pica is precisely one sixth of an inch. (Note: the continental European counterpart to the pica is the *cicero,* which is 7% larger.)

*Piece Fraction* A fraction (such as 9/32) that is not included in the font and must therefore be made up from separate component characters.

*Point* (1) In traditional British and American measure, a point is one twelfth of a pica, which makes it 0.3515 mm, or 0.01383 inch. In round numbers, there are 72 points per inch, or 28.5 points per centimetre. (2) In continental Europe a larger point, the Didot point, is used. The Didot point (one twelfth of a *cicero*) is 0.38 mm or 0.01483 inch. In round numbers, there are 26.5 Didot points per centimetre, or 67.5 per inch. (3) Many photosetters and digital typesetting devices, as well as the PostScript and TrueType computer languages, round the point off to precisely 1/72 inch and the pica to precisely 1/6 inch.

*Quad*   An *em*. Also called *mutton quad*.

*Ranging Figures*   Figures of even height. Synonymous with *lining figures*. Ranging figures are usually *titling figures*, but some ranging figures are smaller than the uppercase letters.

*Raster*   Digital grid. See *hint*.

*Rationalist Axis*   Vertical axis, typical of Neoclassical and Romantic letterforms. See pp 12–13. Compare *humanist axis*.

*Reflexive*   A type of *serif* that simultaneously stops a main stroke and implies its continuation. Reflexive serifs are typical of roman faces, including the face in which these words are set. They always involve a sudden, small stoppage and reversal of the pen's direction, and more often than not they are bilateral. See also *transitive*.

*Resolution*   In digital typography, resolution is the fineness of the grain of the typeset image. It is usually measured in dots per inch (dpi). Laser printers, for example, generally have a resolution between 300 and 1000 dpi, and typesetting machines a resolution substantially greater than 1000 dpi. But other factors besides resolution affect the apparent roughness or fineness of the typeset image. These factors include the inherent design of the characters, the skill with which they are digitized, the hinting technology used to compensate for coarse rasterization, and the type of film or paper on which they are reproduced.

*Rotunda*   A class of blackletter types. See p 200.

RR   Ragged right, which is to say unjustified.

*Sanserif*   From the Latin *sans serif,* without serifs: synonymous with unserifed.

*Scaling Font*   A digital font designed so that the weight and proportions of the letterforms alter in tandem with their size. Handcut foundry type always involves alterations of weight and proportion from size to size. (Small sizes are cut darker and bulkier than larger sizes, so that changes in size involve minimal changes in color.) Linotype and Monotype machine fonts were scaled in a similar way. But many early twentieth-century North American foundry faces were cut mechanically from a single set of patterns. With these faces, as with phototype, there is no difference in proportion from one size to another. Bitmapped digital faces frequently vary in proportion from size to size. Genuine scaling fonts – scalable fonts that allow for changes of proportion on the fly – are a recent development in digital typography.

m

**Serif**  A stroke added to the beginning or end of one of the main strokes of a letter. In the roman alphabet, serifs are usually *reflexive* finishing strokes, forming unilateral or bilateral stops. (They are unilateral if they project only to one side of the main stroke, like the serifs at the head of T and the foot of L, and bilateral if they project to both sides, like the serifs at the foot of T and the head of L.) *Transitive* serifs – smooth entry or exit strokes – are the norm in italic.

There are many descriptive terms for serifs, especially as they have developed in roman faces. They may be not only unilateral or bilateral, but also long or short, thick or thin, pointed or blunt, abrupt or adnate, horizontal or vertical or oblique, tapered, triangular, and so on. In blackletters, they are frequently *scutulate* (diamond-shaped), and in some script faces, such as Tekton, the serifs are virtually round.

(Not all type historians agree that the word *serif* should be used in relation to italic letters. But some term is necessary to denote the difference between, for example, Bembo italic and Gill Sans italic. In this book, the former is described as a serifed italic, the latter as unserifed.)

**Sidehead**  A title or subhead set flush left (more rarely, flush right) or slightly indented. Compare *crosshead.*

**Slab Serif**  An *abrupt* or *adnate* serif of the same thickness as the main stroke. Slab serifs are a hallmark of the so-called egyptian and clarendon types: two groups of Realist faces produced in substantial numbers since the early nineteenth century. Memphis, Rockwell and Serifa are examples.

**Slope**  The angle of inclination of the stems and extenders of letters. Most (but not all!) italics slope to the right at something between 2° and 20°. Not to be confused with *axis.*

**Solid**  Set without additional lead, or with the leading equivalent to the type size. Type set 11/11 or 12/12, for example, is set solid.

**Sort**  Originally an individual piece of metal type. In the world of digital type, where letters have no physical existence until printed, *sort* has become almost synonymous with *character.* That is, it may refer to the pattern or idea instead of its physical incarnation.

**Stem**  A main stroke that is more or less straight, not part of a bowl. The letter *o* has no stem; the letter *l* consists of stem and serifs alone.

*Stempel* D. Stempel AG, the last major typefoundry to operate in Germany. It was founded in Frankfurt in 1895 and acquired punches and matrices from many other German foundries as they closed. The Stempel Foundry ceased commercial operation in 1985. A museum and noncommercial foundry has now been formed from the old core.

*Swash* A letterform reveling in luxury. Some swash letters carry extra flourishes; others simply occupy an abnormally large ration of space. Swash letters are usually cursive and swash typefaces therefore usually italic. True italic capitals (as distinct from sloped roman capitals) are usually swash. (*The Capitals in this Sentence are Examples.*) Hermann Zapf's Zapf Renaissance italic and Robert Slimbach's Poetica are faces in which the swash extends to the lower case.

*Teardrop Terminal* A swelling, like a teardrop, at the end of the arm in letters such as a, c, f, g, j, r and y. This feature is typical of typefaces from the Late Renaissance, Baroque and Neoclassical periods, and is present in many recent faces built on Baroque or Neoclassical lines. Examples: Jannon, Van Dijck, Kis, Caslon, Fournier, Baskerville, Bell, Walbaum, Zapf International, Galliard. Also called *lachrymal terminal*. See also *ball terminal* and *beak terminal*.

*Textblock* The part of the page normally occupied by text. Synonymous with *typeblock*.

*Text Figures* Figures – 123456 – designed to match the lowercase letters in size and color. Most text figures are ascending and descending forms. Compare *lining figures, ranging figures* and *titling figures*.

*Textura* A class of blackletter types. See p 200.

*Thick Space* A space measuring M/3, a third of an em.

*Thin Space* In letterpress work, a space measuring M/5, a fifth of an em. In computer typesetting, sometimes understood as M/6. Compare *mid space* and *thick space*.

| M | M | M |
|---|---|---|
| 3 | 4 | 5 |

*Three-to-em* One-third em. Also written M/3.

*Titling Figures* Figures – 123456 – designed to match the uppercase letters in size and color. Compare *text figures*.

*Transitive* A type of serif which flows directly into or out of the main stroke without stopping to reverse direction, typical of many italics. Transitive serifs are usually unilateral: they extend only to one side of the stem. See also *reflexive*.

*Type Size* See *body size*.

*U&lc*   Upper and lower case: the normal form for setting text in the Latin, Greek and Cyrillic alphabets, all of which are *bicameral*.

*Unicameral*   Having only one case – like the Hebrew alphabet and many roman titling faces. See *bicameral*.

*Versal*   A large initial capital, either elevated or dropped.

*Weight*   The darkness (blackness) of a typeface, independent of its size. See also *color*.

*Whiteletter*   The generally light roman and italic letterforms favored by humanist scribes and typographers in Italy in the fifteenth and sixteenth centuries, as distinct from the generally darker *blackletter* script and type widely used north of the Alps. Whiteletter is the typographical counterpart to Romanesque in architecture, as blackletter is the counterpart to Gothic.

*White Line*   A line space.

*Word Space*   The space between words. When type is set FL/RR, the word space may be of fixed size, but when the type is *justified*, the word space must be elastic.

*x-height*   The distance between the baseline and the midline of an alphabet, which is normally the approximate height of the unextended lowercase letters – a, c, e, m, n, o, r, s, u, v, w, x, z – and of the torso of b, d, h, k, p, q, y. The relation of x-height to cap height, and the relation of x-height to length of extenders, are two important characteristics of any bicameral Latin typeface. See also *baseline, cap height* and *eye*.

# APPENDIX C: FURTHER READING

The study of typography is an ancient and polylingual enterprise, and the recent literature on computer typography is vast. This short list includes only a selection of the more important works available in English.

## C.1 GENERAL HISTORY

Anderson, Donald M. *The Art of Written Forms*. New York. 1969.
DeFrancis, John. *Visible Speech: The Diverse Oneness of Writing Systems*. Honolulu. 1989.
Degering, Hermann. *Lettering*. New York. 1965.
Gaur, Albertine. *A History of Writing*. London. 1984.
Gray, Nicolete. *A History of Lettering*. Oxford. 1986.
———. *Lettering as Drawing*. 2 vols. Oxford. 1970. Reprinted as one vol., 1971.
Knuttel, Gerard. *The Letter as a Work of Art*. Amsterdam. 1951.
Meggs, Philip B. *A History of Graphic Design*. New York. 1983.
Morison, Stanley. *Politics and Script*. Oxford. 1972.
———. *Selected Essays on the History of Letter-forms*. 2 vols. Cambridge, UK. 1981.
Vervliet, H.D.L., ed. *The Book through 5000 Years*. London. 1972.

## C.2 SCRIBAL ROOTS

Diringer, David. *The Hand-Produced Book*. London. 1953. Reprinted as *The Book Before Printing*, New York, 1982.
Knight, Stan. *Historical Scripts*. London. 1984.
Noordzij, Gerrit. *The Stroke of the Pen*. The Hague. 1982.
Wardrop, James. *The Script of Humanism*. Oxford. 1963.

## C.3 TYPOGRAPHIC HISTORY

Blumenthal, Joseph. *Art of the Printed Book, 1455–1955*. New York. 1973.
Bringhurst, Robert. *Shovels, Shoes and the Slow Rotation of Letters*. Vancouver. 1986.

Carter, Harry. *A View of Early Typography.* Oxford. 1969.

*Catalogue of Books Printed in the xvth Century Now in the British Museum.* 12 vols to date, some reprinted with additions. London. 1908–1985.

Chappell, Warren. *A Short History of the Printed Word.* New York. 1970.

Enschedé, Charles. *Typefoundries in the Netherlands.* Translated with revisions and notes by Harry Carter. Haarlem, Netherlands. 1978.

*Fine Print on Type: The Best of Fine Print Magazine on Type and Typography.* San Francisco. 1988.

Johnson, A.F. *Selected Essays on Books and Printing.* Amsterdam. 1970.

————. *Type Designs.* 3rd ed. London. 1966.

Lawson, Alexander. *Anatomy of a Typeface.* Boston. 1990.

Morison, Stanley, & Kenneth Day. *The Typographic Book, 1450–1935.* London. 1963.

Steinberg, Saul. *Five Hundred Years of Printing.* 3rd ed. London. 1974.

Updike, D.B. *Printing Types: Their History, Forms and Use.* 2nd ed. 2 vols. Cambridge, MA. 1937.

C.4   TWENTIETH-CENTURY TYPOGRAPHY

Carter, Sebastian. *Twentieth-Century Type Designers.* London & New York. 1987.

Day, Kenneth, ed. *Book Typography 1815–1965.* London. 1966.

Dreyfus, John. *The Work of Jan van Krimpen.* The Hague. 1952.

McLean, Ruari. *Jan Tschichold: Typographer.* London. 1975.

Morison, Stanley, et al. *A Tally of Types.* 2nd ed. Cambridge, UK. 1973.

Snyder, Gertrude, & Alan Peckolick. *Herb Lubalin.* New York. 1985.

Spencer, Herbert. *Pioneers of Modern Typography.* Rev. ed. Cambridge, MA. 1982.

Tracy, Walter. *Letters of Credit.* London. 1986.

Zapf, Hermann. *Hermann Zapf and His Design Philosophy.* Chicago. 1987.

————. *Manuale Typographicum.* Frankfurt. 1954. Rev. ed., Cambridge, MA. 1970.

————. *Manuale Typographicum 1968.* Frankfurt & New York. 1968.

————. *Typographic Variations.* New York. 1963. Reissued, New Rochelle, NY, 1978.

## C.5 TYPOGRAPHICAL AESTHETICS

Benjamin, Walter. "The Work of Art in the Age of Mechanical Reproduction," in *Illuminations.* London. 1970.
Davids, Betsy, & Jim Petrillo. "The Artist as Book Printer: Four Short Courses." In Joan Lyons, ed., *Artists' Books.* New York. 1985.
Duncan, Harry. *Doors of Perception.* Austin, TX. 1987.
Gill, Eric. *An Essay on Typography.* 2nd ed. London. 1936.
Huntley, H F. *The Divine Proportion: A Study in Mathematical Beauty.* New York. 1970.
Le Corbusier. *The Modulor.* 2nd ed. Cambridge, MA. 1954.
Massin, [Robert]. *Letter and Image.* London. 1970.
Morison, Stanley. *First Principles of Typography.* New York. 1936.
Tschichold, Jan. *Asymmetric Typography.* New York. 1967.
————. *The Form of the Book,* ed. Robert Bringhurst. Vancouver. 1991.
Warde, Beatrice. *The Crystal Goblet.* London. 1955.

*Further Reading*

## C.6 MANUALS & TEXTBOOKS

Adobe Systems Incorporated. *PostScript Language Program Design.* Reading, MA. 1988.
————. *PostScript Language Reference Manual.* 2nd ed. Reading, MA. 1990.
————. *PostScript Language Tutorial and Cookbook.* Reading, MA. 1986.
Dair, Carl. *Design with Type.* 2nd ed. Toronto. 1967.
Itten, Johannes. *The Art of Color,* trans. Ernst von Haagen. New York. 1961.
Karow, Peter. *Digital Formats for Typefaces.* 2nd ed. Hamburg. 1987.
Legros, L.A., & J.C. Grant. *Typographical Printing Surfaces.* London. 1916. Reprinted New York, 1980.
McLean, Ruari. *Thames and Hudson Manual of Typography.* London. 1980.
Martin, Douglas. *Book Design: A Practical Introduction.* New York. 1989.
Roth, Stephen F., ed. *Real World PostScript.* Reading, MA. 1988.

Seybold, John W. *The World of Digital Typesetting.* Media, PA. 1984.

Smith, Ross. *PostScript: A Visual Approach.* Berkeley, CA. 1990.

Tufte, Edward R. *Envisioning Information.* Cheshire, CT. 1990.

————. *The Visual Display of Quantitative Information.* Cheshire, CT. 1983.

*Manuals* Unger, Gerard. *Typography: Basic Principles and Applications.*
*and* Venlo, Netherlands. Undated [*c.*1990].
*Textbooks* Wick, Karl. *Rules for Typesetting Mathematics.* Prague. 1965.

Williamson, Hugh. *Methods of Book Design.* London. 1983.

Wilson, Adrian. *The Design of Books.* New York. 1967. Reprinted Salt Lake City, 1974.

C.7 WORKS OF REFERENCE

*Chicago Manual of Style.* 13th ed. Chicago. 1982.

*Hart's Rules for Compositors and Readers.* 39th ed. Oxford. 1983.

Hlavsa, Oldřich. *A Book of Type and Design.* New York. 1961.

International Organization for Standardization. *Information Processing: Coded Character Sets for Text Communication.* ISO 6937. Parts 1–2 & Addendum 01. Geneva. 1983–89.

————. *Information Processing: 8-bit Single-byte Coded Graphic Character Sets.* ISO 8859. Parts 1–9. Geneva. 1987–89.

Jaspert, W.P., et al. *Encyclopedia of Typefaces.* 5th ed. London. 1983.

Sutton, James, & Alan Bartram. *An Atlas of Typeforms.* London. 1968.

C.8 PERIODICALS

*Fine Print.* Quarterly. 16 vols. San Francisco. 1975–90.

*The Fleuron.* Annual. 7 vols. Cambridge, UK. 1923–30.

*Letterletter.* Semiannual. Journal of the Association Typographique Internationale. Münchenstein, Switzerland. 1985– .

*Typographica.* Irregular, then semiannual. 13 + 16 issues. London. 1949–59; new series, 1960–67.

*Typographische Monatsblätter.* Bimonthly. St Gallen, Switzerland. 1882– .

*U&lc.* Quarterly. Journal of the International Typeface Corporation. New York. 1974– .

# APPENDIX D: STATUS OF DIGITAL FACES

This appendix consists entirely of temporary annotations concerning typefaces listed in Chapter 10. If a face discussed in Chapter 10 is omitted from this appendix – as most of them are – it is safe to assume that, as of 1992, at least one digital foundry supplies the face in more or less complete and serviceable form.

## D.1 SERIFED FACES

*Berkeley* and *Dante*  Small caps and text figures for these faces have not yet been commercially issued in digital form.

*Berling*  Digital versions are now available with text figures, but the small caps are still missing.

*Fairbank Italic* and *Figural*  Not yet digitized.

*Jannon*  Small caps have yet to be supplied for the Simoncini 'Garamond.'

*Joanna*  Text figures and small caps are currently missing from Monotype's digital version. Inauthentic bold weights have been supplied instead.

*Manuscript*  Not yet digitized.

*Photina*  Text figures and small caps – available in the phototype version – have yet to be digitized.

*Poliphilus & Blado*  Text figures and small caps are currently missing from the Monotype digital version.

*Romanée*  A digital version has been announced but not yet issued.

*Trinité*  As of 1992, the digital version has yet to be released.

*Van Dijck*  Text figures and small caps are currently missing from Monotype's digital version.

*Futura*  Text figures, which were part of Renner's original design, have yet to be issued in any form – even in foundry metal.

*Status of*
*Digital*
*Typefaces*

*Gill Sans*  The font as originally issued departs in many respects from Gill's drawings, and a more faithful version would be welcome. In the meantime, Type Unlimited International in The Hague has issued a set of Gill Sans text figures, designed by F.E. Blokland, as a supplement to the Monotype digital fonts.

D.3  SCRIPTS

*Legende*  Not yet digitized.

D.4  TITLING & DISPLAY FACES

*Codex, Cristal, Monument, Pericles, Preissig* and *Romulus Open Capitals*  Not yet digitized.

D.5  BLACKLETTERS

*Claudius, Rhapsodie* and *Trump-Deutsch*  Not yet digitized.

D.6  UNCIALS

All faces listed are available in digital form.

D.7  GREEKS

*Antigone, Attika* and *Heraklit*  Not yet digitized.

*Gill Sans Greek, New Hellenic* and *Porson*  Currently available only for Monotype or Lasercomp equipment.

D.8  CYRILLICS

*Lazurski*  Currently available from the ParaGraph digital foundry, Moscow.

*Manuscript* and *Trajanus*  Not yet digitized.

# INDEX

*Index*

This book was designed by Robert Bringhurst,
set into type by The Typeworks, Vancouver,
and printed and bound by Thomson-Shore,
Dexter, Michigan.

The text face is Minion,
designed by Robert Slimbach
and issued in digital form by Adobe Systems,
Mountain View, California, in 1989.

The captions are set in Syntax,
designed by Hans Eduard Meier,
first cut and cast at the Stempel Foundry,
Frankfurt-am-Main, in 1969.

The fonts used in this book come primarily from the library of
Adobe Systems Inc., with additional fonts and specimens from
FontShop Canada, Giampa Textware, the Golgonooza Letter Foundry,
Linotype-Hell AG, the Monotype Corporation PLC,
ParaGraph International, and several independent sources.